LIVERPOOL PLAYHOUSE:
A THEATRE AND ITS CITY

LIVERPOOL UNIVERSITY PRESS

Liverpool Playhouse:
a theatre and its city

Compiled and edited by Ros Merkin

Title page: Ian Hogg
as Enobarbus and
Jeffrey Kissoon as
Antony in *Antony and
Cleopatra*, directed
by Janet Suzman;
October 2010
(Stephen Vaughan)

First published 2011 by

Liverpool University Press
4 Cambridge Street
Liverpool
L69 7ZU

British Library Cataloguing-in-Publication data
A British Library CIP record is available

ISBN 978–1–84631–747-7

Designed and typeset by Carnegie Book Production, Lancaster

Printed and bound by Henry Ling Ltd, Dorchester

Contents

Introduction

I am wondering whether the Lord Mayor and City Aldermen in solemn company assembled will this day pass a vote of thanks to those energetic citizens to whom they owe the foundations of their theatre. Those first playgoers were laughed at for their mad enthusiasm. They were painfully conscious of the fact that they were not organising anything so important as a new system of docks, but at least they saw to it that the theatre was opened and ready to receive the good ship Civic Pride before she sailed away on the flood tide of prosperity to some other port.*

The vote of thanks from Basil Dean, the Playhouse's first artistic director, on the occasion of the theatre's 21st birthday to the solemn assembled company of sturdy citizens with his allusion to civic pride, does not suggest a note of rebellion. He hints at some ruffling of feathers, playgoers being laughed at for their mad enthusiasm, but this was a very minor ripple compared to the events in the city of 1911 when, according to some, the transport strikes brought the country the closest it has been to revolution. Yet rebellion is precisely the word used by the theatre's first historian, Grace Wyndham Goldie. Liverpool Playhouse was created 'as a result of the rebellion of individuals ... against the *average* quality of the commercial play and the commercial production' and repertory theatres were 'theatres of the left wing, theatres of rebellion.'† In opening its doors, the Liverpool Repertory Theatre (it was to become the Playhouse in 1916) joined a growing movement of revolt which had started in the latter years of the previous century, mostly in London, in a series of clubs and seasons. This developed through the opening of theatres (including the Abbey Theatre, Dublin in 1904, the Gaiety Theatre, Manchester in 1908 and the

Above: Star Theatre of Varieties, designed by Harry Percival for 1898 reconstruction (*The Playgoer* vol. 1, October 1902)

---

*   Basil Dean; quoted in *Daily Post*, 11 November 1932
†   Goldie, 11 and 211

1

Glasgow Repertory Company in 1909*) which aimed to provide a home for a dramatic revival which stood fiercely in opposition to the values of commercialism. The Playhouse joined this opposition to commercialism both in the theatre and in the city itself. In the 1890s Liverpool was confident enough of its future to suggest that:

> [t]his vast city will be the greatest and richest ever known in the world ... London, compared to it, is out of the way ... London, will be our historic city – the city of culture, fashion and intellect. But whoever lives long enough will find the great city on the banks of the Mersey will be the commercial city of the future.†

By 1911, the Playhouse joined a growing band of cultural institutions in the city that aimed to ameliorate the taint of commerce – and challenge London's supremacy not only as the richest city but also as a city of culture, fashion and intellect.

The aims of the repertory movement were laid out in all the programmes of the Playhouse's first season. A repertory theatre:

> is a theatre which seeks to satisfy the ever-widening dramatic taste of the people of our time, desiring also to give adequate expression to the individual life of the city in which it is placed – whose citizens shall control its destinies: An honest attempt to supply the wants of those who love their theatre and desire its instalment amongst the honoured institutions of their country: A theatre which serves and encourages all forms of dramatic art, provided they be worthy of the dignity of a great city – being the servant of the public and not the plaything of any one section of playgoers. It signifies the dramatic renaissance. It is the theatre of the future in this country.

If the movement signified a dramatic renaissance, it was importantly one to be placed firmly at the heart of the city. Built in a spirit of independence fitting for a city that styled itself as "the New York of Europe, a world-city

---

*   These were joined in 1913 by Birmingham Repertory Theatre under Barry Jackson. Both Manchester and Glasgow were to be short lived experiments. Glasgow closed in 1914. In 1917, Miss Horniman, at the Gaiety, dismissed the company and by 1921, despite her appeals to the city to take over the theatre it was bought by a cinema. This left Liverpool as the oldest Repertory theatre in the country

†   'The Future Supremacy of Liverpool', *Tit-Bits*, quoted in John Belchem, *Merseypride: Essays in Liverpool Exceptionalism* (Liverpool: Liverpool University Press, 2000), 4

rather than merely British provincial",* the theatre was from the outset
determined to secure for itself the plays Liverpool wanted to see 'and
not leave themselves at the mercy of London managers, whose primary
concern must necessarily be with the need of the London public.' † And
it was to be owned by its citizens. Whilst Manchester Gaiety could rely
on Miss Horniman's tea fortune and Birmingham could fall back on Barry
Jackson's margarine money (he was the son of the founder of Maypole
Dairies), Liverpool was owned by the people of the city. Money was raised
through £1 shares with the desire to spread the 'ownership' as widely as
possible and the theatre always aimed to maintain a sense of ownership
and familiarity for the audience. The (at the time) unusual inclusion of a
foyer in the theatre fostered a social side to the theatre and in the 1920s,
the *Manchester Guardian* could praise the 'ease and intimacy' of the
'unassuming size' and 'ungilded equipment' of the Playhouse where there
was always a 'pleasant sense that the coming of a new play, like the arrival
of a new infant, is a family event rather than a social occasion.'‡

What this book cannot do is tell the entirety of that story with all its
twists and turns, all its successes and failures. Nor does it focus on what
for many is the theatre's greatest contribution to theatre, the impressive
list of actors who started at the Playhouse and went on to find fame
(although a few, including Patrick Stewart, Rita Tushingham and Patricia
Routledge do appear). Two other books provide detail not found here. Grace
Wyndham Goldie's *The Liverpool Repertory Theatre 1911–1934*, published
in 1935, provides a detailed history of the first thirty-three years. Pelham
McMahon's *An Actor's Place* takes the story on to the closure of the theatre
in 1998. Instead, mostly in the words of those who have worked there, it
aims to give a flavour of the changing times and concerns of a regional
repertory theatre over the last hundred years. It is organised by artistic
directors as they were often the ones (along with the Board or sometimes
despite the Board) who stamped their mark most on the character of the
theatre at any one moment in time. There are, of course, constant concerns
that run throughout the 100 years, not least the vexed question of how
to attract and keep an audience (the theatre was totally reliant on its box
office until the early 1960s when it started to receive a grant from the Arts
Council) and how to foster a more daring theatrical taste at times whilst
maintaining a 'catholic' programme of plays. An even more vexed question

---

*   'Liverpool: Port, Docks, City', *Illustrated London News*, 15 May 1886. Quoted in Belchem, *Merseypride*, 5

†   'Liverpool's Repertory Theatre: A Limited Liability Company', *Liverpool Daily Post and Mercury*, 16 March 1911

‡   *Manchester Guardian*, 6 March 1929

is that of putting the city itself on stage. The theatre always aimed to provide a home for work not produced on the commercial stage but it also always wanted to encourage a new and local school of writing. The Gaiety had been associated with developing the Manchester school of writers (of whom Stanley Houghton and Harold Brighouse were the two most famous exponents) and Liverpool's story of attempting to find its own voice is one of the threads that runs through the book.

Above all, it reminds us of the sense of rebellion, the energy and enthusiasm that fired those first pioneers and whose energy and enthusiasm and rebellion runs like a vein through the theatre's 100 years. For many, the Playhouse is the staid older sister, even the disapproving maiden aunt, of the theatre it is now joined with, the Everyman. This book serves as a reminder that the Playhouse too has had its days of rebellion. It is, as Gemma Bodinetz, the current artistic director, says below, both a safe and a daring space, an old lady with far more spirit than she sometimes gets credit for.

Ros Merkin

A full list of productions can be found on the Everyman and Playhouse website: **http://www.everymanplayhouse.com**

Acknowledgements

Thanks are due to:

The staff at Liverpool Records Office, especially Helena Smart and Roger Hull, for their enthusiastic and cheerful help in locating material in a largely uncatalogued archive and in the middle of a move

The staff at Liverpool Playhouse

Colin Thorpe, Mariko Kishida-Thorpe and Reg Phillips for their help and generosity with locating and digitising images

The Society for Theatre Research for providing funding to digitise images

Everyone who has contributed time, effort and words – and above all to Laura Cockett for being an indispensable research assistant.

The start of the experiment

❝ Will you not help to make this enterprise worthy of you? Will you not see to it that it keeps its flag flying? ❞

JOHN GALSWORTHY, QUOTED IN *POST AND MERCURY*, 12 NOVEMBER 1931

The city ❝ Liverpool at the turn of the century was a city of noticeable contrasts, in attitude quite as much as in physical aspects. Civic pride expressed itself in founding art galleries, libraries and a new university, to say nothing of planning a great cathedral, even while it neglected such domestic issues as slum clearance. At the apex, as it were, of the city's prosperity, there was the rebuilt Adelphi Hotel, its modern wonders, especially the plumbing, proudly displayed to troupes of admiring visitors by young Arthur Towle, about to inherit his father's reputation for railway hotel management … The great shipping families were still the hierarchy of the city's commercial life, its leaders too, in the social round. As Ramsay Muir … wrote later: "In the early years of this century there was a real vitality, a fizz, and a go, in Liverpool." ❞

BASIL DEAN, 77

❝ Liverpool was a thrusting sort of place in those days, and out of the excess of its commercial prosperity was finding time to attend to the higher needs of the soul, although it always seemed to attach its higher educational and artistic problems with a perplexed air, as if its merchant princes and more prominent citizens had been importuned and persuaded by the energetic youthful spirits amongst them on a course of action the final consequences of which it was impossible to foresee. After all, was it merely for a University, a Cathedral, and a Repertory Theatre they had so striven to build upon the sure trading foundations of the clipper ships of their forefathers? ❞

BASIL DEAN, QUOTED IN *POST AND MERCURY*, 10 NOVEMBER 1932

Above:
Professor
Charles Reilly

**Liverpool
theatre
before the
Playhouse**

‘ At this time the most important and fashionable theatre in Liverpool
was the Royal Court. Here had come Henry Irving and Ellen Terry; here
still came H. B. Irving, Martin Harvey and Forbes Robertson. Next in
importance was the Shakespeare. In 1909, W. W. Kelly, that energetic and
enterprising showman, bought a theatre in Paradise Street and called
it Kelly's Theatre. Then there were smaller houses, the Queen's and the
Rotunda, and in Williamson Square, the Star.

The great feature of the year at each of the main theatres was the
Christmas pantomime. Robinson Crusoes and Cinderellas, red nosed Dames
and plump Principal Boys, transformation scenes of incredible length and
ever increasing magnificence occupied their stages from Boxing Day until
well into March … Musical comedy was the passion of the hour. "Lovely
women," said the Liverpool press, "all more or less eligible as peeresses,
bedeck the performances with many beauties of voice and figure and form
a backing so charming that one sometimes wishes the principals out of
the line of sight." … In 1909 Liverpool playgoers could, in a typical week,
choose between Mr Edward Compton in the patriotic play *An Englishman's
Home* at the Court; Mr Forbes Robertson in *The Passing of the Third Floor
Back* at the Shakespeare; *Is Our Navy Ready*, that great aquatic spectacle,
at Olympia; Cecilia Loftus and Bostock's Boxing Kangaroo at the Empire;
The Better Land at the Rotunda; *At Sister's Sin* at the Queen's; *Guilty Gold*
at the Star and, ominously, at the Tivoli "Mr Jasper Redfern's series of
remarkable pictures" foreshadowed the danger of the cinematograph.

The choice was magnificent. But in spite of it there were playgoers in
Liverpool who were envious of the Court Season in Liverpool where *John
Bull's Other Island* and *The Silver Box* were revealing worlds which "that
patriotic play *An Englishman's Home*" had never attempted to envisage. ’

Goldie, 26–7

**Beginnings
of an idea**

‘ I was impressed by the fact that the real life of our country is dominated
by the big cities, which through their schools, their shops and their
newspapers, their theatres, their Art Galleries, shape the outlook of huge
surrounding populations. I was impressed, also, by the fact that the great
provincial cities were being drained of their vitality by the power of
London, so that they had no intellectual life of their own, being far worse
off, in this respect, than the provincial cities of America, of Germany, of
Italy, and even of France. And I thought there was no more worthy aim
that one could set oneself than that of trying to create an independent
intellectual life in these great cities … It seemed merely intolerable
that the theatres of a great city should be no more than booths for the
entertainment of travelling companies from London. We must, if we were

Experimental Season
Strife by John
Galsworthy

civilised, have our *own* theatre, in which we could produce plays that
would affect and criticise our own life instead of being content with the
drawing room (or bedroom) comedies of sophisticated London Society.*

<small>RAMSAY MUIR, PROFESSOR OF MODERN HISTORY, UNIVERSITY OF LIVERPOOL; QUOTED BY GOLDIE, 23</small>

In 1909 the repertory campaign was still in its infancy. But Professor
Reilly was already talking eagerly to all and sundry about the possibility
of having a repertory theatre in Liverpool. Vital, energetic, exuberant,
generous, he was working with enthusiastic zeal for numbers of the many
schemes which were the output of his fertile mind. They were all of them
to quicken life and give it gaiety as well as meaning. And the life that
was to be quickened was, in particular, the life of the city of Liverpool.
The repertory theatre was only one of his schemes but it was among the
most cherished. It was pursued with an untiring, insistent enthusiasm
which met difficulties by refusing to see them. People didn't really want
a repertory theatre? Nonsense. Of course they did. How could anyone not
want to see Shakespeare and *Hedda Gabler* and all those jolly moderns?
And anyway if they didn't like them now they would when the Repertory
Theatre had shown them how good they were. It couldn't pay? That was
nonsense too. If you had enough faith in anything you could always get
money from somewhere to pay for it. And the conversation slipped away
from the difficulties to the marvels that the new theatre would achieve in
the town; to the centre of intellectual activity that it would be; to the gay,
artistic social life that it would promote; to the Greek tragedy, the Shaw,
the Ibsen that its actors would perform … he lavished upon the campaign

for the theatre his insistent faith and his untiring energy. He was, more than any other single individual, responsible for its success.

GOLDIE, 28–9

6 Without him the "Rep" would never have been born ... In the intervals between building his own School of Architecture ... he found time to conduct a voluminous correspondence and to attend countless tea-parties and meetings in aid of the new cause. He insisted that all should know about the coming deliverance from the thraldom of the hated touring company, and if his insistence offended some, what matter so long as our subscription lists responded to his efforts.

BASIL DEAN, QUOTED IN POST AND MERCURY, 10 NOVEMBER 1932

6 As evidence of the ferment of ideas and enthusiasms in Liverpool in the years immediately preceding the war ... the founding of her repertory theatre is a good example ... We had seen enough to make us discontented with the sort of plays we found in the four or five Liverpool theatres ... Why should not Liverpool, then, have a producing theatre of its own and be independent of London? If Manchester had one, and Glasgow was already trying to found one with Alfred Wareing, Liverpool should certainly do the same. Founding things and starting new ventures was in the air those days. Nothing seemed impossible.

When, therefore, I heard from Granville-Barker that he and Nigel Playfair would be visiting Liverpool and would be willing to address a small audience likely to be interested in what a repertory theatre might do for the town, I jumped at the opportunity. I got the University Club to lend me the large dining room for an afternoon meeting ... Granville-Barker was eloquent, Playfair practical, Miss Horniman, for I had persuaded her to come too, scornful of Liverpool. Robert Hield, the editor of the Daily Courier was in the Chair, and Sir Edward Russell, the Editor of the Daily Post, proposed the vote of thanks. The elite and wealthy departed muttering something ought to be done, but did nothing. A little group at the back, however consisting of a chemist's assistant, Oscar Waddington, the owner of small hardware shop, Richard Mason, a young man in the coal trade named Sharman and James Coulton, an insurance clerk, all of whom I had somehow got to know and had invited, stayed behind. They suggested the formation of a Playgoers' Club, not of the usual provincial kind, organised to entertain visiting celebrities, but one designed to educate the public and to back good plays of every kind when and where they could be found ... Within a year we had a thousand members and were, I remember, always having to take a larger hall for our next meeting which is, I think, the best proof that the times were ripe for our venture. *

CHARLES HERBERT REILLY, 141–2

Things moved forward when Alfred Wareing suggested bringing his Glasgow company to the city for a six week trial season. But illness put an end to this plan.

Enter Basil Dean

Aged just 23, Basil Dean had spent three years with Miss Horniman's Manchester Gaiety company as an actor and producing short plays. He received a telegram from Miss Darragh, who had also been with Miss Horniman and had been contacted by Wareing when he knew he could not deliver on his engagement, saying there 'was a chance of doing repertory' in Liverpool, 'please come at once'. * Dean went to Liverpool to help organise the trial season to help the case for establishing a permanent theatre.

* Basil Dean, 72

' Our chances of success seemed flimsy indeed. We knew no one in the city. All we had to go on was the suggestion contained in the Wareing telegram that we should get in touch with Professor Reilly. But we did not know the Professor's address and had to look it up in the telephone book. While Miss Darragh went off to interview him, I was told to see the editor of the *Liverpool Daily Post*. At the newspaper office I met ... Ronald [Jeans], then working in a stockbroker's office, who proved to be the vital link in the chain of interest stretching from the enthusiastic Playgoers' Society and the lively professors at the University right up to the editorial chair of the newspaper, where Sir Edward Russell, veteran journalist and admirer of Henry Irving, still nominally presided. With his approval, egged on by Ronald Jeans, the *Liverpool Daily Post* went all out to publicise and support our plan, pointing out that upon the success of the promised Six Weeks' Experimental Season depended the prospect of a permanent repertory theatre for the city. The rival newspapers soon joined in ... Impressed by the newspaper backing, no less than by Kenyon's offer of five hundred pounds working capital, the original guarantors agreed to transfer their support to our enterprise. ' *

* Kenyon was Charles Kenyon who was offering to back the experiment financially

BASIL DEAN, 74

Rehearsals took place in a small room at the top of Kelly's Theatre in Paradise Street. Actors were gathered from London, plays were found from contacts he had made in his previous three years and scenery was borrowed from Miss Horniman.

6 Work was constantly interrupted by meetings, conferences and interviews as I struggled for a measure of authority over a company of actors brought together for the first time, some of them very senior indeed. 9

BASIL DEAN, 75

At Kelly's Theatre
The Repertory Season by Miss Darragh's Company
Under the Direction of Basil Dean
To promote the Foundation of the Liverpool Repertory Theatre
For Six Weeks
From February 20th to April 1st 1911

The experimental season

John Galsworthy: *Strife* with Harold Chapin: *Augustus in Search of a Father*
Allan Monkhouse: *The Choice* with Stanley Houghton: *Dear Departed*
J. Sackville Martin: *Cupid and Styx*
Hermann Sudermann: *Vale of Content* with Basil Dean: *Mother to Be*
St John Hankin: *The Cassilis Engagement*
John Masefield: *Nan* with J. M. Barrie: *The Twelve Pound Look*

What is a repertory theatre?

6 Repertory Theatres are comparatively new to England; they are mostly to be met with in those continental countries where the Drama may be said to be still a flourishing condition. But the good fortune which has attended the two already in existence in this country – the Gaiety Theatre, Manchester, and the Scottish Repertory Theatre in Glasgow – seems to warrant the attempt to form others.

Primarily a repertory theatre is designed to take the place of the type of theatre only to be encountered in the provinces, which depends for its attractions entirely upon the necessarily haphazard touring system, and consequently can have no ordered relation to the corporate life of the city in which it is placed. It is a mistake to suppose that the plays which attain production in repertory theatres are dull or uninteresting. It should be one of the first aims of such a repertory theatre as it is hoped will shortly be established in Liverpool, to keep the catholicity of the public taste continually in mind. The theatre is the place for amusement and not for sermonising; it should be run at the wish of the patrons; and by its continued good service in the cause of real drama it will achieve just that ennobling influence which a more polemical policy can never do.

The acting in repertory theatres reaches a higher level of excellence even than some of the most celebrated west end of London houses. The reason is obvious. The members of its Company by continual work together before an audience whom they know, with whom they are in personal touch and upon whom they can depend for sympathy in exacting roles become so highly trained, and so welded together that they are able to give performances of a more concerted and more enthusiastic nature than those seen in some of the best theatres in London.

It is designed to make such a theatre a social event; to make it a part of the life of the citizens; a place where men and women of all classes and all shades of opinion may meet and witness the production of plays of the best dramatists, both past and present; a theatre in which they have a personal interest; in which their tastes and criticisms are honestly considered.'

FROM THE BROCHURE FOR THE PRELIMINARY SEASON

' The audience on the opening night, February 20th 1911, represented all aspects of life in the city: the Lord Mayor and his lady, of course, mayors and aldermen of neighbouring towns and boroughs, two visiting judges of the High Court, and, on the social side, representatives of the great shipping families still reigning in the city. Some came partly out of curiosity or in response to editorial indoctrination, and some partly to justify the publication of their names in the list of guarantors. Professors of the University, led by Charles Reilly, sat side by side with leading dramatic critics from London and the North. In one box sat the fifth Lord Derby, that magnum-sized personality whose word was second law throughout Lancashire, and opposite him, Miss Horniman, in her finest brocade and wearing her breastplate of opals, came to watch the inauguration of her first self-governing colony ...

Following that opening night, our tale of unbroken success is briefly told. All concern seemed to be borne aloft upon one great surge of enthusiasm. Crowded audiences were the order at each performance, including the two weeks of *Strife*, this despite the protest of a prominent V.I.P. at being invited to such a "damned Socialist play".* Paradise Street had never before welcomed such a stream of distinguished visitors. Even-hard headed businessmen began to wonder, whether, after all, there might not be some promise for the future in all the enthusiasm. The season closed to deafening applause with distinguished author, John Masefield this time, to give the final nod of metropolitan approval ... I was called, and was able to announce the decision to establish a permanent repertory theatre in Liverpool. (Vociferous cheers.) Professor Reilly was then introduced as the chairman of the proposed company. (More cheers.) The actors were then joined by all the stage staff ... Auld Lang Syne was sung, and everyone trooped out of the theatre, convinced that all that remained was to raise some money and build the theatre as quickly as possible, certainly in time for the autumn!'

BASIL DEAN, 75–7

* Given the unrest brewing among the city's transport workers, Galsworthy's *Strife* was a brave choice for an opening play. Whitford Kane, who moved from Manchester to play the strike leader, Roberts, noted that only those cast as masters were invited to the first night party given by the Earl of Derby. See Rowell and Jackson, 41

From trial to theatre

> ❝ The immediate success of the venture will be the individual responsibility of every member of the audience. ❞
>
> PROGRAMME NOTE, NOVEMBER 1911

Raising the money

From the outset, money for the theatre was raised through £1 shares and a subscription list, not always an easy task.

> ❝ The Liverpool Repertory Theatre is the property of upwards of twelve hundred Liverpool citizens. It is the first English Repertory to be so founded. ❞
>
> PROGRAMME NOTE, NOVEMBER 1911

> ❝ It is proposed that the company should be organised on analogous lines to those which have proved so successful in the various garden suburb or co-partnership tenants' schemes, which aim at public objects on a business footing – namely that the interest should be limited to 6 per cent., and that any surplus after payment of interest should be devoted (a) to increase the efficiency of the theatre by engaging a larger staff, providing better scenery &c.; (b) towards building up a reserve fund … It is an important part of this proposal that the shares should be widely distributed, so that as many persons as possible should feel a sense of personal property and pride in the enterprise. It is proposed that shareholders should receive certain privileges, such as prior rights to book seats for the first nights of new productions. First nights in such a theatre would become attractive social functions, as the Repertory season has shown. Again, it is proposed that there should be occasional receptions in the theatre, at which the shareholders would have opportunities of making the acquaintance of the actors, and a natural and friendly relation would be set up between audience and performer. ❞
>
> 'LIVERPOOL'S REPERTORY THEATRE: A LIMITED LIABILITY COMPANY',
> LIVERPOOL DAILY POST & MERCURY, 16 MARCH 1911

Above: Drawing of the Playhouse used in opening season

12

Securing the theatre

Following the trial season, Basil Dean managed to dispose of Miss Darragh and Charles Kenyon, for, in his words 'hostesses resented this dangerous intrusion into their domestic entourage and set about adjusting their husbands' ideas accordingly, arguing, sensibly enough, that this was a movement best managed by a young man rather than a middle-aged actress of undoubted charm'.* At the same time, work was going on to find a theatre and one day, over lunch at the Adelphi Hotel, a deal was struck by Professor Reilly and Clifford Muspratt with the owner of the Star Theatre.

*Wareing had been leasing The Royalty Theatre in Glasgow and was forced by his ill-health to resign in 1912. Lewis Casson took over the company until the outbreak of World War One when he volunteered for military service and the owners of the theatre decided that escapist entertainment was a sounder wartime offering than repertory. The company found their lease could not be renewed. For more on Glasgow see Rowell and Jackson, p 46–48

'We had all decided that the Star Theatre in Williamson Square, once a music-hall and then a melodrama house, was the one we wanted. Kelly's Theatre … could only be rented and I was determined we should own our theatre and not suffer the fate of Glasgow.* Besides, if the back of the stage was poor, the auditorium was not too big for intimate acting as Kelly's and all other theatres were. The Star held about a thousand. Better still, it was for sale. Indeed the owner, Mr Harris Fineberg, I was told, made a practice of selling it and, with the help of a mortgage, getting it back again. No doubt he hoped to do so in our case, renovated and restored at our expense. His price was £28,000, of which £20,000 could remain on mortgage. The excellent lunch at the Adelphi did not reduce the price. Indeed, it probably stiffened it, as I believe he paid. Anyhow, with never more than a hundred pounds in my banking account, a few thousand more or less did not seem to matter very much. Muspratt and I took up an option. He was younger still but belonged to a rich family and perhaps the figures meant more to him than they did to me. I felt sure the public would subscribe any number of thousands when we brought out our prospectus and told of all the wonderful things we meant to do for the town.'

CHARLES HERBERT REILLY, 143

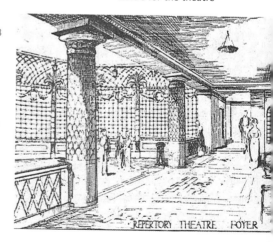

Stanley Adshead's drawing of the foyer, designed as the social centre for the theatre

Fineberg was persuaded to take a good deal of the purchase price in shares, which was just as well when the new company discovered they only had £13,000 subscribed by the citizens of Liverpool. Of this, £5,000 went to Fineberg and the remaining £8,000 was spent altering the theatre, leaving not a penny for working capital.

Redesigning the theatre

‘ The architect chosen to plan the reconstruction was Professor Stanley Adshead, first Professor of Town Planning at the University and a brilliant architect in his own right. A large friendly man with a sense of humour, he provided an excellent foil to the excitable Charles Reilly, whose frequent attempts at interference, he did not hesitate to slap down with firm good humour. ’

BASIL DEAN, 79

‘ The theatre was to open in September and he had about four months in which to buy some property at the back, get a small passage between it and the theatre closed, build a block of new dressing-rooms, a property room and a paint room and, most exciting of all, to re-design the auditorium and turn the beer-cellar under it into a foyer. The old auditorium was a sort of seraglio with half a dozen Moorish boxes on either side. Now it is in a large scale dignified Roman manner with two big boxes only and a ceiling with the loves of Jupiter painted in large roundels by our Sandon Studios friends at, I remember, thirty shillings a Jovian armour. ’ *

CHARLES HERBERT REILLY, 150–1

* The Sandon Studio Society had been founded in 1907 and was a group of painters, sculptors and journalists based at the Bluecoat

The foyer was to be a key feature of the theatre and Dean suggests it was fought for by Charles Reilly.

‘ I found Reilly and Adshead locked in bitter argument over estimates that were far in excess of what had been anticipated. Reilly, waving his silver cigarette case, a favourite gesture when excited, was especially insistent upon the conversion of the old beer cellar into a foyer where people could circulate and discuss the play in the interval. He found an unexpected advocate in myself, for I had been greatly impressed by the *lange pause* of the German theatres, when seemingly the whole audience rose from their seats and hurried to the buffets … to stroll up and down creaking corridors, discussing the play. There is no doubt Reilly was in advance of his time over the foyer … ’

BASIL DEAN, 82

Stanley Adshead (by courtesy of the University of Liverpool Library)

Excitement grows …

‘ For weeks Liverpool seemed to eat, drink and breathe nothing but repertory. Arguments for and against filled the columns of the newspapers. There were lectures, newspaper articles and what used to be called "bun fights" … at which opinions and promises of financial support were eagerly canvassed, the first to be disregarded if they were unfavourable, and the second pursued relentlessly to the moment of signature on the cheque. With the comparative isolation of the Manchester theatre present in my mind I hoped the representation would be as widespread as possible.'*

BASIL DEAN, 'BIRTH OF AN IDEA', *JUBILEE BROCHURE*, 9

… but opening delayed by strikes

'The great strike was on that year. The unemployed were rioting in Liverpool. I remember it well for it was taking place in August during very hot weather. Our theatre was undergoing considerable alteration and renovation … On the site was a store for new bricks for the alterations and we were extremely annoyed when the rioters seized our bricks and made off with them to throw at the police.'

BASIL DEAN; QUOTED IN *LIVERPOOL ECHO*, 2 NOVEMBER 1961

'Williamson Square became the chief battleground between the strikers and the police … We watched with a certain anxiety. As the delay went on and the opening date was postponed we saw the first of January getting nearer and nearer when our mortgage interest was due and with nothing to meet it. However, the gods were kind and the opening was at last fixed for the 11th of November.'

CHARLES HERBERT REILLY, 151

The opening – through the eyes of Basil Dean

The play chosen for the opening was J. M. Barrie's *The Admirable Crichton*, a choice that George Rowell suggests gave a clear indication of the theatre's future policy – and problems. Given the finance from an array of shareholders, their taste had to be considered and 'that taste was inevitably cautious'.*

'At last all was ready, constructional difficulties overcome and the inevitable last-minute delays sufficiently estimated to enable us to fix the opening date. I gave this out, together with the programme for the first half of the season at the October session of the Liverpool Playgoers' Society … The Liverpool

* Dean was referring here to what he saw, rather uncharitably, as the isolation of Miss Horniman and her theatre: 'The Gaiety had not come into existence in response to public demand. Miss Horniman had simply announced her intention of opening in Manchester, because she regarded it as the most suitable city for her experiment. At heart she was not a lover of theatre. She was a "do-gooder" who believed the theatre should educate and uplift the community in which it dwelt: a concept which she called "civilised theatre". Hence the general public regarded the Gaiety productions as lying outside the normal run of playgoing, a foreign body in the corpus of theatrical entertainment.' In 'Birth of an Idea' in *Jubilee Brochure*, 8

* See Rowell and Jackson, 41. Rowell does note that the brave start was by no means reneged on, but there were to be more performances of plays by 'commercial' writers than figured on earlier repertory bills

LIVERPOOL
REPERTORY THEATRE
THE AUDITORIUM

Stanley Adshead's proposed interior for the auditorium, taken from the 1911 brochure. As McMahon notes, the auditorium has been painted in various colours throughout its history; the early cream walls did not prove popular and since the 1930s, dark red, blue or, after the 1968 extension, deep purple have been used

press gave the announcement a warm welcome, except the Liverpool *Porcupine*, which acted up to its title by publishing a column of sarcasm at my expense that brought angry letters from its readers. Two formal openings were decided upon. The first to take place on November 11th would be mainly for our shareholders – there were now 1200 of them – who would be given priority at the box-office; the second, on Monday 13th, would be a civic function presided over by the Lord Mayor. Liverpool society turned out in force on the Saturday night, drawn partly by curiosity to see how its money had been spent, and partly by the unerring instinct of the smart set ever to be in the right place at the right time. Here was a gathering not to be missed, regardless of what took place on the stage. Certainly, the spectacle that awaited them was pleasant enough. The discreet colours of the auditorium (ivory, cerise and gold), the huge banks of flowers massed at vantage points (a gift from a wealthy patron), and above all, the latest fashions of the women, well set off by the white ties and tails of the men; all was fully commented upon in the social columns. The story in the *Liverpool Courier* read like a description of an eighteenth-century rout:

> Society, wearing its prettiest frocks, occupied boxes and stalls and circles. Muspratts, Foxwoods, Holts, Batesons, Willinks were there. The two boxes were occupied – on the one side by the Rathbones and, on the other, by Bowrings. Professors and doctors, student folk and businessmen, journalists and authors, men of law were gathered together to speed the new house of drama. Professor Reilly was the hero of the evening.

A souvenir programme was designed by a member of the School of Architecture in which the hopes and aims of the management were tersely stated ...

The performance began with the National Anthem ... Our patriotic duty done, the red and gold tableau curtains parted to disclose Aida Jenoure, a senior member of the new company, attired as "The Tragic Muse, after Joshua Reynolds", but looking more like a nineteenth-century Britannia slightly gone at the knees, to recite verses especially written for the occasion by John Masefield. The play was ... given in the scenery of the original London production, which took our inexperienced stage-hands so long to arrange, that I had to go in front of the curtain and apologise for the length of the stage waits. This taught me my first lesson in management. In future we must make simple productions of our own ... However, the long waits were no disaster on this occasion since they gave the rank and fashion time to troop into the new foyer to gossip and to admire their surroundings. The quality of the performance received little attention.

Liverpool seemed to give up the entire week-end to contemplation of its latest civic achievement. Throughout Sunday the theatre was thronged with visitors. Parties were led by Professor Reilly into the new foyer, where they collided with similar parties in charge of Professor Adshead, whose ample gestures brushed aside the flatteries showered upon him above the clatter of tea-cups. At Monday's performance all was repeated as before, the social atmosphere increased rather than diminished by the presence of Lord Derby, the city aldermen, the mayors of neighbouring boroughs, and much minor bumbledom, all in full regalia. The banks of flowers were still there, and so, too, was the enthusiasm of the audience.

No sooner had I seen the last of our distinguished guests on their way to the celebration supper in the banqueting hall of the Adelphi Hotel than I heard the sound of a fire-engine approaching the rear of the theatre. I turned back to find the auditorium full of smoke and firemen trailing hoses over our new stalls carpet. A fool had tossed a lighted cigarette into a rubbish-filled wastepaper basket in the manager's office. It took several gallons of water to extinguish the blaze. When I reached the hotel the company was already seated (two hundred and fifteen persons, all of high or middle, none of low, degree). After a hurried word of explanation to the chairman who promptly persuaded the editors present to keep the news out of their papers, I took my place, acutely aware of my sooty shirt front ... Miss Horniman, seated on my right, glanced at my frightened face as I rose to speak. "Cheer up," she whispered. "This is only the beginning." How right she was. *

*Reilly notes that the architect's plans were destroyed in the fire. See Charles Herbert Reilly, 151

BASIL DEAN, 86–8

A poem for the opening by John Masefield

Here in this house, to-night, our city makes
Something which must not fail for our sakes,
For we begin what men have been too blind
To build elsewhere, a temple for the mind.

So many Englishmen, give wealth to build
The great museums with which our town are filled,
Our millionaires compete with so much rage
That all things get endowed except the stage.
Men will not spend, it seems, on that one Art

Which is life's inmost soul and passionate heart;
They count the theatre a place for fun
Where men can laugh at nights when work is done.
If it were only that t'would be worth while
To subsidise a thing which makes men smile;
But it is more: it is that splendid thing,
A place where man's soul shakes triumphant wings,
A place of Art made living, where men may see
What human life is and has seemed to be
To the world's greatest brains; it is the place
Where Shakespeare held the glass to Nature's face;
The place the wise Greeks built by public toll
To keep austere and pure the city's soul;
And now we make it here.

　　　　Oh you who hark,
Fan to a flame through England this first spark,
Till in this land there's none so poor of purse
But he may see high deeds and hear high verse,
And feel his folly lashed, and think him great
In this world's tragedy of Life and Fate.

Tonight our city leads. All you who care
For her fair fame in England keep it fair,
Make this foundation firm, work till it be
Part of her praise on men's lips over sea
That when they name her they will say of her,
'Famous for ships and this her theatre'.

RECITED BY AIDA JENOURE WHO WAS THE FIRST ARTIST TO PERFORM ON THE STAGE

The first season, 1911–12

All shows, apart from *The Cat and the Cherub* were directed by Basil Dean

11/11	*The Admirable Crichton*, J. M. Barrie
27/11	*Justice*, John Galsworthy
22/12	*The Cat and the Cherub* C. B. Fernald, directed by Frank Vernon (one act)
	The Critic, Richard Brinsley Sheridan
22/12	*Katawumpus*, Judge Parry and Louis Calvert (Manchester Gaiety Theatre; matinées)
8/1	*The Perplexed Husband*, Alfred Sutro
22/1	*The Oak Settle*, Harold Brighouse
	The Tyranny of Tears, Haddon Chambers

29/1	*Pillars of Society*, Ibsen
7/2	*The Return of the Prodigal*, St John Hankin
14/2	*Marriages Are Made in Heaven*, Basil Dean
	The Fountain, George Calderon
26/2	*The Honeymoon*, Arnold Bennett
	The Bracelet, Alfred Sutro
18/3	*The Convict on the Hearth*, Frederick Fenn
	The Situation at Newbury, Charles McEvoy
25/3	*You Never Can Tell*, Bernard Shaw
6/4	*Rococo*, Granville Barker (one act)
	The New Sin, Macdonald Hastings
15/4	*A Roman Holiday*, Laurence Hanray (one act)
	The Cassilis Engagement, St John Hankin
22/4	*Tilda's New Hat*, George Paton (one act)
	Dealing in Futures, Harold Brighouse

Stage Right Box
(from *Architecture Illustrated*, 1911)

Transport strikes lasting 72 days paralysed the city; demonstration in St George's Plateau on 13 August, which became known as Red or Bloody Sunday when it was attacked by police; general return to work 24 August

Ground-breaking Post-Impressionist exhibition including work by Picasso, Matisse, Van Gogh and Cezanne alongside work of local artists including Albert Lipczinski (who had an exhibition in the Playhouse foyer 1912); organised by Sandon Studios at the Bluecoat (March)

Opening of Royal Liver Building (work had begun in 1908). It was the second of the three iconic buildings by the pier head; the Mersey Docks and Harbour building was opened in 1907 and the Cunard Building in 1916

Basil Dean, 1911–1913

6 We wanted life to be made more vivid to us by seeing in turn the great dramas of the past, and we wanted to join in the high adventure of new plays which faithfully interpreted the life of to-day. We certainly wanted entertainment, but that was not the first thing. We wanted to laugh more heartily but we wanted to feel more deeply too, and the latter was by far the more important. Of all the producers in turn, looking back I think Basil Dean understood this best. Though he nearly ruined the theatre financially in the two years he was with us, he not only included more serious drama than in the two successive seasons, but with the help of that very genuine artist of the theatre, George Harris, broke what was at the time fresh ground in this country in decorative scenery and lighting effects. 9

CHARLES HERBERT REILLY, 152

6 The troubles attendant upon its birth were many and severe. Looking back over the years it seems that many of those troubles were inherent in the attempt to foist upon a bustling seaport what was in its conception and first constitution virtually a civic theatre before the idea of such an institution had properly caught the imagination of the public … We were pioneering with a vengeance and the work was going to be harder than we knew. 9

BASIL DEAN; QUOTED IN *DAILY POST*, 10 NOVEMBER 1932

First directors of the theatre

Godfrey Edwards, merchant

Robert Hield, editor of *Liverpool Courier*

Ronald Jeans, stock brokers clerk; he went on to become a writer of revues and light comedies in Liverpool and then in London

Clifford Muspratt, director, West Coast Motor Company

George Rathbone, metal merchant

Alec Lionel Rea, junior partner in family's coal factoring company; after World War One he became Basil Dean's partner in ReandeaN, a theatrical production company.

Above: The 'Repertory' Dean, as seen by designer George Harris

Charles Herbert Reilly, Professor of Architecture at Liverpool University and
Chair of Liverpool Playgoers Society
Sir Edward R. Russell, editor *Liverpool Daily Post and Mercury*
John Joseph Shute, cotton broker.

    ❛ We were, in spite of our variety, a party of amateurs entirely ignorant of the practical running of a theatre, and only one or two of us filled with enthusiasm for what is called, often a little derisively to-day, the Repertory Movement. ❜

CHARLES HERBERT REILLY, 150

❛ Professor Reilly, newly appointed Chairman, spent most of his time either pleading the cause of the "avant garde" drama or grumbling at the state of our finances. J. J. Shute, Vice-Chairman ... cast a keen business eye over the seemingly irresponsible ways in which the theatrical profession conducts its affairs. Survival during the difficult years following the first world war was due to his unremitting interest and support.* George Rathbone, calm but indifferent, and Clifford Muspratt, tetchily critical and enthusiastic by turns, but never committed to either emotion for more than ten minutes at a time, represented the hierarchy of Liverpool business. Robert Hield, editor of the *Liverpool Courier*, often absent from the meetings, spent the time trying to pick up the threads from his previous attendance. Alec Rea, Ronald Jeans, who cared so deeply that he would turn deathly pale and inarticulate whenever a policy he believed in was under fire, and Sewell Bacon, proprietor of a fashionable store in Bold Street, from which I cajoled a magnificent set of stage draperies, velvet, thirty feet high, which we used as settings for poetic drama ...

    Battles royal took place in the Board Room every Thursday. The Directors did not select the plays; they merely vetoed them. Suggestions put forward at the behest of the Chairman were usually thought to be too advanced. Commercial plays to redress an adverse verdict at the box office were torn quietly apart by University members. The amount of tension and excitement which the meetings aroused would scarcely be credited out of their context. ❜

BASIL DEAN, 'BIRTH OF AN IDEA', *JUBILEE BROCHURE*, 11

* Charles Herbert Reilly's one complaint about Grace Wyndham Goldie's history of the theatre is that it does not give enough credit to Shute, without whom, Reilly argues, there would have been no successful theatre. 'In each financial crisis of the theatre we turned to Shute. When Dean left us and I resigned the chairmanship, he succeeded me and did things with the Bank of Liverpool that were impossible for me. How much he lent us or guaranteed us will never be known, but it ran into many thousands of pounds, all, I am happy to say, eventually to be paid back.' (Charles Herbert Reilly, *Scaffolding in the Sky*, 154)

Some early productions

❛ In spite of financial stringencies we had no reason to be ashamed of our programme for the first season. We gave plays by Sheridan ... by Galsworthy, who was represented by *Justice* ... and by Ibsen, *Pillars of Society*, in which we obtained such startling effects with our plaster background during the big storm at sea, which we had taken care to make

visible through huge windows at the back, that everybody in Liverpool wanted to see it. We did tremendous business for a fortnight. Even *Porcupine*, which had declared that "Ibsen in Liverpool was tantamount to box-office death", admitted that this was the first commercial success ever achieved by Ibsen in Liverpool. There were comedies by Bernard Shaw, Harold Brighouse and St John Hankin, also by Haddon Chambers and other dramatists not bred in the repertory stable. We also produced new plays by Charles McEvoy and Allan Monkhouse.

BASIL DEAN, 90

Plays for children

' My earliest theatrical recollection concerns Liverpool Playhouse. In my little sailor suit – I never seemed to be out of sailor suits. My father brought me to see a performance of the children's Christmas play, *Fifinella*. This was in the nature of a cultural visit for it was the first time a play had ever been written specially for children and I am glad to say the Playhouse has kept up this tradition ever since. I sat in the stalls but I can recall absolutely nothing of that show. I remember the next one vividly however. It was *Shock-Headed Peter* and I was fascinated by the scene in which the little boy is lifted up and carried away by his umbrella.

WILLARD STOKER, QUOTED IN *LIVERPOOL ECHO*, 2 NOVEMBER 1961

Fifinella by Barry Jackson and Basil Dean (December 1912) – sometimes called "Fluffy Nellie" or the "Girl who could not grow up" – included 14 scenes and a harlequinade. The whole concluded with a grand transformation scene of the salvage of St George's Hall introducing Queen Victoria and Prince Albert on a "real galloping horse". *Shock-Headed Peter* by Phillip Carr and Nigel Playfair was the theatre's third children's Christmas show in 1913 and the theatre, particularly under Armstrong, was to build a reputation for writing for children.

Local writers One of the early aims of the theatre was to discover and nurture a school of local writers to rival the Manchester school developed at The Gaiety. It was to prove to be an unfulfilled ambition for many years.

The Adder by Lascelles Abercrombie, directed by Basil Dean; March 1913

❛[This] was an event. Lascelles Abercrombie had been, for some time, a journalist in Liverpool; he was known as a poet of distinction; and he was now acting as play-reader to the theatre. Was this to be the first product of the local school of drama which was to grow up round the Repertory Theatre? The staging of a new play in blank verse was, in any case, very courageous ... Basil Dean produced the play well in dark curtains with a lurid sunset effect to give the necessary atmosphere ... the play was received as a fine and poignant piece of work ... but one that was difficult for them to accept easily since they were so unused to verse in the theatre.❜

Goldie, 82–3

The first company, from the souvenir programme for the opening

23

A success and a disaster

Hannele: *A Dream-Poem* by Gerhart Hauptmann, directed by Basil Dean; March 1913

6 I put forward ... an idea that I had cherished for some time, Hauptmann's dream play *Hannele*. This was welcomed but when the time came to approve the estimated cost there was sharp argument in the board-room ... We worked out a number of new ideas for the production, some of them I must admit distinctly "Reinhardtian". For instance, I made the figure of Death, shrouded in black gauze, stalk down the middle of the stalls and on to the stage to solemn music (composed by Arnold Clibborn, a Liverpool organist) played by an augmented orchestra. This created quite a hullabaloo among elderly ladies at matinées. There were other effects great and small, such as draped scenes of great height and ghostly lighting designed to enhance the appearance of the child Hannele as she lay in her crystal coffin ...

It was in this production that Gertrude Lawrence and Noël Coward first acted together, appearing as members of the Angelic Chorus ... Gertie was just over fourteen: "Old enough for licence," as she pertly remarked to her new playmate. She suffered her first professional heartbreak, when she discovered that her surname had been spelled with a "u" instead of a "w" in the programme. Noël was a pimply, knobbly-kneed youngster with an assured manner. 9 *

BASIL DEAN, 99–100

* Goldie notes that Coward appeared in the programme as one of the three 'Angels of Light' whereas Gertrude Lawrence had to be content with the 'slightly lower status' as one of the nine who made up the angelic chorus. See Goldie, 84

6 Its production was the most expensive, the most ambitious and most difficult yet attempted in the Repertory Theatre; and it was Basil Dean's greatest triumph as a producer in Liverpool ... It aroused great controversy, mainly between those who thought it irreverent or even blasphemous and those who felt that it was far from being any such thing. 9

GOLDIE, 84–5

George Harris

Dean had been so impressed by Max Reinhardt's London production of *Sumerun*, that he travelled to Frankfurt to meet him. Reinhardt's use of colour, light and movement were to influence the work of Dean and his designer, George Harris, who he had met during the trial season when he discovered they were missing the flower beds for a garden setting.

6 He watched me trying to arrange to flower beds he had brought with him. Then, as my language became unprintable, he added his own salty comments. Soon we began chatting, mocking the silly scenic conventions of the day; the ridiculous foliage borders looking like "washing on the

line", and the flapping landscapes at the back. Should there not be more light and air on the stage? So we tore down the backcloths and threw away the borders, mentally speaking ... And why did scenery always look so flat and dull under the electric light? New painting techniques must be thought out, said George ... for the rest of the season, and for weeks afterwards, we theorised and argued together and worked out plans ...'

BASIL DEAN, 80

' The productions of *Fifinella* and *Hannele* are chiefly memorable to me because they afforded the first opportunities to George Harris and myself of putting into practice the new stagecraft which we had previously worked out together in many a midnight conference. It was upon the success then achieved that we built up the whole of our later work in London ...'

BASIL DEAN; QUOTED IN *DAILY POST*, 11 NOVEMBER 1932.

George Harris

Fifinella was described by Goldie as the outstanding production of the season and proof that 'beauty and an effect of colour, distance and space could be simply achieved'.*

* Goldie, 82

A social centre

' The social atmosphere created by the opening festivities lingered about the theatre throughout the season. When well-known authors came to the first nights of their plays the occupants of the stalls usually wore full evening dress ... The sense of occasion was undoubtedly fostered by Reilly's foyer. At first slightly embarrassed audiences had to be encouraged to leave their seats by switching on blue signal lights at either side of the proscenium, but, eventually, the audience grew accustomed to a social habit that contributed much to the long-term success of the theatre. For many years the interval gatherings in the Playhouse foyer were to remain unique in the provinces.'

BASIL DEAN, 90–1

Dean has to go

Hannele lost nearly £800, and by the end of the 1912–13 season 'disaster was in sight. Changes would have to be made.' Difficulties had never been lacking, nor 'had the clash of strong personalities',* and, in the end, according to Goldie, Dean resigned and Professor Reilly gave up the chairmanship; Dean tells the story slightly differently.

* Goldie, 85

' I knew it was only a question of time before the axe would fall. One Thursday afternoon, after a long and solemn meeting from which I was excluded, the board gave me notice to quit at the end of the season.'

BASIL DEAN, 102

Laurence Hanray, 1913–14

❝ The one thing which seemed absolutely clear in the summer of 1913 was that the theatre could at present afford no more *Hanneles* … There was, in fact, to be, during the coming year, retrenchment and reform. And, in view of the financial position, it is not altogether surprising that, of these retrenchment seemed the most pressing need. ❞

GOLDIE, 86

After Dean's departure, Laurence Hanray, who had been a member of the company from the start and had been responsible for a number of productions in Dean's second season, took charge of productions in what Goldie describes as a transition period.

❝ In the early brochures, in which pictures of the company were printed, he can be seen with a high forehead, a sensitive mouth, a gigantic white collar, and a narrow black tie like a bootlace. He was always word perfect; his performances were always finished, always intelligent, always thorough. ❞

GOLDIE, 73

A real repertory experiment

Financial concerns threatened the theatre with closure by December 1913 and a careful season proved a failure. In response Hanray proposed a revolutionary experiment of 'real repertory'.

❝ Here was reform with vengeance. By the end of the session the theatre seemed established. Whereas in December 1913, *The Daily Dispatch* headed a column "The Liverpool Theatre. Story of a Failure"; in March 1914, the *Porcupine* was issuing a four page "Repertory Theatre Supplement" with "What it has done for our City. Its Aims; Early Struggles; and its Prosperous Present," as its headlines. ❞

GOLDIE, 90

Above: *Masks and Faces* by Tom Taylor and Charles Read, directed by Laurence Hanray; Laurence Hanray as Triplet, October 1913

❝ On Monday January 26th, the "real repertory" experiment was begun. On Monday and Tuesday the Jeans play was given; on Wednesday afternoon and evening, *Twelfth Night*; on Thursday *The Importance of Being Earnest*; on Friday *Two and Two* again; on Saturday afternoon, *Twelfth Night*; and on Saturday evening *The Importance of Being Earnest*.

The system was kept up for the remainder of the season. Normally, in any week, three or four different plays were being performed and one was in rehearsal. There were a number of drawbacks; the strain on the memories of the actors was heavy; playgoers who had not taken sufficient care to find out what was on that night might come to see *Love – and What Then* and find themselves watching *The Tragedy of Nan*; the storing of the necessary scenery caused difficulties ... Still, the system had the advantage of being extremely flexible. It was no longer necessary to drop a successful play at the end of a week; it could go on appearing in the programme as it attracted a public ... A failure could quickly be abandoned since it was no longer necessary to wait until a new play was ready to be staged; and an interesting play could be given for one or two performances a week to the three or more of another with a wider popular appeal. ❞

GOLDIE, 90–1

❝ Since Christmas [1913] the tide has suddenly turned with the Repertory Theatre, and it instantly achieved the success which it undoubtedly deserved long ago. Whether the reason for this abrupt change in public opinion is due to the lowering of the charges of admission, or to the more expert choice of plays on the part of the directors, it is impossible to say. Anyhow, at the present time, the Repertory is an emphatic success, and there is no better patronized nor more popular playhouse. The old impression of "Repertory" meaning dullness and depression has vanished into thin air, and the big audiences who flock to the theatre every evening are emphatic in their expression of cordial approval, whether the fare be sparkling, laughter-laden comedy such as *The Liars* or a passionate and moving drama such as *Nan*. ❞

PORCUPINE, 21 MARCH 1914

A local play

The Riot Act by James Sexton, directed by Laurence Hanray; March 1914

Ronald Jeans, one of the early advocates for the theatre and a director since its opening, was to be one of the theatre's success stories in encouraging local writers although rather than writing with a local voice,

27

An Enemy of the People by Ibsen, directed by Laurence Hanray; Aida Jenoure, Lawrence Hanray, A.C. Rose, George Dewhurst, Eileen Thorndike, F. Pennington-Rush, September 1913

The Liars by Henry Arthur Jones, directed by Laurence Hanray; Frank Snell, Laurence Hanray, Gertrude Sterroll, Olive Wilmot-Davies, Estelle Winwood, February 1914

Two and Two by Ronald Jeans; Estelle Winwood, Eileen Thorndike and J.H. Roberts, January 1914

The Eldest Son by John Galsworthy, directed by Laurence Hanray; Gertrude Sterroll, Eileen Thorndike, J.H. Roberts, September 1913

he went on to have a career that lasted almost 50 years as a writer of intimate revues and light comedies for West End producers including Charlot and Charles B.Cochran. At the Playhouse, 10 of his plays, many premieres, were produced, the last being *Wings Are to Fly With* in 1946 to mark the re-opening of the theatre after World War Two. Another local writer, James Sexton, created more of a stir in the city.

> The play, although in many ways crude, was highly interesting in that it was the first attempt to produce in the theatre a comment on Liverpool life written by a Liverpool author. It dealt with a strike – obviously the Liverpool strike of 1911. In this the author had acted an important part. Here were the events, negotiations and characters as he saw them. Enormous interest was aroused in the town; men outnumbered women in the audience; dockers crowded the gallery. The author was much criticised, less for the quality of his play than for the sentiments he expressed. And he held a meeting in town to defend his attitude. His most determined critics were the suffragettes. The one woman character lied, was disloyal, had a "past", made open love to her employer – and was a suffragette. Here, it was alleged, was an attack on the whole movement.
>
> GOLDIE, 92

Sexton had been the Secretary of the National Union of Dock Workers. The suffragettes were indeed critical of the production and organised a series of protests.

> Soon after the curtain rose Miss Jolley, one of the officials of the Liverpool suffragists, rose and said, "We strongly protest against the performance of this play as an outrage on the women's suffrage movement." She was carried up the stairs of the dress circle, and after making another attempt to speak, was ejected, amid the applause of the audience. A few minutes later a woman in the amphitheatre rose, repeated the protest, and threw suffragist papers over the rail. She, too, was ejected. A third woman, who rose in the dress circle and endeavoured to speak was also put out, and in all six women were ejected.
>
> THE TIMES, 23 FEBRUARY 1914

Sexton was moved to write to the *Liverpool Echo* in defence of his play when they included it in a section entitled 'the period of struggle and excitement' in reviewing Grace Wyndham Goldie's book in 1935. He was concerned that the play would appear as if it had been unpopular, whereas, he was at pains to point out, it had run for a considerable time.

The Riot Act by James Sexton; Laurence Hanray and Arthur C. Rose, February 1914

❝ Apart from the intervention of the militant suffragettes, it was well received by large audiences, including employees and employed concerned. It is true that the docker fraternity crowded the cheaper parts of the theatre, not, however, to disturb or to criticise, but to cheer, notwithstanding the fact that, while extolling their virtues, I did not by any means spare their vices, an attitude which, as a student of economic conditions and as their leader, I considered it my duty to adopt.

The other criticisms … came purely from the highbrows of the local Fabian society and the ILP … who in their ignorance of the true facts, denounced the play in the Press as a gross caricature … The "object lesson" of the play, as my old friend G. B. Shaw, described it in a letter on the opening night of the production was not confined to Liverpool but reached other towns including Blackpool and Manchester (at the Gaiety) …❞

LETTER FROM JAMES SEXTON, *LIVERPOOL ECHO*, 12 DECEMBER 1935

31

A revised version of the play was accepted by Arthur Bourchier for production at the Strand Theatre, London but Bourchier's death prevented its staging.

More disturbances

Playboy of the Western World by J. M. Synge; Abbey Theatre, November 1913

The Abbey Theatre, Dublin came to the Playhouse for a week in November 1913, performing seven plays including the first production in Liverpool of *The Playboy of the Western World*. W. B. Yeats was moved to write to *The Times* condemning what he saw as the police's suppression of the play; following disturbances on the first night, further performances were cancelled. The Abbey Theatre company, however, remained popular in Liverpool and returned in June 1914.

> At the first performance there were shouts and disturbances which prevented the play from being heard. Extra police and commissionaires were obtained. They guarded the entrances to the theatre and, inside, stood round the walls. The gallery was closed. And before the play began the audience was asked to express approval or disapproval only at the end of the act. But already in the first act there were boos, hisses and shrill whistles. During the second act there was a continual uproar ... A man in the pit stood on his seat, began to shout, and was thrown out struggling. Then another. And another. The audience hooted, clapped, hissed, caterwauled.

GOLDIE, 93

World War One and the Commonwealth

How the Theatre Was Saved by Two Women Standing Firm

'You take my life when you take the means whereby I live'*

* This quote from Shakespeare's *The Merchant of Venice* was chosen as the motto for the Commonwealth

In 1914, Madge McIntosh was engaged by the theatre as the new producer; she was an actress who had performed and produced with Alfred Wareing in Glasgow and her appointment coincided with the declaration of war, raising the question of what was to be done with the theatre.

The theatre saved

Every argument seemed in favour of closing it altogether. With every circumstance in its favour, it had only just begun to pay. Under war conditions, with audiences almost certainly reduced it would surely fail. And could the directors feel themselves justified, even, in putting money and energy into a theatre when money and energy might be so much more urgently needed elsewhere? No one knew what conditions in the country generally and in Liverpool would be like in a few months time. There might soon be no directors left to direct and no actors to act. It seemed folly at best, and, at worst unpatriotic for the directors to commit themselves at such a moment to an undertaking which would almost certainly be disastrous.

Arrangements had been made and contracts entered into for the autumn season. But surely war cancelled all contracts? Everyone said so ... So Madge McIntosh, in the empty theatre in August, was preparing an inventory of properties and scenery before packing up to go back to London when an attractive young woman burst into her room. She was a complete stranger. She said, "I'm Estelle Winwood. We can't let the theatre shut." Madge McIntosh looked at her for a moment, and then said, "Have you got any money?" "Not a halfpenny," said Estelle. She asked if

Above: Madge McIntosh

33

Madge McIntosh would stay on and run the theatre if they could keep it going. Madge McIntosh said she would. "I'll come back with a scheme," said Estelle and went off.'

GOLDIE, 94–6

* 'Actors' Commonwealth: A Woman's Clever Brains in War Time', *Daily News and Leader*, 6 May 1915

The scheme she came back with (described by the London press as 'probably unique in the history of the modern stage'*) was drawn up in consultation with Ronald Jeans and the Chairman of the Board and the theatre became a Commonwealth for the next two years. It was run on the lines outlined in a short history produced at the time.

' A successful repertory season, managed and financed on the profit-sharing principle by the artistes and staff of a theatre, is a unique event in modern theatrical history ...

A History of The Liverpool Repertory Theatre Artistes' and Staff's Commonwealth, September 1914 to April 1915

The Commonwealth System

Briefly, the scheme was as follows: That the actors, actresses, attendants, stage staff, orchestra – in fact everyone usually employed in the theatre – should form themselves into a Commonwealth, with Miss McIntosh at the head as producer, and Mr Pigott as business manager.

A minimum living wage was fixed for everyone employed in the theatre, and the Commonwealth reserved to themselves the right of closing

Higgledy Piggledy by Ronald Jeans, directed by Madge McIntosh with the assistance of Ronald Jeans; December 1915 The company on stage playing members of the audience in front of a painted backcloth of the auditorium; it includes Estelle Winwood, Eileen Thorndike, Wilfred Shine, Percy Marmont and William Armstrong as the 'lady' fourth from the right

down should the receipt fail to provide for the payment of the minimum. Salaries were, in any case, to be limited to half the normal, the balance being put aside until the end of the season. The Directors also shared in the Commonwealth, limiting their share in the weekly receipts to an amount sufficient to cover standing charges.

In short, the whole proposition was an offer from the artistes and the staff to shoulder all responsibility, and to carry on, so long as the receipts offered a living wage. In return they asked for no profit, but the chance of earning their normal wage.

Actuated by this new spirit of loyalty and willingness which springs up like magic in a theatre, when each member is his own employer, the Commonwealth started operations on the 19th September, 1914, and the Liverpool public immediately accorded the venture whole-hearted support. Except for a short interval at Christmas when a pre-arranged independent production was staged, the Commonwealth has run on uninterruptedly... The enterprise has been justified by the financial result, for not only has the Company succeeded in paying the weekly sum to the Directors, but the members have been able to draw full normal salaries for the entire period, and hand the Theatre several hundred pounds profit. Needless to say the Commonwealth will start another year's season in Liverpool next autumn. ❜

MADGE MCINTOSH: *A RECORD OF THE LIVERPOOL REPERTORY THEATRE ARTISTE'S AND STAFF'S COMMONWEALTH SEASON, SEPTEMBER–DECEMBER 1914*

❛ The public always admires pluck; and when the Commonwealth entered upon its "great adventure", the Repertory Theatre was crowded to its utmost capacity. ❜

DAILY NEWS AND LEADER, 6 MAY 1915

Hello Repertory by Ronald Jeans, directed by Madge McIntosh; William Armstrong and Estelle Winwood, March 1915

The first Commonwealth season opened on 19 September 1914 with the following verses by John Masefield recited by Madge McIntosh from the stage.

Friends, we are opening at this solemn time
Because, as we believe the stage reveals
Not simply play, but all that is sublime,
Living, and wise in what the nation feels.

Because (as we believe) a nation needs
A temper and support in times of strain,
Beauty for solace when the spirit bleeds,
Laughter for respite to the weary brain.

Because, like you, we wish to play a part
In helping England in the months of stress
To bear the battle with a steady heart,
And by our effort make her troubles less

The spirit of the Commonwealth

For the next two years, the theatre was dominated by the personalities of Madge McIntosh and Estelle Winwood, who managed to deal with all the problems that arose, including opposition from trade unions objecting to the possible minimum wages for their members.

6 When I found myself ... faced with the problem of directing the Commonwealth season, I felt strangely pessimistic as to its ultimate result. Common belief has it that in the routine of theatrical undertakings, self and self only predominates, and that the average actor or actress lives only for self-advancement. The unique success of our season proves the injustice of such a belief, for we could never have brought this, our "great adventure" to so triumphant an issue had it not been for the loyalty and devotion, the total lack of personal aims, of every individual member of company, staff, and orchestra, towards this our Commonwealth. We have been able, thanks to such loyalty, to fill our theatre in these dark days, to keep many people employed, and also to further the advance of the Repertory movement. Mr Granville Barker, who paid us an informal visit in October, was amazed at the overflowing audience, and informed me that we were doing much better business than the majority of London theatres. 9

MADGE MCINTOSH: *A RECORD OF THE LIVERPOOL REPERTORY THEATRE ARTISTES' AND STAFF'S COMMONWEALTH SEASON, SEPTEMBER–DECEMBER 1914*

Liverpool in London

In the late spring of 1915, the theatre was invited to perform a season at the Kingsway Theatre. The visit received a great deal of attention in the press. Undoubtedly the highlight of their season was the premiere of a new play by John Galsworthy.

> It was to have been called *The Full Moon* but this title had already been appropriated so it was re-named, for the worse, *A Bit o' Love*. John Galsworthy, always a most loyal friend of the Liverpool Repertory Theatre, had conducted in Liverpool the rehearsals for *The Fugitive*. He had been impressed by the work of the company, particularly by William Armstrong's acting as Malaise. And he considered allowing the Liverpool Company the production of a new play. He wrote to Madge McIntosh, "Before sending you two new plays I'd like to know two things (1) When have you a date on which you could produce it in Liverpool? (2) What is this scheme for doing a London season of which I've not heard anything? And would Mr Armstrong be with you for it? He is one of the factors that tempts me to send you the longer of the two plays." William Armstrong was eventually cast for the main part of the passionate St. Francis of a clergyman: Madge McIntosh for the wife. They rehearsed their love scenes together at ten o'clock in the morning under the eye of the author in the bar of the Kingsway Theatre ...

GOLDIE, 109–10

Revues

> These revues were the most original productions of the Commonwealth.

GOLDIE, 110

Hello Repertory by Ronald Jeans, music by Laurence Hanray, directed Madge McIntosh, with assistance from Ronald Jeans; April 1915

> Revues of any kind were still rarities. People were still not sure what the word meant. At the Liverpool Empire there had been a sequence of shows, largely spectacle and ballet with a few turns thrown in, which were regarded as revues. Ronald Jeans had watched entertainments of this type ... he thought it would be amusing to write for the repertory theatre a burlesque revue with local flavour ... Audiences were delighted to find that "repertorists" had a sense of humour and could laugh at themselves. And it was amusing to see the familiar members of the company singing and dancing and generally being unexpected. The revue opened with a meeting of the Board of Directors with Harvey Adams representing Professor Wily, William Armstrong as Mr Edify Godwards and Percy Marmont as Mr Thomas Edouin. Arthur Rose, smoking a large cigar and looking like

a Dame in a Pantomime, appeared as Miss A. B. C. D. E. F. Hornblower of the Graveity theatre, Manchester. There was a scene in the entrance hall of the "Middling Wealthy Hotel". This opened with a chorus of charwomen who were scrubbing with their backs to the audience when the curtain went up. Madge McIntosh played Madge Actintosh and Wilfred Shine, admirably made up, was W. W. Kelly, the "Father of the Repertory Movement". There was an amusing burlesque of the Abbey Players with Madge McIntosh as an old Irish woman rocking herself besides her pot and chanting "All Hail, Thane of Cawdor, Ancestor of Harry Lauder" … and there was William Armstrong as an American singer of ragtime songs … The revue was local, intimate and personal.❜

GOLDIE, 104–6

The success of the first revue led to a second for Christmas 1915, *Higgledy Piggledy*. Also by Ronald Jeans, it ended with the company sitting in the front row of the stalls as well known members of the first night audience in front of a backdrop representing the auditorium of the theatre with the effect of the audience looking into a mirror and seeing itself.

The end of the Commonwealth

❛ Although at the end of the Commonwealth's second year the theatre's profits were much greater, nothing had been quite the same. The programme had … been less distinguished. Difficulties had increased. The gloom of a second year of war had settled on the country. The possibility of air-raids kept people at home. Lighting restrictions made night journeys so difficult that for a time the experiment was tried of starting the evening performance at 6.30. Percy Marmont, one of the company's greatest assets, had gone to America. Estelle Winwood … had accepted an offer from Cochran in the spring of 1917. The hard work had had its effect on the producer and on many of the company. The early zeal and the early enthusiasm were waning. Audiences were falling off. And the directors were anxious to re-gain full control of the theatre's policy. So the Commonwealth came to an end. To the courage and enterprise of its founders the Repertory Theatre owes a debt of gratitude … and to them it probably owes its continued existence. For had the theatre closed in 1914 it is doubtful it would ever have opened again.❜

GOLDIE, 111

William Armstrong, 1922–1944

Between 1916 and 1921, the war and its aftermath left the Playhouse with an unsettled existence. A series of producers including Bridges Adams and his wife Muriel Pratt, George Bellamy (for only a few weeks in 1917), Percy Foster (who left to go to war), Lane Bayliff, Gideon Warren, Howard Leslie and Jackson Wilcox passed through its doors. The war also meant an abandonment of some key precepts of the repertory movement with the theatre resorting to long runs; in the 1919–20 season W.W.Jacobs and Louis N.Parker's *Beauty and the Barge* ran for two months and W.J.Locke's *The Beloved Vagabond* for seven weeks. For one heady year (1921–22), Nigel Playfair, who was making his mark as a successful producer in London, took charge promising a return to the original repertory ideals and a Shakespeare season. But, because of his continued London interests, he was a largely absent director (leaving Stanley Drewitt in charge in Liverpool) and left the theatre with a £4000 deficit. Overall, the theatre 'had not yet found a settled way of existence'.* The arrival of William Armstrong in 1922 was to change that.

* Goldie, 112

William Armstrong

❝ One of the most beloved figures in the English theatre … He was mocked, imitated, and adored. At the end of a scene in rehearsal, his voice could be heard from the back of the stalls saying, "Oh! It's so beautiful! So moving!" ❞

MICHAEL REDGRAVE, 84

❝ Dear William. Tall – with a bald, high-domed forehead; heavily built and round shouldered with kind, large, rather protuberant blue eyes … What was the secret of his astonishing success as Producer of the Liverpool Playhouse? I can say in a word – his whimsical and subtly malicious humour. It was a humour that actors relish. It had a tang to it. He was no daring innovator. He had a Board of Directors to placate … And yet nothing trivial came from William Armstrong. No matter how hackneyed the play there was some original twist that was his and his alone.'

A.W.S. (ALFRED SAMPSTER), A TYPESCRIPT WRITTEN AFTER A MEMORIAL SERVICE FOR ARMSTRONG

Problems in finding the right plays

'There had been, it was true, no Shakespeare, no Sheridan, no Ibsen, no Chekhov. But a selection of some of the best works of contemporary English dramatists had been well produced and well-acted. This was not, perhaps, all that some of the theatre's founders had hoped for.'

GOLDIE, 142–3, TALKING ABOUT THE FIRST THREE SEASONS

'The Playhouse has always been more successful in its discovery of new acting talent than in the new dramatists it has encouraged. In my day this was due to the weakness of our finances and to the fact that there were too many people to pass judgement on the manuscripts.'

BASIL DEAN; QUOTED IN *DAILY POST*, 11 NOVEMBER 1932

A number of factors conspired to shape the choices of plays Armstrong could make, including the 'taste of the audience' who, he claimed frequently, were apathetic about a play they knew nothing about.

'We all want to progress in this theatre but we shall never do as much as we should like until we can get people to come to every play. A great number who pride themselves on being Playhouse supporters and say they never miss a play, have no shame whatever in cancelling their seats if a play has not had a very good Press, or is said to be serious or gloomy. We have an extraordinarily loyal upper circle and gallery and pit, but the frequenters of the stalls are not so loyal.'

WILLIAM ARMSTRONG; QUOTED IN *POST AND MERCURY*, 29 NOVEMBER 1930

Changes in playwriting also had an impact on the plays on offer.

'The type of play being written most generally by English authors had been changing for some time past. This change was now clearly reflected in the theatre's programmes. Repertory theatre had been associated in many minds with "repertory plays". For some people this meant plays of exceptional interest, others regarded the name as a synonym for dreariness. But, however interpreted, the term had now become almost meaningless. There was no longer any considerable output of "intellectual" plays of the pre-war type. Back kitchen realism seemed out of date. The standards of the London theatre had altered and numbers of plays which had once have been thought only suitable for repertory were seized upon by London managers. And the new young authors whom repertory had hoped to encourage now needed very little encouragement from anybody. Youth was an asset not a hindrance, in the post-war world. Its typical product, the brilliant, brittle comedies of disillusion, were enormously successful on repertory, as well as London, stages. The distinction between London and repertory plays almost disappeared.

GOLDIE, 160

Hit by the depression

At the same time, external factors intervened, particularly during the 1930s when the depression hit Liverpool very hard; unemployment remained twice the national average throughout the decade and, in consequence, Liverpool was a 'stricken city' with 'boarded-up shops and empty offices' reduced to 'a point of impoverishment' almost unbelievable when compared to pre-war conditions.*

* John Belchem, 39

It has not been an easy season ... because we have had to contend with a great many external conditions beyond our control. The trade slump, for example, is a factor from which we suffer in common with everybody else. Many of our former stalls patrons are now found in the upper circle through shrunken financial resources. It is too early, of course, to say how we shall come out of the season's ordeal in a money sense. At the moment it looks as if we shall find, on the final balance of accounts, that we have at least paid our way. In itself this is something gratifying and notable when one considers the large number of theatres up and down the country which have had to close during the past year due to lack of support. Comedies, of course, are always the most popular and in great demand.

WILLIAM ARMSTRONG, QUOTED IN *LIVERPOOL ECHO*, 14 JUNE 1933

Children's plays

It appears to be a matter of some courage to produce a new play for children. The old classics are dished up again and again; not only because children are innately conservative, but because there will always be a few new ones to come and see them ... It has always been the enlightened policy of the Liverpool Playhouse to produce a new children's play each Christmas – a policy which has already added several novelties to the London programmes.

MANCHESTER GUARDIAN, 27 DECEMBER 1933

While Christmas performances of fairy tales for children became common from the mid-nineteenth century, it was only with the advent of J. M. Barrie's *Peter Pan* in 1904 that other kinds of theatre for children was more generally developed. The Playhouse had made a point of staging

A Hundred Years Old by Quintero Brothers, directed Charles Thomas; Michael Redgrave, in middle, with Lloyd Pearson and Jane Baxter, November 1935

shows for children from its earliest days, often commissioning new work. The production which became a 'signature' for the theatre was Kenneth Grahame's *Toad of Toad Hall* as adapted by A. A. Milne, first produced in December 1929. Later audiences had their chance to see the play, which was revived in 1947 (directed by John Fernald), in 1958 (directed by Willard Stoker), for the Golden Jubilee (directed by William Gaunt) and in 1996 (directed by Richard Williams). Other newly commissioned works included:

1922:	Thackeray (adapted Harris Deans): *The Rose and the Ring*
1923:	Harris Deans: *The Magic Sword*
1924:	A. P. Herbert and William Armstrong: *The King of the Castle*
1931:	Vera Beringer and Enid Bagnold: *Alice and Thomas and Jane*
1932:	G. F. Bradby (adapted Vera Beringer): *What Happened to George*
1933:	Philip Johnson and Howard Agg: *Fun While It Lasts*
1934:	Alec Atkinson: *Ferry Inn*: an adventure in three acts
1935:	Michael Redgrave: *Circus Boy*
1936:	James Laver: *The House That Went to Sea*

1937:   Vera Beringer: *It Might Happen to You*
1938:   Gwendolen Seiler: *The Princess and Mr Parker*

New plays

The theatre did manage to produce a number of new works, including three premieres of plays by J.B.Priestley (*The Roundabout* in 1932; *Duet in Floodlight* in 1935; *The Bad Samaritan* in 1937). In particular, Armstrong was known for promoting new writing through his consistent staging of one-act plays which preceded the main show.

Circus Boy by Michael Redgrave, December 1935. Michael Redgrave appeared in the play as a BBC Official and also wrote *The Seventh Man*, a one act play based on the story of the same name by 'Q' which was performed in May 1935

> ❝ The theatre ... has pursued a definite policy of producing one act plays, thereby giving many a new young author his first audience. ❞
>
> THE PLAYHOUSE 1911–1932; A BROCHURE FOR THE 21ST BIRTHDAY

One of the beneficiaries of this policy was Philip Johnson, from Macclesfield, who was a prolific writer of, mostly, one act plays many of which premiered at the Playhouse.

Afternoon (one act; February 1928)
The Good and the Bad (one act; January 1929)
Derelict (one act; April 1930)
Out She Goes (November 1930)
Queer Cattle (March 1931)
Sad About Europe (November 1931)
Shame the Devil (one act; December 1931)
Send Her Victorious (November 1932)
To-Day of All Days (one act; March 1933)
(with Howard Agg) *Fun While It Lasts* (December 1933)
Lovers Leap (June 1934)
Heaven on Earth (December 1934)
Lovely to Look At (September 1937)
It's Autumn Now (December 1937)

A premiere – and a trip to London

Inheritors by Susan Glaspell, directed by William Armstrong; September 1925

> ❝ So great was the impression made in Liverpool by the play ... that it was decided to try an experiment which had not been attempted since the Commonwealth days. The Everyman Theatre in Hampstead was to be taken for three weeks ... The visit would clearly be a risk. Hampstead was not a very satisfactory place for the experiment. It was a long way from the centre of London ... From the point of view of reputation they would be seen in a courageous experimental work of the type that was associated in people's minds with repertory ... "The big event of the week is the visit of the Liverpool Repertory Company," said the *Sunday Herald*. And the London press in general from the *Times* and the *Morning Post* to the *Field* and *Reynold's News* treated the event as an important theatrical occasion. In Liverpool the company's adventure was watched with something of the affectionate interest of a town for is favourite football team and the Liverpool papers, under the heading "Liverpool Players go to Town, What

London Thinks of the Repertory Company", printed excerpts from the London notices ...'

GOLDIE, 150–2

This was a European premiere, and the Playhouse managed a world premiere of Susan Glaspell's *Alison's House* in November 1930, only 'beating' the New York premiere by a matter of weeks but they were still congratulated by the *Manchester Guardian* on their courage 'and on the success which has rewarded its courage – in handling so fragile a matter' (*Manchester Guardian*, 6 November 1930).

Special matinées

'There is a smaller, more highly intelligent public which demands the experimental type of play. If there is a piece possessing a limited appeal it is staged for special matinees and put it into the evening bill if we find people want to see it.'

WILLIAM ARMSTRONG, QUOTED IN *SUNDAY TIMES*, 30 OCTOBER 1932

Uncle Vanya by Chekhov, directed by Wyndham Goldie; with Pauline Lacey as Marya Vassilyvena Voynitsky and William Armstrong as son, Ivan; June 1930

'Completely in the repertory tradition the theatre decided to celebrate Ibsen's centenary year with two special matinees of *Ghosts* ... Surely the repertory could not neglect the playwright who had been more than any other the inspiration of the repertory movement? But it was felt that a fortnight of Ibsen would be too great a risk. It was disappointing, after seventeen years of existence, that the repertory theatre should still be unable to stage Ibsen without any likelihood of financial success. But Ibsen was less fashionable among the intellectuals now than he had been in 1911. And although his plays would be welcomed, no doubt, by a small, faithful coterie, yet, on the whole, the "advanced" section of the audience was now hankering after the strange new gods of Expressionism rather than demanding Ibsen and Brieux. If Ibsen, then, could not be put on for a fortnight's run why not give a single performance in honour of the centenary without interfering with the regular programme? ... It was decided to give *Ghosts* on two successive Wednesday afternoons ... the producer, in addition to all his usual work and the special effort of this performance, undertook also the part of Oswald.'

GOLDIE, 161–3

The experiment, directed by Wyndham Goldie, was a success, and other special matinées were attempted, including:

Uncle Vanya by Chekhov (directed by Wyndham Goldie; June 1930)

This was not the first time Liverpool had a chance to encounter Chekhov (Armstrong had included three one act plays in earlier years: *The Proposal* in February 1924, *The Swan Song* in March 1926 and *The Bear* in November 1927), but it was the first of his full-length plays undertaken by the Playhouse.

The House into Which I was Born by Jacques Copeau (directed by Wyndham Goldie; June 1932)

This was a world premiere of the only play written by Copeau and the theatre's courage in staging this 'unusual and profound' work was praised by the *Manchester Guardian* (16 June 1932)

> ❛I tried to give Liverpool plays which it would not have seen except for our existence. We tried to break away from the plays done by the ordinary touring companies.❜
>
> WILLIAM ARMSTRONG, QUOTED IN *MANCHESTER GUARDIAN*, 10 SEPTEMBER 1936

Coming of age: 11 November 1932

For the theatre's twenty-first birthday, the Playhouse chose premieres of Allan Monkhouse's *Cecilia* and Philip Johnson's one-act *Send Her Victorious*, two plays by local authors. On the gala night itself they added scenes from *Twelfth Night* with Armstrong as Orsino.

For the Twenty-first Anniversary of the founding of The Liverpool Repertory Theatre

John Drinkwater

Here, in this port of ships, we built a stage,
Where the crusaders of the sea should find,
Their travels done, another pilgrimage
Calling them as crusaders of the mind;
We built a stage, that thereon should be told
All arguments that ever went to school –
We sheltered beauty, crying in the cold –
We built another port of Liverpool

We are of age to-day. We thank you, friends,
Who kept with us the hard, the happy time;
We have dreamt dreams, found vision, heard the ends
Of wisdom manifested in a rhyme;
Together we have learned that all things may
Be fathomed in the splendour of a Play.

‘ Although the Playhouse has succeeded in reaching its Twenty-First birthday, it has always been more or less dependent on its Box Office, and in consequence the Directors have been unable to adventure as much as they would have liked into the realm of plays with frankly limited appeal. It has nevertheless produced several hundred plays, many of them for the first time on any stage, and the greater percentage of them for the first time in Liverpool …’

THE PLAYHOUSE 1911–1932; A BROCHURE FOR THE 21ST BIRTHDAY

The Playhouse Company on the radio

‘ The Playhouse Company was the first repertory company to broadcast a play in the North. This was in 1925 when we did Brighouse's *Lonesome-Like* with Herbert Lomas in his original part of Sam Horrocks. In 1926 several members of the company, myself included, did a radio version of *Peer Gynt* and a year later a broadcast was given of *Faust* … Other broadcasts have been *Everyman*, *The Interlude of Youth* and an act of *Gallows Glorious*, Priestley's *Cornelius* and the Cathedral Scene from *Saint Joan*. In 1926–7 we broadcast from the now extinct Liverpool Station, where, in those days, the producer, the players, the orchestra, the crowd and the sound effects were all in one small studio. Elsie Schauffler's *Parnell*, which we are broadcasting on Wednesday, has caused considerable controversy owing to the author's modification of the historic facts.’

WILLIAM ARMSTRONG, *RADIO TIMES*, 17 JUNE 1938

Jubilee Picture; Front row: (l–r) Sir John Shute; Maud Carpenter, Mrs Denton, Lady Mayoress, Mrs Edwin Thomson, Lord Derby (holding paper); in the middle of the picture is Denton, the Lord Mayor. Behind him is Sir Charles Reilly who is half obscuring William Rushworth. In the back row to the far right are Henry Cohen and William Armstrong; 23 November 1936

The play had been performed at the Playhouse in April 1937, its first production out of London where it had premiered in 1936. For the radio broadcast in June 1938, Armstrong played Parnell.

William Armstrong in Rehearsal 1

❛ I sat alone in a sea of ghostly white-covered seats. The darkened stage, empty but for a couple of packing cases, faced me. I was the solitary, privileged "audience" at a rehearsal of a Playhouse production.

Mr Armstrong, the producer, who is also taking a prominent part in the new play, strolled on to the stage and examined a broken window forming part of the set, which I took to be the room of a dilapidated cottage. Mr Hammond joined him and they discussed it together. "There won't be any glass in it, do you think?" said Mr Armstrong. "How near the front line is it supposed to be?" asked Mr Hammond.

William Armstrong and Wyndham Goldie

*Midsummer
Night's Dream* by
Shakespeare, directed
by William Arnold;
with Robert Donat
and Diana Wynyard;
December 1927

Two more people were called, and the window was pulled to pieces, verbally and actually.

Attention was next turned to the door. "I don't quite like that door, do you?" asked Mr Armstrong. "It looks too much like a room door." "We have a canvas one," said the stage carpenter. "What do you think about trying the canvas one?" said Mr Armstrong. "I think we might try it, don't you, Arthur?"

It was decided to try it.

The lighting then came in for criticism and Mr Armstrong moved to the front of the house. A hidden electrician was asked to put out the "house" lights, and the cleaners in the circle were plunged into darkness. When the blue light was dimmed sufficiently the efforts of Mr "Noises Off" were rehearsed. At last the effect of distant gun fire was obtained and I decided it was somewhere in France.

"Well, we'll make a start," said Mr Armstrong, "but I don't know my lines."

Someone wearing plus four drifted on to the stage and I recognised Mr Williams. He yawned and sat down on one of the boxes.

"Have we got the straw?" said Mr Armstrong.

"It would make rather a mess," said someone. "What about a carpet for now?"

"We must have something," said Mr Armstrong. "I don't want Williams to spoil his beautiful plus fours."

A carpet was produced, the plus fours saved, and the rehearsal began. Mr Armstrong did not know his lines.'

THE PLAYHOUSE AT WORK (1925): E.L.H.

William Armstrong in Rehearsal 2

A description of William Armstrong in rehearsal in 1924 through the eyes of a young dramatist

'For five hours they had been hard at it, yet he was vivacious beyond words. He talked like this: "No, no; you'll kill it if you do it so slowly. That fireplace must come down stage, it is chasing everybody up. No, no; you would have the chloroform ready on the handkerchief, wouldn't you? Don't worry, Constance. Call Tom! Tom! Be quick on that. Again please!

You *are* going to step across there, aren't you? That knitting, you must have it on the left or he'll sit on it. Not so far across, Muriel, a wee step less. Take his arm, but I don't want you to feel as if you are eloping with him.

Oh, I think we must have another line there. "Let's go" would do. Try that chair. No, I can't see you. That gramophone is distracting; try a fibre

Youth at the Helm
by Hubert Griffiths,
directed by William
Armstrong; Michael
Redgrave as Randolph
Warrender, Rachel
Kempson as Yvonne
and Lloyd Pearson
as Chairman of
the London and
Metropolitan Bank;
August 1935

needle and close the lid. That bell is just too late. No, you must be on the other side, Clarky. What's the matter? Why are you laughing? Cheer up, Tiny.

Just a little moment of feeling there – on the word *life*. Try taking the hand at the end of the sentence. No that won't do. Can't we have the curtain on *that* line and transpose it somehow? No? A pity. Thank you all for a good day's work. Dear me I feel half asleep."

GOLDIE, 205–6

William Armstrong resigns

6 He had a wonderful flair not only for choosing a play but also for choosing people, and a still greater flair for getting the best from them once he got them into the company.9

EDWIN THOMPSON; QUOTED IN *DAILY POST*, 24 OCTOBER 1944

6 Although Armstrong was not the creator of the Liverpool Playhouse he took it over when it was not prospering ... As he ran a self-supporting theatre he rarely attempted innovations which might be disastrous, so the Playhouse sometimes seemed less enterprising than, say, the Birmingham

Repertory Theatre, but Armstrong was working to a policy designed to keep a good regular theatre alive in Liverpool with the best plays that could be found, mainly after first productions in London.'

MANCHESTER GUARDIAN, 6 OCTOBER 1952: AN OBITUARY FOR ARMSTRONG

1931   All, except two plays, were directed by William Armstrong.

22/1	*The New Hangman,* Laurence Housman
	The Constant Wife, W. Somerset Maugham
11/2	*The Forest,* John Galsworthy
5/3	*The Fascinating Foundling,* G. B. Shaw
	Queer Cattle, Philip Johnson
24/3	*The Five Leverets,* Griffiths Humphreys
	Count Albany, Donald Carswell
14/4	*Mademoiselle Diana,* John Pollock (one act)
	Art and Opportunity, Harold Chapin
6/5	*Chee-Chee,* Luigi Pirandello, directed by Wyndham Goldie
	The Circle, W. Somerset Maugham
27/5	*Brains and Brass,* Anthony Armstrong
10/6	*The Anniversary,* Anton Chekhov, directed by Wyndham Goldie
	The Man with a Load of Mischief, Ashley Dukes
3/9	*Screening the Screen Scene,* Margaret Drew (one act)
	The Swan, Franz Molnar
23/9	*Rizzio's Boots,* Hal D. Stewart (one act)
	The World of Light, Aldous Huxley
9/10	*The Road of Poplars,* Vernon Sylvaine (one act)
	See Naples and Die, Elmer Rice
4/11	*Strife,* John Galsworthy
	The Twelve Pound Look, J. M. Barrie
25/11	*Sad About Europe,* Philip Johnson (one act)
	By Candle Light, Captain Harry Graham
26/12	*Something to Talk About,* Eden Phillpotts
	Shame the Devil, Philip Johnson (one act)
	March Hares, H. W. Gribble
	Alice and Thomas and Jane, Vera Beringer and Enid Bagnold (matinées)

Maud Carpenter

❛ No one person can make a theatre. The vital thing is teamwork – from the callboys and cleaners upwards. ❜

MAUD CARPENTER, QUOTED IN *DAILY POST*, 9 JULY 1962

❛ The Maud Carpenter story is the whole story of the Playhouse and it is also a considerable part of the story of Liverpool. ❜

SIR CHARLES TRUSTAM, CHAIR OF THE BOARD, SPEECH ON THE OCCASION OF
MAUD CARPENTER'S RETIREMENT; QUOTED IN *DAILY POST*, 9 JULY 1962

Maud Carpenter started work at the theatre during the Experimental season in 1911, becoming a junior box office assistant when the theatre opened. After five years as assistant manager, in 1923 she became manager and licensee and in 1945 was the first woman to join the Board. She remained at the theatre until 1962 and was vice-president to the Board until her death in 1967.

❛ To each of us Maud meant something special … She had a gracious dignity crowned by good looks and in my youthful innocence based on William Armstrong's affectionate way of addressing her I assumed they were at least engaged if not married … The actors and actresses she regarded as her children, many of them somewhat wayward ones. The staff were her members of the household over which she presided. Together they existed to look after the audiences and it was to their service that her real life was dedicated. Everything about our theatre, its productions and its operation must be for their good and their comfort … She was critical of all inefficiency and bad work … Her stand against much modern play-writing was strong in that she could see no point in bad language, immorality or irreligion for its own sake. ❜

JAMES RUSHWORTH, IN MEMORIAM, 22 JUNE 1967

❛ She was often brutally frank, but only if the occasion demanded it, and I doubt if she ever made an enemy. ❜

LORD COHEN, MEMBER OF BOARD FOR THIRTY YEARS, CHAIR FROM 1948 TO 1963; QUOTED IN *DAILY POST*, 19 JUNE 1967

‘ I think the great thing about her was her astonishing grasp of the importance of the theatre's relationship with its audience. She had such a remarkable warmth for the audience, and seemed to know them all by name or if not by name, by sight. I don't think any other manager of a theatre has had this personal quality to link herself so strikingly and with such affection to a theatre. I think we probably disagreed with each other quite possibly more often than we agreed with each other, and yet we had a very strong mutual respect …’

JOHN FERNALD; QUOTED IN *DAILY POST*, 19 JUNE 1967

‘ William was greatly helped in the Playhouse by his co-partner, Maud Carpenter. A shy bachelor himself, he was "Mother's boy" to her, and he cuddled in to her warm and generous personality. Maud – a Lancashire lass – with lovely Vandyke hands and a flair for management. Soon the business of the theatre was in those hands and "William and Maud" ran the theatre. It was, in those nineteen thirties, a perfect combination.’

MEMORIAL SERVICE BY A.W.S. (ALFRED SAMPSTER),
A TYPESCRIPT WRITTEN AFTER A MEMORIAL SERVICE FOR ARMSTRONG.

‘ No matter how good you were … you still almost genuflected when you passed Maud. She had this curious effect upon people, no matter who you were: Lord Mayors, they came and went, but Maud Carpenter was still, as somebody once said, "the unofficial Lady Mayoress of Liverpool". And she had a terrific influence upon everybody … she thought she was a theatre manager, which she was, although she didn't really know anything about theatre, curiously enough. She used to make all sorts of mistakes like she couldn't remember titles of plays. She'd always get mixed up somewhere or other and she'd pronounce them wrongly. In fact, so much of this went on they became known as "Maudisms" … the sets had to be nice and the costumes had to be nice, otherwise Maud would have something to say in that curious way … She ruled them, Lord Cohen even was scared of Maud at times. They all were … Maud was exactly what Lillian Bayliss was to the Old Vic. Just like that. A dedication to the theatre which meant the Playhouse came before everything with Maud.’

RONALD SETTLE, QUOTED IN *MCMAHON*, 30–1

Ronald Settle was asked to write a biography of Maud after her death but it was never finished.

❛ She always sat every three weeks at the back of the Stalls, to watch the new production, and she came round afterwards with her choice comments … we were doing Ibsen's *The Doll's House* and the final thing in the play is where Nora is leaving her husband and she walks out and you hear the front door slam, and the tabs come down. She came backstage and said, "Very nice, Eileen [Herlie], very nice indeed, but you know, as soon as I heard that door slam I knew I'd seen it before."❜

HAROLD GOODWIN, QUOTED IN MCMAHON, 29

❛ The Playhouse had a Matriarch Manager who knew very little about theatre but could read a play list and say, 'they'll come to that, they won't come to that, they'll hate that' etc. It's a gift of sorts but it meant she only ever wanted to do what 'they'd come to'. She was also credited with an exact knowledge of the social standing of every patron and this could be seen – almost like a comic turn – every night of the week as she greeted them in the foyer, running from a neat curtsey and full title for the very important down to a bleak, wordless crease of the lips to those she considered fit only for the gallery. At some point she had been made a member of the Board. The result was that, from then on, after every Board meeting, the other members (all male) would secretly sneak off to the bar at the Adelphi Hotel to discuss the things they didn't want her to know.

Maud's instinct sometimes memorably let her down. John Fernald wanted to do *The Seagull*. Maud thought it was a nice title. Mythology has it that it was a memorable production. It also emptied the theatre. A year or so later John did a children's Christmas show called *The Silver Curlew*. Maud had no objections – it sounded nice. A few days before it opened she said to John, 'What's a Kaloo?' 'It's Curlew, Maud,' he replied. 'It's a bird.' Maud looked stunned. 'If I'd known it was one of those bird plays we'd never have been doing it,' she said.❜

ANTONY TUCKEY, ARTISTIC DIRECTOR

1911

War and the Old Vic

When war broke out, the Playhouse had just opened its season with Cecil Roberts' aptly named *Spears Against Us*, which closed after four performances. They reopened in late September, starting shows at 6.30, and for a season struggled on presenting plays that were necessarily of a 'lighter nature than usual'. Business was not good, however, and at the end of the season, the blackouts and a wave of sickness, 'which seemed to have made Liverpool one gigantic nursing home', closed the theatre with a loss.* May 1941 saw seven nights of intensive bombing that devastated many Liverpool landmarks; bombings led to in excess of 4,000 fatalities during the war.

* Daily Post, 16 November 1939

The theatre remained closed until 1942, when the Old Vic, who had been bombed out of their London home and had already transferred its headquarters to Burnley, took it on as their temporary home.

A.R.P.

❛ Should an Air Raid Warning be given during the performance the audience will be notified from the Stage. Members of the audience will then have the opportunity of either remaining in their seats or taking advantage of the Air Raid Shelter in Messers. George Henry Lee's basement … the entrance is opposite the Stage Door of the Theatre. The Directors of The Playhouse wish to express their appreciation of Messers. G. H. Lee's generous help in this matter. When the "All Clear" Signal is given and the audience again seated then the performance will be resumed. ❜

Notice in wartime programmes

The Old Vic at the Playhouse

❛ When the second World War brought heavy bombing to Merseyside, the Directors deemed it wise to close the Theatre, but having withstood raids, in 1942 it was re-opened, not with the usual resident company, but with the Old Vic Company, who had been bombed out of their London home – Maud Carpenter remained as Manager and Licensee – the Old Vic occupied the Theatre until 1946 and enjoyed considerable success despite wartime

55

Lot's Wife by Peter Blackmore, directed by William Armstrong; September 1939 'Under present conditions, the Producer has thought it advisable to curtail as far as possible the realism of the volcanic eruption at the end of Act 1.' (Programme note)

conditions. They brought many distinguished artists, and several talented Producers including Tyrone Guthrie, who was Administrator of the Old Vic, Peter Glenville, John Moody and Eric Capon. The choice of plays differed in some respects (being mostly classics) from those to which the Playhouse audiences had been accustomed, but the audience differed too. The wartime audience was mainly composed of young people in uniform, the majority of them strangers to the city, and, in many cases, seeing "live" plays for the first time. Many of the "regulars" had been bombed out of their homes and had evacuated, others were engaged on important war work which left them little time for theatre-going, especially with transport difficulties and early openings.'

MAUD CARPENTER, *THE PLAYHOUSE, LIVERPOOL: A SHORT HISTORY*, PUBLISHED FOR THE LIVERPOOL FESTIVAL OF BRITAIN CELEBRATIONS, 1951

The Old Vic opened on 4 November 1942, initially for a 14-week season, as part of a policy 'to re-establish first-class repertory in the country as a whole' (*Daily Post*, 17 December 1942).

The Old Vic at the Playhouse: *Point Valaine* by Noel Coward, directed by Peter Glenville; October 1944 (John Vickers)

' Liverpool was not just a haphazard choice for the experiment. It was chosen because the Liverpool Playhouse has the finest unbroken record of any repertory theatre in the country; because the theatre was available and the directors were anxious to re-open; and – perhaps most important of all – because Liverpool offered the advantage of a ready-made public which has supported repertory for over a generation. '

DAILY POST, 17 DECEMBER 1942

John Fernald, 1946–1949

> ❛ The Company always feels like this is Liverpool's theatre, but it is also a national theatre. ❜
>
> JOHN FERNALD, QUOTED IN *DAILY POST*, 5 JULY 1948

Three eventful years

❛ My three years at the Playhouse were professionally the happiest and the most productive of my life. They were years of aspiration, of pretensions perhaps, which were not all justified. Yet they were years mercifully free from any thoughts of expediency, during which a single motive dominated our thoughts – to reach out for the highest possible standard of achievement. Whatever we did ... we did under the stimulus of an ideal. It was a simple ideal, even, it might be said by laymen, a simple minded ideal, but it is an ideal common to all theatre artists who respect their calling. We believe that we should only do plays by authors who wrote not merely for the exploitation of a market, but from an inner compulsion to create and to explore. We believed that the power of an actor should come from a continuous distillation of a true feeling within himself. With Stanislavsky as an example, though not as a model, we believed in "honest" acting, devoid of tricks and short cuts, unadulterated by ambitions towards selfish or solo playing. We believed in the importance of the corporate ideal of the "team".

The "Playhouse" of the immediate post-war years presented a unique opportunity ... The war had seen the theatre closed and then after a time temporarily occupied by a distinguished but alien organisation – the "Old Vic". Liverpool it seemed was ready for a change. A new post-war generation was eager for new ideas. And first class highly experienced performers could be found, men and women who had worked with me in London before the war, and whose careers the war had interrupted. We were all ready to start our professional lives over again, and to come to Liverpool to do it.

As I look back on the time I can realise where we failed to take our opportunities and where, in part, we succeeded. Two practical ambitions

Alice in Wonderland
by Lewis Carroll
(adapted by Clemence
Dane), directed
by John Fernald;
December 1946
(Burrell and Hardman)

Alice in Wonderland
by Lewis Carroll
(adapted by Clemence
Dane), directed
by John Fernald;
December 1946
(Burrell and Hardman)

quickly became definite in my mind. The first was to try to make the Playhouse the "National Theatre of the North". The Playhouse could become, I believed, a place where anyone interested in the theatre would be sure, over a period, of seeing the best representative drama of the Western world. Shakespeare, Shaw, Ibsen, Chekhov and all the "great" dramatists were to be the mainstay of the programme. And, as befitted a "National" theatre, new plays, plenty of them, if possible by northern authors, were to break exciting new ground.

The first ambition was never achieved. Though we did Shakespeare and the modern classics, sometimes well and sometimes badly, we never discovered a playwright of originality and power. It was not for want of trying. Eight new plays were produced, none of which had any importance; yet, at the time I believed in them with fervent sincerity. We even organised a competition for new playwrights; but this had no more success than usually characterises competitions of this kind. The simple truth was that the post-war years were barren years for playwrights. Only Peter Ustinov (whose *The Indifferent Shepherd* was one of our better productions) relieved the drab theatrical horizon of that epoch.

The other ambition was to make something happen which can never happen on the West End stage, but which is, I believe, the duty of repertory theatres to attempt, since it is within reach of most of them. This was gradually to create a company of actors which, through unity of aim and understanding of each other's methods, could become a truly expressive instrument, capable of rising to any opportunity which might come to it: a company, in short, of the type of the Berliner Ensemble or the Moscow Art Theatre. It is easy for a producer to imagine he is building such a company, when in fact he is only hoping for the best in backing his intuitions: his intuitions can be wrong and I was no exception. None the less the year 1948 saw a company which, after considerable trial and error, had become something of which any director could be proud. The production of *The Cherry Orchard* which went from the Playhouse to the St James's Theatre, London, in June of that year remains the company's memorial. London critics, who tend to forget that it is possible to have a high standard outside the metropolis, were astonished to discover that a "provincial" staging of such a difficult play could challenge comparison with star-led London productions. The Liverpool company, in their finest hour, with their fame drawing a visit from Queen Mary at the last performance, became part of theatrical history.

The Playhouse actors of that time varied greatly in experience and ability, but they were united in what is perhaps an unusual ambition among actors. They did not seek to become stars, but to play their part to the last ounce of effort in the creation of a balanced orchestrated artistic effect ...

For me, the Playhouse was an experience vital to my development as a director, and I shall always be grateful to it ... I learnt that though my ambitions for the Playhouse were not yet realised, yet they were not yet impossible ambitions. Someone can, and I believe, will achieve them. Playhouse audience are no different from other audiences. They will accept what is less than the best if they must; but they will grasp hungrily, if a patient and cunning policy directs, at wider horizons and at deeper experiences than a simple policy of box-office expediency might suggest. Someday, I hope and believe, the National Theatre of the North may be discovered to be a thriving reality on our door-step, in Williamson Square.

JOHN FERNALD, *JUBILEE BROCHURE*, 29–30

Chekhov at the Playhouse

The Three Sisters by Chekhov, directed by John Fernald; May 1947

❛ It is perhaps odd that *The Three Sisters* should only now be achieving its Liverpool premiere nearly fifty years after it was written; yet the fact is a significant comment on the vast change which has come over the theatre-going public in recent years. Two decades have passed since *Uncle Vanya* was put in the bill at the Playhouse for a few special matinees – the only form of presentation possible at a time when public support for Chekhov's works was everywhere notoriously small. The experiment was not considered worth repeating and no major work of Chekhov was produced in Liverpool until 1942 when the Old Vic Company put on *Uncle Vanya* again and shortly afterwards *The Seagull*. By this time audiences had come to understand the Russian genius, and performances of his plays had ceased to be "experimental" ...'

JOHN FERNALD, PROGRAMME NOTE

Fernald then directed *The Cherry Orchard* in April 1948 and in June the British Theatre Group, whose home was at the St Jame's Theatre in London (run by Basil Dean), hosted an eight-week Repertory Festival. Along with Sheffield, Birmingham and Bristol Old Vic, Liverpool Playhouse went to the capital and performed *The Cherry Orchard* to great critical acclaim. During this time, the British Theatre Group toured the theatres performing Ted Willis' *No Trees in the Street* appearing at the Playhouse at the end of May 1948.

' London is being treated to a very healthy reminder that the theatre in this country doesn't begin and end with it, as Londoners are too apt to imagine ... Chekhov is a hard test through which these players come with colours flying.'

PUNCH, 23 JUNE 1948

Earlier productions of Chekhov

10/2/1925	*The Proposal* (one act); directed William Armstrong
09/3/1926	*The Swan Song* (one act; English premiere); directed William Armstrong
25/11/1927	*The Bear* (one act); directed William Armstrong
11/6/1930	*Uncle Vanya* (Special Matinees); directed Wyndham Goldie
10/6/1931	*The Anniversary* (one act); directed Wyndham Goldie
30/3/1943	*Uncle Vanya*; directed Norman Marshall (Old Vic)
26/4/1943	*The Seagull*; directed John Moody (Old Vic)
29/4/1947	*The Bear* (one act); directed John Fernald

Fernald went on to direct *Uncle Vanya* in April 1949 and then the Playhouse audience had to wait until April 1961 until the playwright appeared again with Frederick Farley's production of *The Seagull*.

New plays

' Can you explain why Liverpool unlike Manchester and Dublin has never produced a school of dramatists of its own? I really don't know. We gave

The Cherry Orchard by Anton Chekhov, directed by John Fernald; April 1948

The Silver Curlew by Eleanor Farjeon, directed by John Fernald, set design by Paul Mayo; December 1948 (Burrell and Hardman). 'It is a truly fine tribute to the special position the Playhouse holds among the theatres of the country that it should have been offered the opportunity to produce this play for the first time.' (John Fernald, programme note)

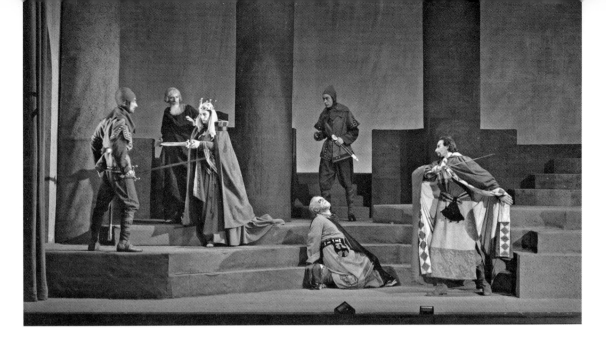

them every encouragement. Ronald Jeans did some outstanding work but it is true that no school ever did develop. I wonder whether it is because Liverpool is a seaport, with so much coming and going making for an unsettled life?

BASIL DEAN; QUOTED IN *DAILY POST*, 1 JUNE 1948

One of the functions of a Repertory Theatre is to encourage new dramatists by providing them with a shop window, for to-day it is more difficult than ever for new writers to convince commercial managements that they have something worthwhile to offer.

JOHN FERNALD, PROGRAMME NOTE, MARCH 1947

Despite the problem of developing a school of new writers, Fernald re-opened the Playhouse with Ronald Jeans' contemporary comedy about the difficulties of two post-war families sharing a flat. If he was not to discover, in his own words, any plays of importance, it did not prevent Fernald from trying. Premieres included:

10/9/1946   *Wings are to Fly With* by Ronald Jeans
1/10/1946   *Jassy* by Ronald Gow (from novel by Norah Lofts)
07/4/1947   *Boy Duster* by R.W.Earp
10/6/1947   *One Flight Up* by Hugh Miller and Ronald Simpson
25/11/1947   *The End of the Song*, Joyce Dennys
17/5/1948   *The Human Touch* by J Lee-Thompson and Dudley Leslie
27/9/1948   *Unknown Victory* by Neil Grant
22/12/1948   *The Silver Curlew* by Eleanor Farjeon
15/3/1949   *The Whirligig of Time* by David Monger

Playhouse Revue

Party at the Playhouse: A New Revue by Terry Bowen-Jones, Jenny Laird and Ronald Jeans; music by Ronald Settle; devised and produced by John Fernald

The Playhouse did not ignore a more light-hearted feel at times; Clemence Dane's adaptation of *Alice in Wonderland* was produced for Christmas 1946, the first Christmas play for six years, and Fernald also dipped his toes, at least once, in the Playhouse's tradition of home-made revues, a tradition that had been upheld even during the war with a production of *Repertory Rations: A Topical Revue* by Alfred Francis and Maud Budden in November 1939.

' Like the proverbial comedian who has the illusion that he can play *Hamlet* (and whose case really calls for a psychoanalyst) the Playhouse Company and I are the victims of a "complex". We have a sneaking feeling, despite having achieved some success over the modest problems of *Sleep No More* and *King Lear*, that our talents will never be truly recognised until we triumph over the monumental difficulties of a revue ... But Christmas is on its way: some indulgence, some levity and some irresponsibility may be forgiven, and so we invite you ... to join us for some fun. '

JOHN FERNALD, PROGRAMME NOTE

' I'm grateful to the board of directors for giving me my fling. I have certainly flung! '

JOHN FERNALD, QUOTED IN *EVENING EXPRESS*, 27 JUNE 1949

Interior, 1932

Gerald Cross, 1949–1951

❝ We have avoided producing plays which, although we knew they would draw large audiences, would nevertheless be unworthy of presentation at the leading repertory theatre in this country ... On the other hand we cannot produce plays if the audience which they attract are so small that the financial stability of the theatre is gravely threatened. What we hope to continue to do is to produce a variety of classics, whether old or modern, with the work of contemporary authors, so that the theatre-goer is familiar with what is best in other countries. ❞

SIR HENRY COTTON, QUOTED IN *DAILY POST*, 6 DECEMBER 1949

Shakespeare

According to Goldie, Shakespeare 'was always a risk, a difficult business' for a repertory company. There were those who wouldn't come because they associated Shakespeare with school; others who thought Shakespeare should be reserved 'for the quiet of the study' rather than submitting his poetry to 'the rough usage of the stage'. There were others who felt 'it to be sacrilege to perform his works, without months of preliminary study, a producer of European fame, a company who are less actors than archangels.' They could not 'give themselves the pain of watching the imperfections of a hurried repertory production.'*

* Goldie, 184

Yet, the Playhouse had not ignored Shakespeare, although 8 of the 20 Shakespearean productions up to the time Gerald Cross took to the stage as Richard II in 1950, had been performed by the Old Vic company. Those staged by the Playhouse itself had included two *Twelfth Night*'s, the first opening on Boxing Day in 1913 and the second, directed by William Armstrong, in 1936, with Rachel Kempson as Viola and Michael Redgrave as Malvolio as well as John Fernald's productions of *King Lear* (1947), *Julius Caesar* (1948) and *The Tempest* (1949). With the arrival of Cross, the argument became less whether to stage Shakespeare and more how to stage his plays and the theatre took its place alongside a number of companies experimenting with methods of staging.

King Richard II by Shakespeare (with Gerald Cross as Richard), directed by Michael Macowan; February 1950

' To-day Shakespearean scholars, and the best minds in our theatre, are agreed that most of the plays can only have their full force if they are allowed to flow on uninterrupted between scenes. The open platform of Shakespeare's theatre, with its curtained alcove and upper balcony, took no account of change of place or lapse of time. When this is vital to the action, words convey it. We have therefore tried to devise a simple setting suggestive of the period and atmosphere which we hope will assist the audience's imagination without confining it ... we have not attempted to embroider the play with invention, business or striking effects. We hope that it will speak for itself ...

To preserve the formal and placeless nature of the stage, and to try and capture some of the intimacy between actors and audience of the Elizabethan theatre, the front curtain will not be lowered during the performance, and the orchestra pit is occasionally used for exits and entrances. '

MICHAEL MACOWAN, GUEST PRODUCER, PROGRAMME NOTE

A European premiere

The Beaver Coat by Gerhart Hauptmann, directed by Gerald Cross; October 1950

' This is the first time that this comedy by Gerhart Hauptmann has ever been done in England. Two of his serious dramas, *Lonely Lives* and *Hannele* were done in the 1912–1913 season here by Basil Dean and since then none of his work has been seen.

The Beaver Coat has been specially translated for the Playhouse by Eric Colledge of the University of this city. It happened that one day Mr Colledge read me, for amusement's sake, a translation which he made ... I found it so entertaining that I asked him to let me have a version to submit to my Directors; and here is the result. It will be something of an occasion for us, for the widow of the distinguished author and her son, the present Dr Hauptmann, consider the presentation of this play important enough to make a special journey from the Continent to Liverpool to come and see it. The play is a comedy of character and situation arising from what we should nowadays call black market activity. '

GERALD CROSS, PROGRAMME NOTE

The cast included Peggy Mount as Mrs Woolf and Beryl Bainbridge as Adelheid Woolf.

Exterior 1949
(L Turnock)

The Bonesetter of Crosshall Street by William Hywell, directed by Gerald Cross; April 1951

Writing the city

❛ This play should be of particular interest to a Liverpool audience, for what it presents is local history. The street of the title is the street of that name in this town, where dwelt the Evan Thomas of the play, a collateral ancestor of the famous Sir Robert Jones, whose name we still hear mentioned with affection. The time of the play is that at which the Royal College of Physicians and Surgeons first began to feel obliged to prevent the operation of unorthodox and unrecognised practices.❜

GERALD CROSS, PROGRAMME NOTE

The cast included Peggy Mount and Cyril Luckham as Evan Thomas.

Starting out: Beryl Bainbridge

❛ I joined the Liverpool Repertory Company at the age of sixteen … The war was over but the city was still a quarter in ruins. The streets were full of ex-soldiers with missing limbs, ex-pilots whose burnt faces were as waxen as Halloween masks; on the bomb sites purple foxgloves bloomed.

It always surprises me that reviews of novels I have written to do with that time of wine and roses always remark on the squalor of the period; they refer to the "seedy theatrical company", place emphasis on the fact that the characters bath but once a week. I can only suppose that such critics are either too young or too privileged to know what life was like over forty years ago, and that they have little knowledge of the history of provincial theatre.

To be a member of the Playhouse Company was to have "arrived". We were special, not least because we were "three weekly". Scarcely a day passed without Maud Carpenter – that redoubtable lady who had begun her career serving beer in the slush bar of Kelly's Theatre in Paradise Street and whose reputation as a manger of the Playhouse Theatre equalled if not excelled that of Miss Horniman in Manchester – lecturing us on the way we should dress and conduct ourselves. She spoke with passion about "our" audience, "our" patrons, without whom the theatre could not survive. All those years ago, when I was a small cog in that great company, there was a producer (nowadays called a director), a scenic designer (helped out by students from the Arts School), a wardrobe mistress, a stage manager plus two assistants (the latter unpaid), a property master, a lighting man, a manager and front of house assistant,

Westward Journey by Eve Morganti, directed by Gerald Cross, set design by Paul Mayo; September 1949 (Burrell and Hardman)

three or four scene shifters, two pianists, a rat catcher and a door man. On top of that there were the actors, twelve in all. Any extras needed were recruited from the University or the local Amateur Dramatic Society.

At the back of the theatre was the green room, filled to the roof with stuffed birds, bits of china, old furniture; we warmed our kettle and our tins of beans on an open fire surrounded by a nursery guard on which hung our damp clothing. On first nights it was standing room only, on every night after that there was but a handful of empty seats. *

BERYL BAINBRIDGE, foreword in G. WALTER GEORGE *THE LAND WHERE YOUR DREAMS COME TRUE*

1951		
	29/1	*Rookery Nook*, Ben Travers (revival), directed by Gerald Cross
	20/2	*Night's Lodging*, C.E. Openshaw, directed by Gerald Cross
	13/3	*All's Well that Ends Well*, Shakespeare, directed by Gerald Cross
	3/4	*The Bonesetter of Crosshall Street*, William Hywell, directed by Gerald Cross
	24/4	*The Moon is Down*, John Steinbeck, directed by Gerald Cross
	15/5	*That Lady*, Kate O'Brien, directed by Gerald Cross
	10/8	*Henry IV*, Pirandello directed by Michael Macowan (Festival of Britain Production)
	31/7	*The Sun and I*, A.R. Whatmore, directed by Michael Macowan (Festival of Britain Production)
	21/8	*The Way of the World*, William Congreve, directed by Gerald Cross
	2/9	*Design for Living*, Noël Coward, directed by Gerald Cross
	11/9	*Dear Brutus*, J.M. Barrie, directed by Gerald Cross
	2/10	*The Little Foxes*, Lillian Hellman, directed by Willard Stoker
	23/10	*Venus Observed*, Christopher Fry, directed by Gerald Cross
	13/11	*Winterset*, Maxwell Anderson, directed by Willard Stoker
	04/12	*Nothing but the Truth*, James Montgomery, directed by Willard Stoker
	21/12	*The Glass Slipper*, Herbert and Eleanor Farjeon, directed by Willard Stoker

Willard Stoker, 1951–1962

' The future of the theatre must surely lie with the playwrights, which brings us to our rather sad point. Where are the wits of yester-year? With the passing of Shaw and Bridie we seem to have lost inspiration. When the repertory companies come to consider their programmes, what have they to fall back upon? Creaking vehicles for erstwhile film stars which have tiptoed out of the West End and are eagerly awaiting customers; far-fetched farces which have been fashioned for clowns, and which merely demand a company of comic understudies; the ever ready revival and the dreaded classic.'

WILLARD STOKER, QUOTED IN *DAILY POST*, 4 DECEMBER 1951

Summer revues

One of Stoker's contributions was to build on the theatre's tradition of creating local and topical revues and he wrote and directed six which were staged at the end the seasons. Ronald Settle contributed both original music and arrangements of classics.

June 1955   *Spring Quartet* (based on the music of Schubert and set in Austria)

May 1956   *Themes and Variations* (based on the music of Tchaikovsky; set in Petrograd 1917)

June 1958   *The Londonderry Heir* (based on the music of Chopin and set in Scotland)

June 1959   *Williamson Square Dance*: 'The rather feeble pun in the title of our revue is intentional! We hope it will be an inducement to all those teenagers who regard the Playhouse Company as a bunch of "Squares", for our players are eager to try out their all-round versatility ...' (Willard Stoker, programme note)

Williamson Square Dance by Jill Fenson, Terence Bowen and Ronald Settle, directed by Willard Stoker; June 1959

71

La Vie Parisienne
by A. P. Herbert and
A. Davies Adams, directed
by Willard Stoker;
(Coronation production)
with Patricia Routledge,
June 1953

The Druid Circle by John
van Druten, directed
by Willard Stoker; with
Patricia Routledge,
April 1953

June 1960   *I Remember, I Remember* (set in Ormskirk in 1909)
June 1962   *Reflections in the Square* (Stoker's farewell production)

Starting out: Patricia Routledge

  'A year after graduating in English from the University of Liverpool, I auditioned for Willard Stoker on a bright, late spring afternoon in 1952 and was taken on as an unpaid Assistant Stage Manager for the 1952–3 season. (I believe that previously a premium had to be paid for this apprenticeship.) It was still a prestigious repertory company, (some of the resident staff still spoke glowingly of "the days of William Armstrong") and it was able to provide a varied programme of plays – Shakespeare, Coward, Maugham, Lonsdale, Guthrie, Bridie, Sam Spewack, Emlyn Williams – each production playing for three weeks; a luxury enjoyed by only two other repertory companies: Manchester and Birmingham.

  An ASM in those days was a general dogsbody and you knew your place! I can honestly say that I began my professional life sweeping the stage. On my first morning I was assigned the task of cleaning out a dusty, chaotic space full of discarded furniture, old props, boxes of scripts and cobwebs – an area that was to become the actors' green room. The duties of an ASM were multiple and various: attending all rehearsals; occasionally undertaking the hazardous responsibility of prompter; assisting the designer in buying and sometimes making props; preparing stage food and drink when necessary; working the panatrope for sound effects and music; which involved placing the needle on the exact spot of the vinyl record then judiciously bringing up the volume and, most important of all, "calling" the actors to be on stage in time for their entrances. This entailed running the length of backstage corridors (since there was no tannoy system), knocking on dressing room doors, giving the summons to "Mr" or "Miss" so-and-so and waiting for the acknowledgement that they had accepted the "call".

  The ASM was answerable to the Stage Director, in this case a brilliant, acerbic and volatile Irishman, Charles Blair, who would take the rap for anything his ASM had failed to do and then carpet the offender with extreme patience and sensitivity. The Stage Manager (a kind and courteous Andrew Sachs at that time), would also help keep the ASM on track.

  The hierarchy of the company was as follows: Leading Lady, Leading Man, who were each obliged to provide their own basic wardrobe: a couple of evening dresses and a suit for the leading lady and dinner jacket and one good suit for the gentleman; senior character actors, male and female, two ingénues and two junior character actors. Other roles would be filled by visiting actors and (fortunately for me) the ASM. Lighting then was very unsubtle, so make-up (skin-tone Leichner sticks 5 and 9 with Lake

As You Are by Hugh Mills and Wells Root, directed by Willard Stoker; April 1956 (Withers) 'Lancashire playgoers will appreciate the North Country humour and the faithful reproduction of characters so faithfully observed in this comedy. It seems to us that people from the North of England have a particularly dry kind of humour that is essentially local – though the long run of the play in London seems to indicate that some of our humour is acceptable to Southerners.' (Willard Stoker, programme note)

Liner for wrinkles and shadows, together with wigs, until Wig Creations came along) was fairly crude. Ticket prices ranged from a shilling (5p in today's money) to seven shillings and sixpence (37½p), and during the intervals (usually two) tea would be served in the stalls, the danger being that the rattle of china on trays could well cut across the focus of the ensuing scene!

After three months I was called into the general manager's office (the formidable, legendary Maud Carpenter), who enquired as to whether I "liked being here at the Playhouse". "Oh yes, Miss Carpenter," I unhesitatingly replied. "Well," she said, "You seem a sensible sort of girl, would you like to come into the company? I'll pay you £5 a week." "Oh yes, Miss Carpenter!"

It was a season of great opportunity for me; playing a variety of roles (to some of which I was unsuited!), watching, learning, finding a discipline, realising how much the practical, technical contributions of stage management are essential to the whole; making mistakes, making progress, facing disappointment and relishing the thrill of being part of live theatre.

PATRICIA ROUTLEDGE, ACTRESS

The Americans in Liverpool

❝ Some loyal followers protested that too many American plays were being presented. ❞

GUARDIAN, 7 FEBRUARY 1959

While Stoker did offer the audience a number of new English and European writers, he also did more than his predecessors to introduce the audience to American writers. While William Armstrong had favoured Eugene O'Neill, the first Arthur Miller play, *Death of a Salesman*, appeared in 1954, followed by *The Crucible* in March 1957. Elmer Rice helped Stoker on a trip to America to establish new contacts, the *Post* claiming that if this 'bold' move succeeded, 'Liverpool will have the prospect of witnessing, from time to time, worthy American plays for the first time in Britain ... It is considered a constructive variant to the repertorial necessity of so often playing second fiddle to London.' (*Daily Post*, 17 January 1957). Some of these new American productions included:

The Druid Circle by John van Druten; directed by Willard Stoker; April 1953
Another Part of the Forest by Lillian Hellman; directed by Willard Stoker; September 1953
Death of a Salesman by Arthur Miller; directed by Willard Stoker; May 1954
Late Love by Rosemary Casey; directed Willard Stoker; September 1954
The Wooden Dish by Edmund Morris; directed by Willard Stoker; May 1955

Starting out: Rita Tushingham

❝ My mother, Enid, used to go to every production at the Playhouse and she would often take me with her. That was my introduction to this beautiful theatre; I wanted so much to be on that stage. I discovered that the Playhouse had positions for student assistant stage managers so I

The Crucible by Arthur Miller, directed by Willard Stoker; Richard Briers is centre stage, behind the table, March 1957

started on the long road of writing letters to the director – at that time – Willard Stoker. I wrote over twenty letters asking him if I could join the Playhouse in any capacity. My perseverance was eventually rewarded; I was given an appointment for an interview with him. The Christmas show *Toad of Toad Hall* was about to start rehearsals and they needed extra backstage staff for the production.

The interview went well. He was warm and friendly and offered me the job of student assistant stage manager – a dogsbody. I started work the next day on the great wage of a £1.00 a week. Thank goodness I lived at home!

The company had such a variety of personalities, friendly, welcoming, aloof. I quickly learned their likes, dislikes, superstitions, when to talk and when not to talk but most importantly their favourite mug to drink tea from and how many spoonfuls of sugar they took. There was a gas ring under the stage and a very old burnt out kettle, I'm sure health and safety would have had a field day if they had been around then! Sometimes it was remarked that the tea had a slight burnt taste to it. I blamed it on the tea.

I worked with the stage manager and did just about every back stage job that I was physically able to do – props, costumes, sweeping the stage – a must to make you humble – doing the book, prompting, calls for the actors – no tannoy system.

I had to go up five flights of stairs and by the time I had got to the top flight it was time to start again but I couldn't have been happier!

Rehearsals for *Toad of Toad Hall* were about to start. The cast list went up on the board. To my delight I was given two roles – a rabbit and the back legs of a horse, a role that I found easy to overact in. I graduated from animals to many a maid and got my big opportunity in an end of season

Deep are the Roots by Arnaud d'Usseau and James Gow, directed by Willard Stoker; Harry Baird played the hero who 'returned from the war with a mind of his own and a strong disinclination to remain the under-privileged protégé of the Big House.' (*Guardian*, 1 October 1959); September 1959

Thark by Ben Travers, directed by Willard Stoker; with Rita Tushingham as a maid, September 1960

production, *I Remember I Remember*. Willard wrote a sketch for me about a rather ungainly girl whose father was an inventor and invented a box that made people disappear. One evening the sketch was going along as planned. I duly got into the box. The door was closed. I stamped on the floor to give the cue to open the trap door under the box but it would not open, I had to keep saying, "I'm still here, I'm still here." In the end, the only solution was a blackout leaving the audience very confused as to the reason for the sketch.

During my time at the Playhouse I was fortunate enough to be cast as Jo in the film *A Taste of Honey*. All the company were so supportive of me. I learned so much from my time at Liverpool Playhouse, what it takes to put on a production, dedication, professionalism, tantrums, tears, hysteria, everyone loving and hating everyone but always with good humour and the show was always right on the night! For me it was the best training ground ever, preparing me for my future career and to be able to do this in my own home town was a bonus. The Liverpool Playhouse will always have a special place in my heart.*

RITA TUSHINGHAM, ASSISTANT STAGE MANAGER AND ACTOR

Classics – re-done

She Stoops to Conquer by Oliver Goldsmith, directed by Willard Stoker; March 1952

To be performed in modern dress: This production is not intended to be in the nature of a "stunt". Perhaps from a surfeit of study, there are playgoers who regard the classic plays with faint disfavour – for them so many uncut little volumes will only attract attention by their odour of musty neglect. We would like to show these misguided few that humanity does not change in particulars … Thus it seemed sensible to suppose

77

that if the situations perpetrated by Goldsmith were re-created in the background of 1952, then perhaps everybody would come to appreciate the humorous simplicities that are so often concealed by the conceits of the "period" production.*

WILLARD STOKER, PROGRAMME NOTE

The Golden Jubilee

'Here in this house tonight, our City makes
Something which must not fail for all our sakes,
For we begin what men have been too blind
To build elsewhere, a temple for the mind.'

So fifty years ago, this House was hailed;
Today we greet a House that has not failed.

Fifty full years, eleven spent in war,
Of countless genius dead, still sorrowed for,
Pageant and wreck of many million lives …
What ship, of then, exists? But this survives.

In every enterprise of man, the first
Half century of struggle is the worst …
Later reward comes, with acquired power.

I saw the tree set, you behold the flower.

May that remembered Stage ring with your cheers …
Rare harvest to you this next fifty years.

LINES COMPOSED BY JOHN MASEFIELD, POET LAUREATE, TO COMMEMORATE THE
GOLDEN JUBILEE OF THE PLAYHOUSE, SPOKEN AT THE GALA BY JENNIFER HILARY

Below left: *Williamson Square Dance* by Jill Fenson, Terence Bowen and Ronald Settle; directed by Willard Stoker; June 1959

Below right: *Reflections in the Square* by Willard Stoker, Ronald Settle and Jill Fenson, directed by Willard Stoker; June 1962

Diary of Anne Frank by Francis Goodrich and Albert Hackett, directed by Willard Stoker; with Thelma Barlow as Anne Frank, September 1957

The Double Dealer by Congreve, directed by Willard Stoker; l–r: Thelma Barlow; Denis Edwards, Caroline Blakiston, David Cameron, October 1957

Juno and the Paycock by Sean O'Casey, directed by Willard Stoker; with John Thaw as Joxer Daley, November 1960

Celebration by Keith Waterhouse and Willis Hall, directed by Bernard Hepton, who directed two productions while Stoker was away; April 1962 'Presenting the people to the people reaches the end of the line when *Celebration* by Keith Waterhouse and Willis Hall takes the stage in Liverpool. Northern industrial town off stage faces Northern industrial town on stage: the real thing sees itself in a distorting mirror.' (*Guardian*, 18 April 1962)

The Bells adapted by Leopold Lewis from *The Polish Jew* by M Erchmann-Chatrian. (a double-bill with *Lady Audley's Secret* by C.H.Hazlewood), directed by Willard Stoker; Richard Briers as Mathias played in the style of Henry Irving's original performance, May 1957

The Rivals by R.B.Sheridan, directed by Willard Stoker; March 1956 (Withers). This was Stoker's second attempt at a contemporary staging of a classic play

‘ The taste of citizens in the drama, whether those of the audience or the board of directors, is seldom adventurous. A theatre which is dependent upon their goodwill makes only cautious moves towards new writing and new thoughts. And no new school of playwrights has in fact grown up – as was hoped – round the Playhouse ... Once again there is a new stir in the drama. Once again a new type of play is being staged at the Royal Court Theatre ... Once again there is a new school of playwrights ... They get their first showings in London, not in Liverpool. Can Liverpool's citizens create a climate of interest with a standard of acting and production which will make new playwrights feel honoured that their plays should be staged first in Liverpool Playhouse? Or must a citizens' theatre be content with the "good drama" which its citizens love? ’

GRACE WYNDHAM GOLDIE, JUBILEE OF A CITIZENS' THEATRE, *GUARDIAN*, 11 NOVEMBER 1961

‘ The Repertory Theatre has created in Liverpool an interest in the drama that goes far beyond the confines of the city itself. Can a citizens' theatre do more than that? ’

GRACE WYNDHAM GOLDIE, JUBILEE OF A CITIZENS' THEATRE, *GUARDIAN*, 11 NOVEMBER 1961

The end of an era

‘ Two years ago the Liverpool Playhouse celebrated fifty years of existence with a Jubilee season graced by Royalty and honoured by the City ... It was a happy occasion not to be marred by too close or searching a look at the future, but in the minds of many present there must have been the thought that the celebrations marked the end of an era. This was symbolised most dramatically perhaps by the subsequent changes to the Board and the Direction of the Theatre. Lord Cohen after 25 years on the Board retired from the Chairmanship, which he had held for 12 years; Miss Carpenter sought a well-earned retirement after 50 years' work in the Playhouse and Mr Willard Stoker relinquished his appointment after eleven successful but very strenuous years as Producer. It would be very understandable that some Patrons should say, "The Playhouse will never be the same again." Nor would it. ’

JOHN T. EDWARDS, CHAIRMAN, 'THE FUTURE PLAYHOUSE', *LIVERPOOL REVIEW*, 1963

Golden Jubilee celebrations; Basil Dean with Dulcie Bowman, Jennifer Stirling and Prudence Drage

Bernard Hepton, 1962–63

❝ I do not agree that [the theatre] is here purely for entertainment. It is here to hold some sort of mirror up to the way we live; it is here as a social force.❞

Bernard Hepton, quoted in *Daily Post*, 29 October 1962

❝ A year peppered with critical success but which put the theatre in the red.❞

Guardian, 5 April 1967

❝ *The Fireraisers* did raise a few eyebrows. The play is a humorous, if rather surreal case for not living one's life in blinkers. The notices in both Liverpool newspapers which covered it were diametrically opposed – one passionately for, the other passionately against. We had them both enlarged and displayed at the front of the theatre. And the correspondence in these papers went on and on, and on, from all sections of the community, for and against, so at least it caused more than a ripple. It seemed to upset people, even if they hadn't seen it. But it was bad box-office, and that is what mattered.

My tenure as Artistic Director lasted but one year, towards the end of which I was told by the Board of Directors to change my selection of *Luther*, by John Osborne, because "we don't want another *Fireraisers*". As the extra actors had been engaged, the sets and costumes already decided and being made ready, I refused and offered my resignation. I am glad to say that *Luther* was a big success. It was becoming obvious that I was not the person the Board wanted as Artistic Director, and when my contract expired, I left. Before my appointment I was given to understand that I would have a free hand, within reason, but it soon became plain that my

Man for All Seasons by Robert Bolt, directed by Willard Stoker; with Bernard Hepton as Thomas More; November 1962 (Colin Thorpe)

selection of plays had to be vetted by the Board. That and managerial difficulties were very disappointing.

The 1960s is a long time ago. Things have changed, I hope for the better.'

Bernard Hepton, Artistic Director

The theatre's first grant

'Up to now the Playhouse has not received any subsidies. But in the past week, it was announced that the Arts Council have decided to make a grant of £5000 to the theatre. This, I feel suggests that the choice of plays should not be considered purely from a box office point of view.'

Bernard Hepton, quoted in Liverpool Echo, 2 April 1963

The photo-call

'Every three weeks, the night before each play opened to the public, the company would assemble for the final rehearsal, and I would be there to take the promotional shots. As you might expect the atmosphere could be tense and stressful. Taking over from Edward Chambre-Hardman in 1962 was initially intimidating. He had a well-established reputation that enabled him to command the stage, and his photo-calls could take up to half a day. He tended to produce monumental, statuesque, and very high-quality images, but by 1962 both the theatre and the times required

The Fireraisers by Max Frisch, directed by Bernard Hepton; February 1963 (Colin Thorpe)

Opposite: Back row (l–r): Terence Lodge, Leslie Lawton; front row: Richard Kay, Inigo Jackson and Peter Needham

Below: Rosemary Leach played Anna

a new approach, one that would capture the energy and spontaneity of live performance.

I had two basic approaches to making the shots. One was to range around the stage and theatre invisibly, shooting at decisive moments. The director would run the rehearsal and I would catch what I could. But this was not always effective because the stage is large and the action might be spread across it. Sometimes it was better to condense in order to create cinematic shots, to set up specifically for the image. I would arrange actors into the frame to try and depict a particular moment in the play, or represent the atmosphere or theme of a play more generally. At other times I would combine the methods, directing the actors to run through a particular section having arranged them into the shot. This allowed me to combine candour and careful composition.

It must be said, some directors were far from keen to give the necessary time, and this was understandable given the pressures they were

under. But mostly, both directors and actors were very publicity-savvy. They understood the need for promotion, and perhaps unsurprisingly, many enjoyed posing for the camera! In general they were cooperative and if not, the director would tend to insist on seriousness. I remember Bernard Hepton, Patrick Stewart and Ian McKellen being particularly gracious. Anthony Hopkins was more reserved, tending to save himself for performance, but still he was very responsive. The images of *The Playboy of the Western World* were all contrived to illustrate a dramatic moment in the play, and Hopkins would switch from a quiet detachment to an authentic interpretation of the character at a moment's notice. Ken Dodd was also memorable. He had a comic charisma that commanded the stage – and to be honest the rest of the cast didn't seem entirely happy to be up-staged!

Among my favourite images is that of King Lear holding Cordelia in the centre of the stage. In a sense it represents my interest both in theatre and photography. It's a dramatic moment in which the character comes to a moment of self-realisation; photography is, in some ways, all about seeing and catching a fleeting moment, trying to represent what is essential and significant.

Once the shoot was over, I would race back to the studio, develop and print the shots, and return them to the theatre the next day for the opening night. It was demanding, particularly as I was working full time in the day, producing different types of photography for a wide range of clients. But the Playhouse work was stimulating, and enabled me effectively to have a solo exhibition every three weeks.'

COLIN THORPE, PHOTOGRAPHER

Luther by John Osborne, directed by Bernard Hepton; March 1963 (Colin Thorpe)

Resignation

6 As far as the Policy of the Playhouse is concerned regarding plays there has been no substantial difference of opinion between the directors and myself. But as far as the running of the Playhouse is concerned we have had differences of opinion, and under the circumstances I feel I cannot continue to stay on. 9

BERNARD HEPTON, QUOTED IN *LIVERPOOL ECHO*, 2 APRIL 1963

6 Although the theatre has lost money this season, it is perhaps some comfort to know that this is fairly general over the country and not just peculiar to Liverpool. But given a realistic and courageous outlook, there is little reason why this theatre should not be one of the leading theatres in the country, and achieve once again its past greatness. But this is impossible without the co-operation and support of the audience ... My contact with some of the audience has been most stimulating and I say this in particular reference to the young people we have entertained here on Saturday mornings. It has been a year of development for me and for this I am grateful. 9

BERNARD HEPTON, QUOTED IN *LIVERPOOL ECHO*, 30 MAY 1963

King Lear by Shakespeare, directed by Bernard Hepton; with Inigo Jackson as Lear, April 1963 (Colin Thorpe)

Ronald Settle and Joan Ovens

Ronald Settle became the Music Director in 1944 and was joined at the piano by Joan Ovens in 1949. They were to provide music before, after and during the shows and intervals until 1970. Settle also composed music for many shows.

6 One Summer afternoon 17 years ago, when the Old Vic were in residence at the Playhouse, Noel Willman came to see me. He had come on behalf of Tyrone Guthrie and Peter Glenville to ask me if I would consider an invitation to become the new Music Director of the Playhouse. "We want to make a feature of the music," he said. I was to take over from Harold Stone … After some deliberation I decided to try it for "the season", stipulating that I would like either an orchestra of ten, or just two pianos. For reasons of economy, the two-piano suggestion was accepted, and two Bechsteins were soon installed in the orchestra pit.

My first real problem was to find a suitable partner for the second piano and here I was indeed fortunate in obtaining the devoted services of Thomas Haines … who remained with me at the Playhouse until his death five years later. Finding a worthy successor to Tommy – as he was affectionately known to everyone in the theatre – I was fortunate again in deciding on Joan Ovens …

During these 17 years of the two-piano reign the music programmes have included almost the entire repertoire of published two-piano works, and covered a range of styles from Bach to Boogie Woogie, Scarlatti to Shearing, and Pergolesi to "Pops". Just as the Repertory movement in the theatre is not fulfilling its true artistic mission unless it presents the early classics of Shakespeare and the Restoration Period, plus a reasonable proportion of new contemporary plays – even if they do not appeal to the box-office – so, in my opinion, should the musical programmes introduce a certain amount of newly composed music. This we have done, and much of the music was in fact receiving its first public performance in Liverpool. 9

RONALD SETTLE, SILVER JUBILEE BOOKLET, 1961

Ronald Settle at the piano for the *Little Mrs Foster Show* by Henry Livings, directed by David Scase; November 1966 (Colin Thorpe)

The end of an era

In November 1970, it was announced that after Ronald Settle had been at the theatre for 26 years (and Joan Ovens for 21) and after providing music for over 250 productions and writing five musicals and three revues, the pianos were to go, victims of a cost-cutting exercise and a sign of changing times. By then, the Playhouse was one of the few remaining theatres in the country to have musicians performing before the curtain rose and during the interval. At the same time, the practice of serving tea to the audience at their seats at matinées also ceased.

David Scase, 1963–1967

⁶ While we hope to do everything in our power to encourage young people to come to our theatre, it is not our intention to do anything to disturb the wonderful relationship we have with our older audience … Our audiences still seem to be resisting modern trends in writing and presentation.⁹

JAMES RUSHWORTH AT AGM; QUOTED IN *LIVERPOOL ECHO*, 17 DECEMBER 1965

From Manchester to Liverpool: Patrick Stewart

⁶ I had not intended to leave the Manchester Library Theatre, where I was very happy and where I had been playing leading roles, play after play, for the first time in my short career. But David Scase, the Artistic Director, for some reason never explained, decided to take over the Liverpool Playhouse. I have always imagined it was because The Playhouse was a "real" theatre with a long distinguished and colourful history, whereas, The Library Theatre was a cramped, bland, municipal space in the basement of Manchester City Central Library. Anyway, I was only at The Library Theatre because of David. I had wanted to work with him from the moment I left The Bristol Old Vic Theatre School four years earlier and so when he asked me and a few other actors to make the move with him I had no hesitation.

I loved the theatre and I admired Liverpool immediately. I had never even visited the city before but I feel in love with its steep streets, its vistas, its buildings and architecture and its people. Quite different from Mancunians. To a Yorkshireman they seemed more foreign. There the city and its people clung to the Western edge of Northern England, with that broad, iconic, inviting river suggesting ocean voyages, exotic peoples and languages. For the first half of the one year I worked at The Playhouse I lived in a spacious flat in a big old house in Birkenhead on The Wirral and I crossed the Mersey every morning on the ferry. But long before the Liver Building got close I would gaze to my left, downstream to where the river opened up to the Irish Sea and fantasise about sea journeys. As a child, *Treasure Island* had been my favourite book and I was always dreaming about sailing off into the unknown.

The Birthday Party by Harold Pinter, directed by Tony Colegate; l–r: Warren Clarke as McCann, Colin Welland as Stanley and David Scase as Goldberg; March 1966 (Colin Thorpe)

Dr Angelus by James Bridie, directed by David Scase; Patrick Stewart as Dr Cyril Angelus and Peter Needham as Dr George Johnson, January 1964 (Colin Thorpe)

The Entertainer
by John Osborne,
directed by David
Scase; November
1963 (Colin Thorpe)

David had brought with him from Manchester, as well as myself, Cynthia Grenville, Desmond Stokes, Charles Thomas, Helena De Crespo. We were the core of the Library Company and a quite diverse group of actors. Cynthia was massively experienced, with a big range. Desmond too had done a lot of work and just before leaving Manchester he had played Davies in *The Caretaker* with me as Aston and Charlie Thomas as Mick. Charlie was a young actor right out of Rose Bruford School and David had employed him – ever a man for economies – as an ASM as well as actor. He had great natural talent and the RSC headhunted him before that Liverpool season was over. Charlie was doing brilliantly with the RSC but tragically died soon after on an RSC overseas tour. He was the first colleague I had lost and it was years before I could accept his death. I was to encounter Harold Pinter's great play decades later when I too played Davies on Broadway and though Aiden Gillen was brilliant and got a Tony Nomination, echoes of Charlie were everywhere in the play. Helena was a lovely, unusual actress, idiosyncratic and unique. I had quite a crush on her but she was dating another actor in the company so ...

In that first Liverpool production, Alun Owen's *The Rough and Ready Lot*, were also Jon Lauriemore and Peter Needham. Jon was a very handsome, dashing, intelligent actor who was to partner another gorgeous young actress who joined us later, Gilly McIver. I was keen on her too but ... . Oh hell, it was all acting and sex in those days.

There were so many highlights in the Playhouse season; *A View From the Bridge* with John Slater, Brendan Behan's *The Hostage* and a wonderful *A Midsummer Night's Dream* with John as Bottom. In that production I played Oberon for the first time and fell in love with the role and the play. I was to play Snout the Tinker five years later in the legendary Peter Brook "white box" *Dream* but I understudied Alan Howard as Oberon/Theseus and went on several times. Because I only stayed one season at The Playhouse, as I had at The Library, I saw it very much as an important stepping stone in my journey up the British Repertory Theatre ladder. I left Liverpool and went to Bristol for two seasons and from there, at last, into my beloved Royal Shakespeare Company. But what helped to win that place as an Associate Artist at the RSC was the experience, technique, love of language and the sheer excitement of being on a stage, all acquired on the great regional repertory stages of Sheffield, Manchester, Liverpool and Bristol. Today that journey isn't possible and it is a great loss.❜

SIR PATRICK STEWART, ACTOR

Opposite: *The Hostage* by Brendan Behan, directed by David Scase; September 1963 (Colin Thorpe). Patrick Stewart as Pat and Cynthia Grenville as Meg

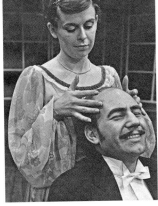

Far left: *Hindle Wakes* by Stanley Houghton, directed by Tony Colegate; March 1964 (Colin Thorpe). Jean Boht as Fanny, Desmond Stokes as Christopher Hawthorn and Cynthia Grenville as Mrs Hawthorn

Left: *Heartbreak House* by George Bernard Shaw, directed by David Scase; April 1964 (Colin Thorpe). Helena de Crespo as Ellie Dunn and Patrick Stewart as Boss Mangan

Below: *The Long, the Short and the Tall* by Willis Hall, directed by David Scase; October 1965 (Colin Thorpe). The cast included William Kendrick, Tony Colegate, Brian Miller & Steven Berkoff

Below: *A Midsummer Night's Dream* by Shakespeare, directed by David Scase; February 1964 (Colin Thorpe). John Slater as Bottom (surrounded by Christopher Reich, David Colling, Desmond Stokes, Michael Frances, Howard Rawlinson)

Below: *The Little Mrs Foster Show* by Henry Livings, directed by David Scase; November 1966 (Colin Thorpe)
The action of the play takes place at the Liverpool Playhouse. 'Playing here in *Semi-Detached* confirmed a feeling I'd been nursing that you don't need to pretend a play is real for it to be true. We faced you and told you the story; we didn't pretend you weren't there ... So Mrs Foster is a show; the actors will be playing the story for you as truly and as entertainingly as they know how. There's even a game of Bingo, so don't say I don't give value.' (Henry Livings, programme note)

Below: *Summer and Smoke* by Tennessee Williams, directed by David Scase; October 1963 (Colin Thorpe) Helena de Crespo as Alma Winemiller and Charles Thomas as John Buchan Jr

The Hostage by Brendan Behan, directed by David Scase; Helena de Crespo as Teresa; Jon Laurimore as Monsewer; Malcolm Reid as Leslie; Patrick Stewart as Pat. The rest of the cast included Cynthia Grenville, Jennifer Stirling, Charles Thomas, Michael Frances, Philip Hedley, Desmond Stokes, Sonia Francis, Jean Boht, Peter Needham and David Collings, September 1963 (Colin Thorpe)

'What a talented Director can do with a good young Company has been brilliantly shown by the recent Playhouse production of *The Hostage* of which the *Daily Telegraph* wrote, 'By any standards David Scase's production is first class theatre. There would be little wrong with the Repertory Theatre in this country if all companies were to emulate Liverpool.' (John T. Edwards, 'The Future Playhouse', *Liverpool Review*, 1963)

Starting out: Philip Hedley

Pinocchio by Brian Way and Warren Jenkins, directed by David Scase; l–r: Peter Needham as a policeman, Patrick Stewart as Gepetto, Malcolm Reid as Pinocchio and Cynthia Grenville as Fairy; December 1963 (Colin Thorpe)

❛My year at the Liverpool Playhouse was one filled with constant activity and discovery. My job was to be one of three Actor/Assistant Stage Managers, a hybrid position which has unfortunately disappeared from repertory theatre. What better experience could there be for a recent graduate from a drama school than servicing a huge range of plays by prompting in rehearsal, cueing the effects during the show, operating the sound, finding props, assisting on fit-ups, making tea and occasionally appearing in small parts?

We worked from 9.30am to 10.00 or 11.00pm. It didn't seem like long hours, more like hundreds and hundreds of exciting, short hours crowded into your day, with the pleasure of presenting a show in the evening. My day was made more busy by taking it upon myself to prepare huge fruit salads at lunchtime, with the contents bought cheaply at the friendly market next door. I sold them to actors and staff at the cost price of half a crown.

Right: *The Quare Fellow* by Brendan Behan, directed by David Scase; Anthony Hopkins as Donelly, September 1964 (Colin Thorpe) 'To present a Behan play each season would be a joyous prospect for the audience and the company in any theatre. Just one year after our production of *The Hostage*, we now approach *The Quare Fellow* and in doing so sadly reflect that these are the only two full-length plays written by the late Brendan Behan.' (David Scase programme note)

The Scandalous Affair of Mr Kettle and Mrs Moon by J.B. Priestley, directed by Caroline Smith; Peter Clay as George Kettle, Jean Boht as Delia Moon and Antony Hopkins as Henry Moon, May 1965 (Colin Thorpe)

Top left: *Playboy of the Western World* by J. M. Synge, directed by David Scase; Anthony Hopkins with Vivien Jones, Lynda Marchal, Jean Boht, Margaret Peacock, Cynthia Grenville, March 1965 (Colin Thorpe)

Top right: *Sparrers Can't Sing* by Stephen Lewis, directed by David Scase; Anthony Hopkins and Margaret Jones, September 1964 (Colin Thorpe)

Middle left: *A View from the Bridge* by Arthur Miller, directed by David Scase; John Slater as Eddie, Patrick Stewart as Mr Alfieri, February 1964 (Colin Thorpe)

Middle right: *The Rough and Ready Lot* by Alun Owen, directed by David Scase; Patrick Stewart as The Colonel and Cynthia Grenville as Chica, August 1963 (Colin Thorpe)

What a feast of plays there was to work on too. In the best tradition of what was then called "provincial rep" and is now called "regional, building-based, producing houses", we presented in the one season plays by Shakespeare, Shaw, Coward, Bridie, Harold Brighouse, Arthur Miller, Tennessee Williams, Alun Owen and John Osborne.

Perhaps the greatest success of the season was *The Hostage*, which was drawn from the rumbustious talent of Brendan Behan by the ground-breaking director, Joan Littlewood, whose irreverent way of working sent a huge blast of fresh air through British theatre. The new artistic director of the 1963/4 season was the much-loved, no-nonsense David Scase, who had been a crucial member of Joan Littlewood's company Theatre Workshop in the Fifties. He brought the right paradoxical mix of truthful realism and up-front entertainment to the production.

The backstage staff were all proud of the contribution our stage-manager, Jean Boht, made to the show. She was a popular local actress who played several major roles in the season, including a scene-stealing Miss Gilchrist in *The Hostage*. She chose the last night to up-date the lyrics of her song, "Don't Muck About With The Moon!" by including a reference to the news of the day, which happened to be about Harold MacMillan's shoe-horning of Lord Home into the job of prime minister. This was in the best tradition of Theatre Workshop, but not of the Lord Chamberlain, and Jean was severely reprimanded for endangering the theatre's licence.

At the end of the season, when we had time to take breath because we were no longer rehearsing during the day, I sat on a bench in Williamson Square at the front door of the Playhouse and reviewed my year there. I thought of the contribution of one of the leading actors in the company, Patrick Stewart, and of his industrious commitment to an astonishing range of roles. I knew I could never match this display of versatility or talent as an actor.

However I also saw that I had brought a similar enthusiasm to organising and occasionally directing the Saturday morning workshop presentations for young people, which company members would give up precious spare time to appear in, every month or so. On that bench I resolved to become a director.'

Philip Hedley CBE, ASM, 1963–64

'Many of the plays of the kind that I would like to do have been refused in Liverpool. There is a stubborn rearguard in the make-up of audience – not only at the Playhouse. Maybe it needs an entirely new style of director, somebody like John Neville with the kudos to make people come along and accept something new in spite of themselves.'

David Scase, quoted in *Guardian*, 5 April 1967

Kay Gardner, 1967–1969

6 Considerable care has been taken in the selection of a new director of productions. We have not yet found the right applicant. We therefore asked our administrator, Miss Kay Gardner, who has had a long experience of directing, to continue in charge of productions, assisted by an associate producer and guest directors. It was felt (indeed it has already been proved) that this would bring larger audiences and interesting productions which would not only reflect current theatre thinking but also be acceptable to our audience old and new. We are able in this way to bring to Liverpool young directors of standing to produce plays of their choice, and to give them opportunities to develop their work in this way. 9

JAMES RUSHWORTH, QUOTED IN *DAILY POST*, 29 MARCH 1968

Kay Gardner did direct a number of productions during her two years, including *Tinker's Curse*, Thackeray's *Vanity Fair*, *A Kind of Loving* and a version of *Romeo and Juliet* which Gillian Reynolds in the *Guardian* noted as impressive in its technical scope and ambition.* She also presided over a series of guest directors, including Meredith Edwards, Graham Woodruff, Alan Vaughan Williams and David Jones, whose production of *The Diary of a Scoundrel* introduced Penelope Keith to the Playhouse audience. However, the excitement of this period focused less on the stage and more on the extension of the theatre.

* Guardian, 8 November 1967

Extending the Playhouse

6 The Playhouse goes "Mod": Liverpool's theatreland will soon be moving into the jet age. 9

LIVERPOOL WEEKLY NEWS, 9 JUNE 1966

The year 1968 saw the opening of the most significant alteration to the theatre, the addition of a circular glass and steel tower at the side of the Victorian theatre. It was a strong and confident architectural statement designed by Ken Martin, the project architect at Hall, O'Donahue & Wilson, a statement which, in the words of James Soane, worked on the urban

A Kind of Loving by Stan Barstow (adapted Stan Barstow and Alfred Bradley), directed by Kay Gardner, her final production; January 1969 (Colin Thorpe)

* Pamela Buxton, 'James Soane's Inspiration: Liverpool Playhouse Extension', *Building Design*, 12 March 2010

level because from outside, 'you see people spilling into and animating the edge of the square — while from within, you come out of the "black box" of the theatre into the city. In that sense, the presence of people provides both the spectacle and the audience — it is in the spirit of the theatre.'*

    ❝ We had to make the new part an entity without butchering the original, that was an entity in itself. We could not make it look like the old building ... the two buildings will relate. ❞

JAMES O'DONAHUE, QUOTED IN *LIVERPOOL DAILY POST*, SUPPLEMENT, 3

    ❝ The effect will be the union (literally) of the old and new – an effect which, it is hoped, will have an important impact on prospective audiences. ❞

LIVERPOOL WEEKLY NEWS, 9 JUNE 1966

A new theatre: the practicalities

    ❝ The original building, flanked by Williamson Square and Houghton Street, remains structurally unchanged. Outside and in, attractive redecoration and vital improvement to heating, lighting and toilet facilities combined with re-positioning of the lighting and sound control at the back of the auditorium are some of the essential points of modernisation ... The new building with its outstanding contemporary design blending perfectly both with the old theatre and the next door Ravenseft development, occupies

Duchess of Kent on the gala night for re-opening of the Playhouse with a production of *Man and Superman*, 29 October 1968

an area as large again as the old one and houses on the ground level the new Booking Office, Foyer and cloakroom. On the first floor the Playhouse Restaurant and above that the Redgrave Room and the Star Buttery and Bar. In conjunction with the old stalls bar and coffee bar these areas provide greatly increased facilities for patrons and with access to the auditorium at all levels via the main staircase the whole audience can mingle as they choose ...

Backstage spacious workshops and scene painting facilities replace the old makeshift area ... On the stage itself two bulky corner obstructions have been cleared to enlarge the stage ... Dressing rooms have been rebuilt and extended and showers are available for artists and staff together with a new green room and small kitchen attached ... At the top of the building much needed administrative offices and a Board room flank the entrance to a large rehearsal studio. With an area equal to that of the

The Lyons Mail newly adapted by George Rowell, directed by Alan Vaughan Williams; September 1968 (Colin Thorpe)
'The intriguing choice of a rumbustious Victorian melodrama for the start of the season is not accidental. Miss Gardner explains that the choice was made deliberately to underline the fact that the Playhouse is not severing its links with the past.' (*Liverpool Daily Post* Supplement for re-opening)

105

Restaurant after the redevelopment
Extension April 1967 (Elsam M Cooper)

Building the extension, September
1967 (Elsam M Cooper)

stage, this welcome addition can be used for experimental work, Playhouse
Club meetings, and performances for young people. *

LIVERPOOL PLAYHOUSE REDEVELOPMENT BROCHURE

Open all day!

*Centrally situated, Liverpool Playhouse makes the ideal rendezvous to
meet your friends. From morning coffee right through to a late meal
after the show, you can find it at the Playhouse! The Scene is Williamson
Square!*

LIVERPOOL PLAYHOUSE RE-OPENING BROCHURE

Catering facilities included: The Redgrave Room above the Restaurant,
named after Sir Michael Redgrave; the Playhouse Restaurant, on Circle level,
with 'a full Grill-room menu'; the Star Buttery Room at the top (the name
perpetuating the Playhouse's original name) offering a Buttery Service 'for
play-goers in a hurry'; the Stalls Coffee Bar and Licensed Bar. Between
them, they offered food and drink from 10.30 in the morning until after
the show. These extensive facilities suggested a real attempt to make the
theatre a social centre, somewhere 'where young people could come during
their lunch breaks and so acquire the habit of going to the theatre itself in
the evenings'. (Liverpool Playhouse Re-opening Brochure)

' We hope it will make theatre-going far more attractive ... A visit to the Playhouse will now be much more of an "occasion" for patrons. '

KAY GARDNER, QUOTED IN *LIVERPOOL WEEKLY NEWS*, 9 JUNE 1966

The re-opening Although the theatre had not been officially closed during the three-year rebuild (work had been confined to extended summer closures so as not to lose the 'goodwill' of the audience), completion of the work was greeted with three gala nights and a redevelopment brochure extolling the virtues of the refurbished building.

' The re-opening of the Liverpool Playhouse in September was more than a local event; it had a significance throughout the theatrical world and wherever there is concern and interest for the theatre. '

Drawing of the Exterior, 1969 (E. Scott Jones)

LORD GOODMAN, CHAIR OF THE ARTS COUNCIL, *LIVERPOOL PLAYHOUSE* RE-OPENING BROCHURE

Drawing of the theatre
after the redevelopment,
showing two views of
the entrance, ticket office
and foyer 1969
(E. Scott Jones)

The Playhouse resurgent: a progressive policy

❝ Now that our building programme is completed we are seeking to develop the full potential of the new complex and it is our policy and intention to cast the net wide … We are concerned to encourage new authors as well as writing on matters of regional interest. We want to give you the opportunity of seeing the best and even the unfamiliar both modern and classical. We believe it is part of the job of a theatre such as ours to dig and delve for forgotten treasures as well as to mint new coin …

This is an era of argument and assertion especially among young people. We want young audiences to know that in our Theatre they can enlarge their theatre going experience by means of talk, discussion and constructive critical analysis with our actors and directors.

The introduction of special Monday Night programmes also caters both for the serious student and the more avant-garde playgoer by giving us opportunity to present for one or two performances only, more way-out writing, the unusual classic or the specialist production …

Our new attitude to the world and our City is evident in the new appearance of the Playhouse, which combines the charm of the "old look" of the Victorian Age with the workmanlike and efficient "new look" of the Twentieth century. This makes the Theatre very symbolic of our society and the age in which we live. The blending of old with new preserves the beauty of the past …❞

JAMES RUSHWORTH, LIVERPOOL PLAYHOUSE RE-OPENING BROCHURE

Antony Tuckey, 1969–1975

> ❝ Time brings its changes, new men new faces, mean new – or at least different – ideas. But it would be wrong and superficial to think that any changes in Playhouse policy are due solely to a set of new men and new ideas – the position is more complex and more interesting than that. What is really happening is that the conditions in the Theatre generally have changed fundamentally since the Playhouse was opened fifty-two years ago and, if the future Playhouse is to be healthy, it must adapt itself to those changed conditions. ❞
>
> JOHN T. EDWARDS, CHAIRMAN, 'THE FUTURE PLAYHOUSE', *LIVERPOOL REVIEW*, 1963

> ❝ When I did my first interview I was shown round the Playhouse. The auditorium was a wonderful, friendly, red and gold. When I came back it was a hideously daunting purple and white. Grandiose, aloof, almost hostile. I was honestly shocked. Who had decided this was a good idea? The architect I was told. The audience should never, of course, think about it but every aspect of the building they are visiting should be welcoming. I can think of no colour more daunting or unsympathetic than purple (later I was told that James Rushworth had dreams of it becoming the "Royal" Playhouse: just at the time when sensible souls were starting to wonder if we needed a royal family at all). ❞
>
> ANTONY TUCKEY, ARTISTIC DIRECTOR

Antony Tuckey, the man

> ❝ Dick Tuckey was a tough-minded individualist, he had already proffered his resignation before he had signed his contract … He balked at the idea of submitting his choice of plays to a play-reading committee of the Board. Henceforth, he would do the choosing. The Arts Council supported him. The tendency to dig in his heels where he felt a matter of principle was concerned was not to lead to an easy relationship with the Board, but no-one who met him could deny he was a man of stubborn integrity, a professional with high standards, a man who was by nature courteous and diffident. ❞
>
> VOAKE

Black Spot on the Mersey by Ray H. Dunbobbin, directed by Antony Tuckey; March 1970 (Colin Thorpe)

Borstal Boy by Brendan Behan (adapt Frank McMahon), directed Tomas MacAnna; September 1971 (Colin Thorpe) This was the English premiere of work that started at Abbey Theatre, Dublin

Right: *Breaking the Silence* by W.J. Weatherby, directed by Antony Tuckey; Sheila Scott Wilkinson as Christine, October 1969 (Colin Thorpe)

Far right: *The Contractor* by David Storey, directed by Sue Wilson; April 1974 (Colin Thorpe) 'It's a very technical play involving putting up a marquee and taking it down ... I went off and found a firm in Surrey where they were erecting tents in mid-winter. I worked with the men for a couple of weeks. At least when I got that show on the stage I understood the principles of putting up a tent.' (Sue Wilson; quoted in Voake)

Right: *Comedy of Errors* by Shakespeare, directed by Antony Tuckey; Sheila Scott Wilkinson as Luciana, November 1969

Above: *Brainwaves* by Andrew Dallmeyer, directed by Andrew Dallmeyer; March 1973 (Colin Thorpe)

Above right: *Coriolanus* by Shakespeare, directed by Antony Tuckey; Michael Gambon, March 1970 (Colin Thorpe)

Right: *Happy Days* by Samuel Beckett (a National Theatre Tour); Peggy Ashcroft, November 1974

Below right: *In Celebration* by David Storey, directed by Barry Kyle; Michael Gambon as Andrew Shaw, January 1970

In His Own Write based on nonsense fables, verse and puns by John Lennon with Adrienne Kennedy, and Victor Spinetti, directed by Antony Tuckey; March 1969 (Colin Thorpe)

❝ He was smashing to work for. He took responsibility. He didn't hang over your shoulder. At the same time, he was there if you got into trouble. Everyone knew he was honest and wouldn't be pulling the wool over your eyes. He never did things for the greater glory of Dick Tuckey. ❞

Caroline Smith, associate director 1974–75; quoted by Voake

New work *In His Own Write* by John Lennon, directed by Antony Tuckey; March 1969

❝ "I was bored when I believed the nastics were still booming us led by Madolf Heatlump ..."

In His Own Write is really a fragment of autobiography; a crazy montage of the images and influences that surrounded the author while he grew up in Liverpool in the 40s and 50s. It creates a landscape that most of us have passed through at some time of our lives; a world in which comic book characters and film and television heroes assume a greater reality than the people we mix with every day.

The play is an adaptation of John Lennon's two books *In His Own Write* and *A Spaniard in the Works* ... The play becomes a kind of journey, a journey of growth: about the beginning of things, childish at first and then more serious as ME began to appreciate the wonder of words and of himself.'

Although, entirely lacking in pomposity, the play has a serious underlying theme. ME is essentially the product of the last 30 years and at moments some of the pain of growing up in the post-war world peeps through the crazy energy and zest for life.

PROGRAMME NOTE, ANTONY TUCKEY

In His Own Write, which had been adapted by Victor Spinetti for the National Theatre, was performed as part of a double bill with Peter Shaffer's *Black Comedy*.

Breaking the Silence by W. J. Weatherby, directed by Antony Tuckey; October 1969

The Merchant of Venice by Shakespeare, directed by Antony Tuckey; Geraldine Newman as Portia and Teresa Campbell as Nerissa, March 1972 (Colin Thorpe)

My third production at Bristol had been a play called *And People All Around* by George Sklar. It dealt with the Deep South Freedom Summer and the Klu Klux Klan murders of Civil Rights workers. While researching it I read Bill (W. J.) Weatherby's docunovel *Breaking the Silence*. When I was appointed to the Playhouse I contacted him about adapting it for the stage. The story of an ex-*Guardian* journalist's – from the north-west – encounter with the racial tensions in America seemed an

interesting choice. Bill recommended I get a friend of his, Laurence Dobie, who had several plays to his credit, to do the adaptation. I met Laurence but he declined the offer. He seemed charming but stressed. So Bill said he'd do it.

When the Board found out what the play was about some of them raised (yet another) outcry: "we have absolutely no problem with black people in Liverpool; this could cause trouble" etc. Ten years later Toxteth erupted – I don't think the play was responsible.

Forty years ago finding good black actors could be a problem. Bill told me of a young American actress he had seen on the fringe in London who he thought would be very right. Well, God was smiling on the Playhouse that day. Sheila (Scott-Wilkinson) came to see me, proved ideal and agreed to do the play (it may not even have been written at that time). She may have been influenced by the offer of *Comedy of Errors* to follow. Shakespeare was rare for black actors then ... but I don't know that. She, along with a lovely actor called Alfred Bell, carried the play brilliantly and although the box-office was a modest 50%, the show was much praised; we even went to London for a TV excerpt. 9

ANTONY TUCKEY, ARTISTIC DIRECTOR

A Night at the Indian Empire by Charles Chilton, directed by Antony Tuckey; April 1973 (Colin Thorpe) 'Not a disaster but a major disappointment. Charles Chilton had initially been hugely enthusiastic, said there was a wealth of material but suddenly wobbled. We started rehearsals with about half the script and then got it day by day, the last few pages literally during the last week of rehearsal ... An attempt to get Liverpudlians to contribute memories got absolutely nowhere – surely some of them must have had their share in the Raj'. (Antony Tuckey, artistic director)

6 In 1968 I had just finished my studies at the London Drama Centre and concluded a couple plays at the Royal Court Theatre in London and a six-month run as one the original cast members in the West End Production of *Hair* when Dick Tuckey invited me to audition for several plays including *Breaking the Silence*, a play about the 60s' Civil Rights Movement in America, Martha, in Albee's *Who's Afraid of Virginia Woolf* and Luciana in *Comedy of Errors*. As a young actress I was so excited about going to Liverpool to be a part of such a prestigious theatre company. My impressions of the people and the city were most inviting and friendly. They warmly welcomed me into the community enthusiastically. Being an American I remember how much I had been moved by the remnants of the bombed out buildings left over from the war. I equated the hardships and struggles of the war with the Civil

Saved by Edward Bond, directed by Barry Kyle; November 1969

The Lancashire Twins by Carlo Goldoni, adapted and directed by Antony Tuckey; May 1971 (Colin Thorpe)

Rights Movement of the sixties and my portrayal of a young African American girl in *Breaking the Silence* who had to find inner strength to cope with her unsettling circumstances. This must have been, I surmised, how the British people overcame their immediate struggles of the aftermath of the war. They also had to gain the fortitude to triumph over their dire circumstances, in order to gain self-resilience to win.

I loved rehearsing in the airy rehearsal room of the Playhouse and better yet performing on the large Playhouse stage. I remember my first chopstick experience in Liverpool at a Chinese restaurant where the cast would go for a nosh after rehearsals. During my tenure in Liverpool I was also introduced to the Cavern, the notably energetic club where the famous Beatles had gotten their start. It was in Liverpool where I first ate fish and chips and peas out of newspaper. It was in Liverpool where I contemplated the overcast haze of the city's grand waterfront. It was in Liverpool where I met people of true grit like Dick Tuckey who I believe was a genuine visionary with a quiet rebellious spirit. He had a heart of gold and a talent to match. His foresight to cast an African American actress in the part of Martha in *Who's Afraid of Virginia Woolf* and Luciana in *Comedy of Errors* was colourblind casting and a tribute to the Liverpool Playhouse and to Dick Tuckey. It was a finite moment in the sixties for the British theatre and an awaking to the many possibilities of a new and thoughtful experience for an audience.

SHEILA SCOTT-WILKINSON, ACTOR

Causing a stir

Saved by Edward Bond, directed by Barry Kyle; November 1969

Saved had premiered at the Royal Court, London, in November 1965 and had caused controversy. The reader for the Lord Chamberlain (to whom all plays had to be submitted prior to performance) had demanded 54 changes and after deciding it was 'a revolting amateur play by one of those dramatists who write as it comes to them out of a heightened image of

115

* See Dominic Shellard, *British Theatre Since the War* (London: Yale University Press, 2000), 140–6

their experience. It is about a bunch of brainless, ape-like yobs with so little individuality that it is difficult to distinguish between them ... They are all moral imbeciles ... The writing is vile and the language and conception worse.' The artistic director of the theatre, William Gaskill, had been taken to court and fined by the Lord Chamberlain.*

❝ In a letter to *The Observer* Sir Laurence Olivier said "*Saved* is not for children but it is for grownups, and the grownups of this country should have the courage to look at it". **We would, however, seriously warn some of our patrons that if they feel *Saved* is not for them, they should not come.**❞

SEASON BROCHURE, 1969–70

Three Months Gone by Donald Howarth, directed by Ian McKellen; January 1972 (Colin Thorpe)

❝ It is only when we are prepared to avoid simple "moral" outrage at sex and violence in art, that we will be able to get it in proportion, and look beyond it. There is far more sensationalism in *King Lear*, and there is more than a stoning scene in *Saved*.❞

BARRY KYLE, PROGRAMME NOTE

❝ *Saved* was my second production. Ian Talbot who played Len was a warm and very popular personality and it probably helped. After the first night, the Bishop of Liverpool Cathedral (Protestant) was invited to discuss the play onstage with Dick Tuckey and myself. He was decent about it. But the mood in the theatre about the production was a little tense. The famous scene where a baby was stoned received no stylisation from me. I had real stones. And rather preposterously I had one of the stoners wear a tee-shirt which said GOD IS LOVE (not in the text.) On the whole the show was tolerated, attracted a small audience in a short run, and the most concerns it generated were about whether my stones would damage the proscenium arch.❞

BARRY KYLE, TRAINEE AND ASSOCIATE DIRECTOR, 1969–72

Black Spot on the Mersey by Ray H. Dunbobbin; directed by Antony Tuckey and Barry Kyle, March 1970

❝ The history of the Irish Potato Famine has been told many times, but the retribution for political mismanagement in Ireland was paid in full by Ireland's second capital, Liverpool.❞

RAY H. DUNBOBBIN, PROGRAMME NOTE

❝ Ray Dunbobbin rang me to say he had an idea for a play which would fill the Playhouse for a month. I was, I fear, a little cynical but I asked

The Bacchae by Euripides (trans Philip Vellacott), directed by Antony Tuckey; Ian McKellen as Pentheus, April 1969 (Colin Thorpe)

him to come and tell me about it. Like many authors he talked at length before leaving his baby with me. It was a piece about Father Nugent, a remarkable Roman Catholic priest, who did much for destitute children following an influx of thousands of poor Irish. His work resulted in a close collaboration with a Church of England clergyman, Rev. Lester, and the play suggested that this was why Liverpool never had the same degree of religious hatred as Ulster. However, my own researches when doing the play suggested that in the second half of the nineteenth century, the Liberals in the city – who had never really been able to make a majority on the council – did a deal with the Catholic Church for their support. This increased the Liberal vote and provided a political base and mouthpiece for the Roman Catholics in the city. But we had no time to introduce that, though I did a lot of rewriting … Yet again there were Board members who feared there would be riots consequent on this production. In fact there was one complaint. It was from the Roman Catholic secretary of the Board. The decorations and banners for Nugent's funeral were, he said, in bad taste. Alas, they were taken direct from illustrations in the local papers. Ray Dunbobbin was right about one thing: it filled the theatre and I'm not being facetious when I say they were told from the pulpit to attend … which Ray had also said would happen.'

ANTONY TUCKEY, ARTISTIC DIRECTOR

Happy Days … and others

'In 1974, the National Theatre asked if we had a week where they could premiere Beckett's *Happy Days*, starring Peggy Ashcroft and directed by Peter Hall. We had – and if we hadn't we'd make one.

A few days after the show I was introduced to a lady at some function. "Ah," she said, "I want a word with you. How could you put on such dreadful rubbish?" I told her politely (though mentally wishing she was buried well over her neck in sand) that I didn't think I could honestly apologise for bringing to the Playhouse a NT production of a play by a great writer, starring our greatest actress and directed by Peter Hall. "Well," she replied. "You jolly well ought to."

It was a conversation that seemed to epitomise all the problems facing the Playhouse in the early 70s. This, after all, was the swinging city of half the world's dreams, a fabulous new cultural frontier, "the centre of consciousness of the human universe", I think Alan Ginsberg called it.

A Tide in the Affairs of Women by Philip Martin, directed by Antony Tuckey; January 1975 (Colin Thorpe) 'Set in Liverpool in 1975 this exciting new play by local author Philip Martin takes a savage, but humourous look at the lives of five women. Definitely for Adults only.' (Programme note)

Well, maybe some of it was all that, but the rest was wholly, conservative – left as well as right – resentful of its new-found fame and happy to rubbish the Beatles, Gerry, the Poets, the Cavern and everything connected with that fertile period.

Being blunt, there was much to mistrust. A Probation Officer I got to know, said, "I'm sure Liverpool 8's great if you can have a pad on Rodney Street. For the unmarried mother round a couple of corners, it's a hell on earth."

It would be tedious to name all the plays that some of the Playhouse Board and Public thought would cause problems (*Breaking the Silence* might give rise to racial discontent, *Black Spot on the Mersey* might cause sectarian violence, *Borstal Boy* was an unhappy and unnecessary reminder of the bad times in the 30s, even Neil Simon's *The Odd Couple* ("Two men setting up house together?") was regarded with grave suspicion). Looking back, most of the plays seem uncontroversial. But even an enjoyable 1920s' style *Merchant of Venice* caused outrage. "When I go to the Philharmonic," wrote a patron, "I don't expect to see musicians in 1920s bathing costumes". The logic of this criticism escaped me, but I could at least write back, "nor do they wear knee-breeches and powdered wigs to play Mozart – though either garb would be quite good fun".

The need for a space to present more "way out" plays led to the creation of The Playhouse Upstairs. Even this didn't happen without controversy. The opening play was to be Howard Brenton's satire *Christie in Love*. The programme was nodded through at a Board Meeting, but a member took it upon himself to buy and read it. He sent it to the Chairman saying he was "appalled". The Chairman was also "appalled". A special meeting was called and I was told to withdraw the play. I pointed out that play-choice had been established as my prerogative and I couldn't do that. So a motion was passed ordering me to do so. Constitutionally I could not refuse, so I agreed and the following day resigned. This caused some panic (I'm not sure whether it was a passionate desire to keep me or fear of what the press might say – I'll flatter myself and say a bit of both). The Arts Council became involved and many phone calls and Special Meetings later *Christie* was performed Upstairs to tiny audiences and without a whiff of controversy. I remained at the Playhouse and the Board Member who had caused the – *wholly unnecessary* – problem and who had made the Chairman (a really good man lost in the cultural upheaval of the period) look a fool, remained on the Board.

But Upstairs was founded and many excellent productions followed, including Athol Fugard's *Sizwe Bansi is Dead* with John Kani and Winston Ntshona – its only showing outside London – and an evening no one who saw it is likely to forget (but it contained male nudity so maybe the battle above had to be fought?). And, of course, our commissioning of Alan Bleasdale's *Fat Harold* and its brilliant production by Caroline Smith launched the theatre career of Liverpool's most significant playwright.

I have a huge muddle of memories. Of marvellous colleagues, some of them quite mad; of Ian Talbot's irrepressible Trufaldino in *The Servant of Two Masters*, my first production; of Sheila Scott-Wilkinson's bruised but radiant Christine in *Breaking the Silence*; of Ken Dodd – yes, of course, for his Malvolio – but also for his gentle and intense interest in how a play is put on; of Caroline Smith's production of David Hare's *Slag* which guaranteed a successful future for Upstairs; of the Technical Rehearsal for *Days of the Commune*, which began at 9.00 in the morning and continued almost without break until 4 the following morning and began again at 9.00 … ah, those Happy Days before overtime. "What are you doing under the stage?" I once asked a couple of Acting-Assistant Stage-Managers (remember them?). "Digging a way out," they replied.

I knew how they felt. (And I guess Beckett's title was intended to be ironic?)

ANTONY TUCKEY, ARTISTIC DIRECTOR

A resignation

I resigned over *Christie in Love*. An emergency board meeting had been called because a board member had read the script (long after it had been board approved). I remember the phrase he used to depict the play negatively: "a gratuitous insult to the people of Liverpool." I was in rehearsal with it. It's a dark and Rabelaisian sketch about the sex murderer Christie. Anyway, it was not possible to justify *Christie in Love* by citing moral gravity, in the way *Saved* had been justified. I said privately to Dick that if the Board banned the play then it opened up serious issues about censorship, and that he might want to make clear to the Board that he would have to consider his position. More than a bit cheeky of me. We had our one and only argument with each other on the subject. I remember breaking down in his office and saying I'd resign if the Board banned it. Dick was more pragmatic. He thought the better strategy was to keep the Board onside. Anyway, they forced a withdrawal of the production, although I was already in rehearsal. I

The Prime of Miss Jean Brodie by Muriel Spark (adapted by Joy Presson Allen), directed by Ian McKellen; Barbara Ewing as Miss Brodie, May 1969 (Colin Thorpe)

resigned. After I left Dick and I never met, or talked, again. We have not to this day; something I greatly regret. *9*

BARRY KYLE, TRAINEE AND ASSOCIATE DIRECTOR, 1969–72

Christie in Love had been scheduled to appear in the Studio in January 1972 but was postponed and appeared in November of that year, directed by Antony Tuckey.

Diamond Jubilee

Prologues, said Ibsen in the 1880s,
Are out of date, no matter what the date is.
But though a prophet, how could he forsee
This Playhouse and its diamond jubilee –
Time for a fanfare! And may we suppose
A fanfare's better said in verse than prose.
For in the year that George the Fifth was crowned
Came the dramatic tones of the Mersey sound –
As notable as that sound yet to come,
The shard-borne Beatles with their rousing hum:
A Playhouse, like the turning of a page
In the advancing history of the stage
To a new chapter with a youthful Dean,
Making new values, helping change the scene
Of England's drama, and enduring still
(In spite of man's propensity to kill)
Through sixty years, out-riding two long wars:
An open space progenitive of stars.

Great change has come upon the world, it's certain,
Since Masefield's prologue first rang up the curtain.
1911 – when audiences all
Dressed for the theatre as for a ball,
And actors not so long before were taken
To be mere vagabonds and Godforsaken.
But now an audience of straightened means,
In tasselled ponchos and in splitting jeans,
Look from their lowly station up toward
The Knights and dames, or even (with luck) a lord.
True that the actors, labouring to please,
To put the clapping-classes at their ease,
Will condescend from their exalted state
To let the audience participate.
And, for this purpose, there's been much endeavour

To bring the audience and stage together,
Abolishing whatever comes between 'em,
Such as the footlights, curtains and proscenium;
By theatre in the curve, or through the gaps,
Or by actors sitting in our laps.
And, as that didn't seem to be enough,
By everybody stripping to the buff –
A bonus from promoters of the Arts
To let the audience learn the actors' parts.
But whether this can bring us any nearer
To mutual understanding, or make clearer
What you and I and time are all about
Is something some of us take leave to doubt.

For though a fashion may express a need
It withers all when turned into a creed.
And can we learn he nature of the vine,
Drinking the dregs while we ignore the wine,
If all the world's a stage, the stage is worth
Making as rich and various as the earth;
In sound and colour, dark and light together,
Their bruising metal and dancing feather.

And this was what the Playhouse then believed
And for a span of sixty years achieved.
So may this diamond Prologue prophesy
Forty years on to our centenary

CHRISTOPHER FRY

Twelfth Night by Shakespeare, directed by Antony Tuckey; Diamond Jubilee production with Ken Dodd as Malvolio, November 1971

❛ This proved to have every ingredient necessary for a huge success; Kenneth himself earned the highest praise and the whole Company gave performances of great talent and strength. Business was over 90% and it is, I think, fair to claim that we celebrated our jubilee with considerable style. Having said that, the Artistic Director must reflect, with some wry feelings, that, in his opinion, the *Comedy of Errors*, *The Taming of the Shrew* and *The Merchant of Venice* were all better, more original and more entertaining productions. They averaged less than 60% between them! ❜

ANTONY TUCKEY, ARTISTIC DIRECTOR'S REPORT, 1971

121

Twelfth Night by Shakespeare, directed by Antony Tuckey; Ken Dodd as Malvolio with Brian Coburn as Sir Toby Belch, John Webb as Fabian, Norman Henry as Sir Andrew Aguecheek; November 1971 (Colin Thorpe)

Disagreements

❛ The Chairman reported that the Board members had discussed the current production *Three Months Gone* and in varying degrees disliked it. They considered it very bad programming coming so soon after *Lighthearted Intercourse*. They did not wish to see anything like this in the Playhouse again. They were satisfied that it was not what the theatre's patrons wanted and the Board did not want to offer it to them.

Mr Tuckey said that he agreed that the programming was not good following on so soon after *Lighthearted Intercourse*. He continued that any contemporary playwright includes passages of the type in *Three Months Gone* in their plays and if the Liverpool Playhouse is to stage contemporary plays then we must face these types of passages. He felt that to make any hard and fast rule to exclude such plays would create problems. ❜

BOARD MEETING MINUTES, 7 FEBRUARY 1972

Lighthearted Intercourse by Bill Naughton, directed by Antony Tuckey; December 1971 (Colin Thorpe)

❛ *Lighthearted Intercourse* by Bill Naughton ... offended many people with its subject matter; so much so that the real point of the play was lost to them, namely that unemployment is a destructive force that enters into every corner of people's lives, brutalises them and destroys their happiness. This was the reason for its inclusion in our programme as this lesson from the 1920's seemed only too sadly relevant 50 years later ... *Three Months Gone*, well directed by Ian McKellen, and played by a largely visiting Company, again caused a great deal of offence to a section of our audience. The play, dealing as it does with the loneliness and unhappiness that lies beneath our 20th century prosperity again seemed to me most relevant. ❜

ANTONY TUCKEY, ARTISTIC DIRECTOR'S REPORT, 1971

Donald Howarth's *Three Months Gone* was performed in January 1972 and *Lighthearted Intercourse* had been directed by Antony Tuckey in December 1971.

A Tide in the Affairs of Women by Philip Martin, directed by Antony Tuckey; January 1975

Philip Martin

❛ In spite of its clumsy title, his was possibly the best play written about Liverpool at that time. No larky scousers or laments for Back-Buchanan Street but three embittered and wretchedly poor young women who plan to rob two "rich" older women in a posh part of the city, not realising that they too are at the end of their means. It ends in a double killing as the robbery goes wrong. Philip Martin also wrote *Lord Nelson Lives in Liverpool 8*, performed in the Studio, the story of a gentle black guy who hero worships Nelson, goes to the Isle of Man for a holiday, is unjustly accused of a crime and birched, and on his return finds himself a race hero and takes up a leadership role.'

ANTONY TUCKEY, ARTISTIC DIRECTOR

Antony Tuckey leaves

' His resignation was received with very real regret … He has personally directed about sixty productions and to each he has brought care, imagination and professionalism. Some of his best work has been for children and of the classics. His inborn modesty conceals a determination, not to be confused with stubbornness. He has built up the audience in recent years by pursuing a play policy he has passionately believed in. At times some of our audience may have been offended. But in retrospect they have all appreciated his sincerity and will to succeed.'

CHAIRMAN'S STATEMENT TO THE AGM, 28 JULY 1975

' Antony Tuckey embodied a real respect for the institution of Liverpool Playhouse. He used to call the Chairman of the Board, James Rushworth, Sir. I assumed for a while you always called Board members Sir! He looked both ways as an Artistic Director. He understood the audience, and tried to please the middle class folks from the Wirral, and yet also encouraged young audiences and new plays. All that and run a 3 weekly Rep. Dick Tuckey was a smart theatre tactician as well as a genial and likeable leader.'

BARRY KYLE, TRAINEE AND ASSOCIATE DIRECTOR, 1969–72

Who's Afraid of Virginia Woolf? by Edward Albee, directed by Antony Tuckey; Sheila Scott Wilkinson as Martha, June 1970

Studio 1

The making
of the Studio:
Playhouse
Upstairs

‘ The second production in the studio was David Hare's *Slag*, three women, saying and doing things rarely, if ever, said and done by women on the stage before. We opened with almost no tickets sold and had to paper the first performance. Next day there was a rave review in *The Guardian* and, by the time the second performance commenced that evening, the show was sold out. Such is the power of the press!

A year or so later we did a popular comedy called *A Girl in My Soup* in the main house and Heathcote Williams *AC/DC* in the studio – probably the most bizarre play ever written – and Ken Campbell was in the cast! Both sold out and the whole theatre was heaving. It was a memorable three weeks.

However. Why Playhouse Upstairs?

There was I felt a need for a small space where such plays could be performed. Our Main House had to pursue a fairly conservative policy in order to achieve the 50 to 60% box-office necessary for survival. The Everyman, often brilliantly empty under Peter James, was packing them in under Alan Dossor with a series of beautifully acted and directed robust social comedies. The lack in the city's theatrical life was a space where new names, Brenton, Hare, Heathcote Williams and others could be seen. The Upstairs programme would be limited; perhaps 5 productions playing, at most, 15 weeks in the year. ’

ANTONY TUCKEY, ARTISTIC DIRECTOR

**Starting out:
Caroline Smith
and Alan
Bleasdale**

The first studio production had been a version of *King Lear* directed by Barry Kyle in December 1971, but the 'official' opening of the studio came in January 1972 with a double bill of C.P. Taylor's *Allergy* and Howard Brenton's *Heads*.

Above: *The Mersey Ferry Boat Show* by A.J. Kelly, directed by Tim Albery; March 1977

‘ My first involvement with the Liverpool Playhouse was in 1962 when I went there as a trainee director. At that time the Artistic Director was David Scase. The things I remember most about those days were, firstly, what turned out to be a very talented resident company. It included Anthony Hopkins, Linda Marchal (later to become the writer Linda La Plante), Stephen Berkoff and Jean Boht among others. David had a good eye for spotting potential. The second memory is of the open antagonism that existed between the General Manager, Mr Hamilton Moore and David. As far as we, who stood watching and listening, could gather it was basically because David was trying to do plays by playwrights like Brecht, which the Manager, somewhat patronisingly, didn't feel his audiences could cope with. It resulted in David leaving earlier than expected.

It was a very different story when I went back to Liverpool in 1974 as associate director to Antony Tuckey. The General Manager was now Chris Bullock who was wonderfully supportive to the things the artistic side was trying to achieve. There was trouble of course ... but this time with the Board of Management. However Dick (aka Antony Tuckey) fought hard and was finally allowed to make several innovations. Most notable of these, as far as I was concerned, was the creation of studio seasons in the old rehearsal room. The plays we did there were many and varied. The one I personally most enjoyed being involved with was *Fat Harold and the Last 26* by Alan Bleasdale. Set somewhere in Liverpool, it was about a bus driver, who with all his passengers loses his way in the fog. A slim premise, but a very funny and telling play. This was Alan Bleasdale's first stage play which the Playhouse commissioned for the princely sum of £200. Again and again the Everyman Theatre have been given the credit for discovering and doing Alan's first play. Actually, it was the Playhouse. Alan obviously had a great deal of talent, but this was his first play, and he had things to learn, particularly about structure. Thus he manfully stood by and allowed his play to be chopped up into little bits and sellotaped together into a new structure. The play was greeted by a wonderful review from Robin Thornber, which put Alan on the map as a new young playwright.

Other plays I really enjoyed doing in the studio were *Yers Owd Pool* – about Liverpool in the 1930s, and following that success, *Yers Owd Pool Goes to War* – about Liverpool in World War Two. Both docu-dramas were researched by Ray Herman and co-written by him and the company. With six actors and the help of songs and music from the period we managed, I think, to create many nostalgic memories for the older members of the audience and an enjoyable education for those too young to remember. The thing both sections of the audience seem to respond to in both plays was the recognition of the "Scouse Spirit" which somehow overcame the many obstacles the people of Liverpool were confronted with.

CAROLINE SMITH, ASSOCIATE DIRECTOR

Lucky Liverpool

❛ Each year Thames Television award a bursary to writers to work for twelve months with a professional company. This year one of the recipients of the award was Alan Bleasdale who now becomes resident dramatist at the Playhouse. We have already produced two of his plays ... and one of them, *Fat Harold and the Last 26* has just been staged in London at the New End Theatre.

Frank Marcus ... reviewed this recent production in *The Daily Telegraph* on January 4 1976: 'We hear a lot about regional theatres these days, the term 'provincial' having been dropped because of its patronising sound ... The accepted criterion of justification for regional theatre is the degree to which they deal with indigenous issues. Local industrial problems are probed, local history is unearthed, and the inhabitants are subjected to constant interrogation on a great variety of issues. All this well-meaning activity is designed to give the population a sense of identification with 'their' theatre ... The prospect of sitting in a converted morgue in Hampstead in order to see a play set in a bus depot in Liverpool on a foggy night seemed less than propitious. In the circumstances it turned out to be a hugely enjoyable experience. It did not surprise me that the author, Alan Bleasdale, knew his subject and his speech idiom inside out. What was surprising was the assurance with which he organised his material ... and his surprising sense of humour ...'

Alan Bleasdale is now writing his first play for the main auditorium and is also going to be responsible for all literary aspects of the Playhouse and will make regular contributions to the programme, read new scripts and look for new writing talents as well as contributing more original work for both the Playhouse Upstairs and the main auditorium. Lucky Liverpool indeed – and Lucky Playhouse! ❜

PROGRAMME NOTE, JANUARY 1976

Fat Harold went to the New End Theatre in London and the Nuffield Theatre in Southampton (where the setting was changed) and then to the Shaw Theatre in London, still set in Southampton. Bleasdale's second studio play, *The Party's Over* (directed by Sue Wilson, November 1975) was set in a remand home and tickets at the Playhouse sold out.

Merseyside Miscellany, directed by Tim Albery; November 1976

❛ "It is commonplace to hear that talent will always find a way. It is not true. The few who emerge as artists have often been helped by the most unlikely stroke of luck in the way of human contacts." (Ted Hughes)

127

Jason, Gin and Southport by Catherine Hayes, directed William Gaunt; the cast was Leslie Schofield, Miranda Forbes, Ian Mackenzie, Polly Hemingway and Jenny Tarren, March 1978 (Colin Thorpe)

Hitting Town by Stephen Poliakoff, directed by Bob Cartland; with Dean Harris and Pamela Blackwood, March 1977

I am working in the theatre today simply because of Caroline Smith, who was associate director at the Playhouse in 1975. Without my knowledge, Robert Cooper, my producer at Radio Merseyside, gave Ms Smith a copy of the only play I had ever written – a half hour radio play. On the strength of that she commissioned me ...

Most people who write in the isolation of their bedroom or back kitchen will never have the luck that I had. Some of those writers deserve to be given a chance to be heard. However, in the theatre of the financially barren mid-seventies, the opportunities are few and far between. So, when Leslie Lawton suggested that I compile an evening of plays by writers who had never had their work presented on stage before, I naturally welcomed the idea.

In June of this year, Joe Riley announced in the *Liverpool Echo* that we were searching for new material, short in length, limited in cast, for

Merseyside Miscellany. Two weeks later, I was sitting in front of over fifty scripts, but most were lamentable, several were over two hours long and many had enough characters to make *War and Peace* seem like *Krapp's Last Tape.*

Slowly, the standard of work improved and we started to get pieces that had been specially written within the confines that we had set. When Tim Albery, the director of this production, arrived at the Playhouse in August, we were soon down to four scripts by three writers, Catherine Hayes, Lesley Clive and Paul Sonabend. Much later Frank Dagnalls, who knew nothing of *Merseyside Miscellany*, pushed a very funny and topical sketch through my letterbox in the hope that I could find a place for it on local radio. One of Ted Hughes' "most unlikely strokes of luck".

Little Sandra by Catherine Hayes, directed by Tim Fywell; Sarah Webb as Sandra. The cast also included Brenda Fricker as Mrs Tranter, March 1980

Skirmishes by Catherine Hayes, directed by Tim Fywell; Kate Fitzgerald as Rita and Eileen O'Brien as Jean, April 1981 (Colin Thorpe)

There were other scripts from other writers that we could, at a pinch, have presented tonight, but we were constantly aware of the danger of putting work on stage that is not ready for production. We may be doing that tonight, and if we are, it is our fault, not the writers involved. What we do hope, above all else, is that at least one of the plays is so well received that this time next year the writer will be commissioned for a studio production in this theatre of his or her first full length piece.

Opposite: *Merseyside Miscellany* directed by Tim Albery; November 1976

"A great proportion of people have some talent, given the right conditions for it to show itself. It mightn't be much – not enough to justify them throwing up all other ambitions in the hope of becoming an artist. But even the tiniest spark is very important to the person who has it, and very important to the rest of society … Here and there, of course, we will find someone with real talent." (Ted Hughes)

ALAN BLEASDALE, PROGRAMME NOTE

Merseyside Miscellany presented: Catherine Hayes: *Life's Simplest Tasks*; Leslie Clive: *Tie-Up*; Paul Sonabend: *Play without a Play*; Frank Dagnalls: *One Man, One Bus, One Missing*; Paul Sonabend: *Significance*. Catherine Hayes' *Jason, Gin and Southport* was commissioned for the studio in the following season.

Skirmishes by Catherine Hayes, directed Tim Fywell; April 1981

Starting out: Catherine Hayes

The Liverpool Playhouse changed my life. Or perhaps, Alan Bleasdale and Tim Albery did. They were the people who asked local writers to send them scripts in the hope of producing an evening of one-act plays in the studio, or Playhouse Upstairs, to give it its official name. This was a small, dark, low-ceilinged room and, for me, the most exciting space in Liverpool bar none. You went there to see new plays, old plays, foreign plays, entertainments, one-offs, and other peculiarities that didn't find a home on the main stage. You could arrive for a 7.45 performance, see it, have a drink, and go back in for something completely different at eleven o'clock. Fantastic.

Everything about the Playhouse was fantastic in those days, the late seventies/early eighties. A golden age, if you like, when there seemed to be constant theatrical toing and froing between Liverpool and London. Bill Gaunt took over from Leslie Lawton as Artistic Director and the theatre continued to be a place of excitement. I learnt various things there: every show is different every night; something normally goes wrong but usually the audience doesn't notice; no matter how many people are entranced, someone's bored stiff; in a perfect world the audience would be included in the cast list.

I wrote a play called *Skirmishes* which did very well on the Upstairs stage. It's a black comedy and it got lots of laughs every night except for one night (oh, OK. There may have been other nights, but let's stick to the one). The play started well but a very pleasant-looking lady in the front row couldn't stop laughing. She laughed and laughed. All the time. No matter what the actresses were saying. No matter what was happening on

Judgement by Barry
Collins, directed by
William Gaunt and
Tim Fywell; Patrick
Malahide, November
1979
'The man, Vukhov, is
a fiction; so, broadly
is the story he tells.
Certain details,
however, are factual
... the Germans left a
number of captured
Russian officers locked
in a cellar. Two of the
prisoners managed
to stay alive by
killing and devouring
their companions.'
(Programme note)

Starting out:
Tim Fywell

stage. She just kept laughing. She was thoroughly enjoying herself. Laugh, laugh, laugh. Giggle, giggle, giggle. Before long, no-one was watching the performance anymore. All eyes were on her. Mine in particular, I was giving her daggers. To no avail, though. The play died in front of us. One person entranced, ninety-nine bored stiff. What can you do?

That's the attraction really. I love going to the cinema but, at its best, nothing can touch a live performance. Few things fire your imagination more than the blackout before the curtains open. A film will run its course. It'll repeat itself flawlessly every showing. Your influence is zero. Box office takings aside, it doesn't actually matter whether you're there or not. In the theatre, though, you're integral and during my association with the Playhouse, it seemed to me that the theatre was integral to the city. Things meshed together and we all profited. It was the beginning of the most exciting time of my life. *)*

CATHERINE HAYES, WRITER

Skirmishes was also performed in the main house in January 1983 and she was one of the theatre's Thames television writers in residence. Her other plays were:

Jason, Gin and Southport, directed by William Gaunt, February 1978
Little Sandra, directed by Tim Fywell, March 1980
Marrowfat Peas for *The April 1st Show*, directed by George Costigan, Janet
    Goddard and Willy Russell, December 1981

(Bill Gaunt phoned me and said, "Can you start on Monday?"

I arrived at Lime Street station for the first time on the Monday morning early train. The man in the newsagent's told me where the Playhouse was – "Just over there." Everyone knew it.

I was directing Patrick Malahide in *Judgement*, a three and a half hour monologue by Barry Collins about a Russian Army Colonel who had to cannibalise his fellow men in order to survive during the siege of Leningrad. Three and a half hours and just a week to rehearse. I divided the play up into pages. We had 12 to 15 pages to get through in a day. Luckily Patrick had already learned it. We rehearsed morning noon and night. At one point, working with just one actor and one chair, I started hallucinating and called Patrick "Roger". He was so wired by this time that he screamed and threw the chair (the only prop) at me. We got through that and the show was a big success.

My next show in the studio was *Little Sandra*. It starred the brilliant, erratic, volatile Brenda Fricker who told me: "You're too good. You're on my case. I don't like you." I remember auditioning a 16 year old

Manchester schoolgirl called Joanne Whalley for the title role, and having to turn her down – regretfully – because she was just too beautiful for the part – she looked like a movie star.

Then I did *Skirmishes*, also by Catherine Hayes, an intensely haunting play about two sisters looking after their dying mother, with varying degrees of love and resentment. It starred Eileen O'Brien and Kate Fitzgerald as the sisters. Catherine – an only daughter who lived with her own Mum at the time, had divided herself in two – the devoted daughter, and the flighty one who has escaped the claustrophobic nest – and written a lacerating, brilliant play. Willy Russell and Alan Bleasdale were in the audience on press night. Alan came up to me and said: "No-one can write family dramas like Cath Hayes." The production was funny, savage and emotional – we revived it with a starry cast in London subsequently but it didn't have the raw power of that initial Liverpool production.

TIM FYWELL, DIRECTOR

Late-night shows

It is with some reluctance that I report on the general success of the Late Night Shows – *Dilys*, *Ashes* and *Oh, Coward* in particular. Reluctance because they are now established as a normal part of Playhouse business which means for quite a few of us the longest working days in the history of the British Theatre and it means at any one time we have six shows in performance and/or preparation. However, on Saturday October 7th 1976 I stood squashed half way up the stairs while literally hundreds of

The Party's Over by Alan Bleasdale, directed by Sue Wilson; November 1975

people swarmed around me. Both *Robin Redbreast* and *Miss Julie* had been playing to capacity and another capacity crowd was gathering for Dilys Watling's late night show ... The resultant crush was every theatre's dream – in other words we were busy.*

LESLIE LAWTON, ANNUAL STATEMENT TO THE BOARD, JULY 1977

The After Hours Late Shows at 11 continued in the 1977–78 season and included Leslie Lawton in his one man show, *My Turn*.

Ashes by David Rudkin, directed by Antony Webb; Jenny Oulton and Leslie Lawton, March 1976 (Colin Thorpe)

The audience up there is changing ... Dare I say it? OLDER faces are appearing and we have at last broken down the image of either an exclusive "club" theatre, an experimental semi-amateur theatre mainly catering for students or a den of iniquity where nudity and four-letter words are obligatory ...

LESLIE LAWTON, ARTISTIC DIRECTOR'S STATEMENT TO THE AGM FOR 1977–78 SEASON

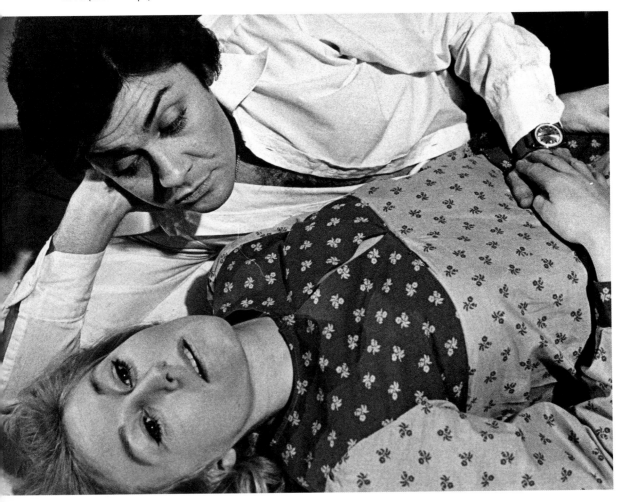

Leslie Lawton, 1975–1979

❛ Where Dick Tuckey looked like a Roman centurion steadfastly manning the frontier, Leslie reminded one more of Tony Curtis. Flamboyant, larger than life, he swept into the Playhouse a one-man PR agency. ❜

Voake

The view from the Artistic Director

❛ My first professional theatre work was at the Liverpool Playhouse in 1962/3. I was in the very lowly position of Male Assistant Stage Manager (my female counterpart was Jean Boht) and combined menial stage sweeping, tea making duties with playing small roles. So it was with some trepidation that I returned only 12 years later as Artistic Director. I inherited the building at an interesting time. The Everyman was regarded as the more exciting and contemporary of the City's two "repertory" theatres and had already successfully transferred several of its productions to London. In engaging a 32 year old "whizzkid" Artistic Director to succeed the rather staid and intellectual Antony Tuckey the Playhouse board seemed to be throwing down the gauntlet to the seemingly more youthful Everyman.

It was clear that my main purpose was to shake off the blue rinse, Wirral commuters dominated image of the building. The trick was to build up a new audience without losing too many members of the old one in the process. I felt that the answer lay in the Playhouse Upstairs. The studio theatre had a regular little audience which was probably shared by our rivals in Hope Street. A considerable percentage of this audience would never descend to the main house just as the main house's respectable regular audience would never dream of climbing up to the studio. I could see that my task was to mix things up a little. And so I resolved to schedule "studio" work in the main auditorium and some lighter fare upstairs.

But first I had to increase the main house audience figures which were distressingly low and financially disturbing. I pulled in a few favours from actors and writers with whom I had worked in London theatre and television. I felt we could worry about forging a more "local" image later – let's just get larger numbers visiting us regularly first. My first company included a host of familiar TV faces – Anne Stallybrass, Marius Goring, Ken Farrington, William Lucas, Rhoda Lewis, Michael Elwyn, Barbara Flynn, Geoffrey Hughes, Glyn Owen, Elisabeth Sladen, Dilys Watling, Alfred Marks, Ian Ogilvy and Peggy Mount. The box office was busier than it had been for many years.

The first season's playlist was not revolutionary or in any way experimental but it proved to be very attractive to large numbers – Pinero, Priestley, Tennessee Williams, Shaw, Strindberg, Alan Bennett, Jean Genet, Orton, Ayckbourn, Shaffer, Rudkin and Storey were the reliable playwrights whose work graced my first year's programme. And there were two new plays from Willis Hall, a British premiere from the Irish writer Hugh Leonard and two specially written pieces from our resident writer Alan Bleasdale.

The Christmas season saw a box office record breaking run of the musical *Cabaret*. This became an annual tradition and *My Fair Lady, A Funny Thing Happened on the Way to the Forum* and *The Wizard of Oz* were subsequent yuletide hits. Our output over the next few years was extraordinary – 28 in house productions every 12 months with an average of 16 performances each week (In the Main House, Playhouse Upstairs and Upstairs Late Night) plus late night jazz concerts etc. in the Main House. And all of this with a staggeringly pared down regular staff – four office staff, three technicians, seven stage management and a total of seven personnel covering workshop and wardrobe. Don't ask me how that overworked little group managed to produce such consistently good work but somehow they did.

Boys in the Band by Matt Crowley, directed by William Lucas; Leslie Lawton, Colin Farrell, Richard Norton, Hugh Ross, March 1977 (Colin Thorpe)

Comedians by Trevor Griffiths, directed by Brian Howard; Norman Rossington as Eddie Waters and Jonathan Coy as Gethin; March 1978
'The experiment of mixing up the audiences really came unstuck just after *Streamers*. The problem was Trevor Griffith's *Comedians*. People walked out very angry. It lost a big section of the public for quite a long time.' (Leslie Lawton, quoted in Voake)

Children's Day by Keith Waterhouse and Willis Hall, directed by Leslie Lawton; with Alan Rothwell, John Jardine and Muriel Barker, July 1979

Audiences grew in numbers but were often mysteriously fickle. In one season we played to near capacity with *King Lear, Bedroom Farce* and *Privates on Parade* but emptied the theatre with Shaffer's *The Royal Hunt of the Sun.* Unanimously enthusiastic reviews did nothing to improve business – a valuable lesson!

This was something of a Golden Age for the British regional theatre with an energetic and committed roster of Artistic Directors at the helms – Nottingham (Richard Eyre), Birmingham (Clive Perry), Leeds (John Harrison), Bristol (Richard Cotterill), Glasgow (Giles Havergal), Manchester (Michael Elliott, Casper Wrede and Braham Murray).The idea of public subsidy for regional arts establishments seemed to be an accepted concept at long last and, although there were inevitable problems such as the upkeep of the buildings, both new and old, there was a feeling of some security. The Playhouse's subsidy, from the local authorities and the Arts Council, mostly went towards the running of what was by now an old building with on-going housekeeping difficulties. We were very dependent on the box office income for the basic financing of the actual productions. To me, and I suspect most of the Artistic Directors of my generation, this seemed entirely correct. Did we suspect, I wonder now, that this was a halcyon period with a fast approaching end in-sight? Within a decade we were all fighting for survival thanks to funding cutbacks, spiralling costs, new union demands for fairer pay and better working conditions

Confusions by Alan Ayckbourn, directed by Tim Albery;
Leslie Lawton played 4 different roles,
Sept 1977 (Colin Thorpe)
Top left: Gosforth in *Gosforth's Fete*
Left: Harry in *Drinking Companion*
Below: Waiter in *Between Mouthfuls*
Above: Ernest in *A Talk in the Park*

Cabaret by Kander and Ebb, directed by Kim Grant; Leslie Lawton with two Kit Kat Klub Girls, December 1975 (Colin Thorpe) 'He caught all the razzmatazz and decadent glitter of the club; one felt that he himself would have been happy as a music hall entertainer' (Colin Voake)

which inevitably led to increased staff and shorter working hours. And the battle to attract audiences away from the ever increasing demands on their leisure time and disposable incomes.

But when I left the Playhouse in 1979 (tempted by the challenge of "saving" the beleaguered Royal Lyceum Theatre in Edinburgh) we were still sailing through calm waters and there was a good, solid regular Playhouse audience once again. And an audience which had, indeed, changed over my tenure In particular there was less of a "divide" between the Playhouse and Everyman clientele. We now both shared a large section of our audience which had always been my aim. And even as long ago as 1979 I was promoting the "unthinkable" idea that one day the two theatres might combine their administration and artistic talents and run the two theatres under one umbrella. It is comforting to know that I turned out not to be as daft as some people supposed I was! 9

LESLIE LAWTON, ARTISTIC DIRECTOR

Bleasdale on the main stage

Down the Dock Road by Alan Bleasdale, directed by Brian Howard; March 1976

The choice of *Down the Dock Road* was one part of an attempt by Lawton to look for a new and younger audience, helped by the closure of The Everyman in 1976 for a rebuild.

6 In the 60s and 70s there was a useful relationship between theatre and television. Thames Television organised and financed trainee theatre director and writer schemes. At the Playhouse the first beneficiary of the latter secondment was a local schoolteacher who had already had some success ...

Alan Bleasdale had been a binman and a steel worker and had taught in the Remedial Department of a school on an estate and at a large comprehensive in Halewood and had been an Education Officer in the Gilbert and Ellice Islands of the Western Pacific.

He had established himself as a writer of some talent, wit and observation with his Scully stories which appeared in *The Listener* and the *Liverpool Daily Post*. His first stage piece was *Fat Harold and the Last 26* in Antony Tuckey's final season in the Playhouse Upstairs. Fortuitously for me Henry Cotton, the visionary Chairman of the Board urged me to see it. I was bowled over by the confidence of the writing and, when his Thames "apprenticeship" came to an end I urged him to stay on as Writer in Residence.

Alan's next play was *The Party's Over,* a slight but touching account of life in a Liverpool Remand Home. But I was worried at the time that most of the new writing was small cast, intimate "Studio" stuff. Where was the new work for the big stage coming from, I wondered? I commissioned him to write a "big" play for the Playhouse with no restrictions on cast size or technical requirements. At the same time stressing the desirability of a) writing, as all young writers should, about what he really knew and b) writing something relevant to the local audience.

It was a gamble (like most worthwhile ground-breaking theatrical events) as in my first season we had fared very badly with a play about football which I had, wrongly, assumed would be a big hit in a city so steeped in the lore and lure of the game.

Alan took me at my word. One of his earliest jobs had been as an Insecurity guard on Liverpool Docks. He used this experience vividly and created *Down the Dock Road*, a funny, moving and clearly accurate portrait of the men who he described as "quite special in the folklore of this city".

It was an instant success and brought in a new audience that even the more experimental and progressive Everyman Theatre had never managed to attract.

By 1975 *Scully* had become a best-selling novel and I asked him for a stage adaptation which he delivered in 1980. It then became a TV series and it is in this media where he has since earned many awards for his brilliant work including *GBH* and, of course, *Boys From The Black Stuff* which I would like to think owed something to what he learnt from his experience down the Down Road – both the actual one and the Playhouse representation!

LESLIE LAWTON, ARTISTIC DIRECTOR

In 1970, I was an Insecurity Guard on Birkenhead Docks during my Easter and Summer holidays from school, where I was earning £17 a week after tax and deductions as a fully qualified school teacher. I needed money because I was getting married at the end of the year, and a friend of mine gave me a phone number, said there was some easy money to be earned and told me to use a false name.

For a total of ten weeks I became Alan Grant, was in charge of security on a number of ships, was paid five pounds a day in my hand, and was never asked for my Insurance Cards or proof of identity. I was working for a small but bona-fide security firm, and I could have been straight out of prison, borstal or a bomb-making society.

The dockers were very suspicious of me at first. I wasn't an old age pensioner, I wasn't crippled, I didn't slip off down the Dole with the others to sign on, and I wasn't on the rob. It was only when it dawned on them that I actually was an innocent abroad, and when I told them my monthly salary was equal to their weekly wage, that I became accepted.

The suspicion and surliness vanished and I was allowed to see the warmth, weird immoral honesty, wit and camaraderie that really does make – in my experience – the Liverpool docker someone quite special in the folklore of this city. The very nature of the job, and the battles the men have fought against management, through the overlapping generations, no doubt makes this inevitable, but nevertheless for someone like myself, wrapped in the manners and gentle debate of staffrooms, it was an experience never to be forgotten ...

ALAN BLEASDALE, PROGRAMME NOTE

141

Franny Scully's Christmas Stories by Alan Bleasdale, directed by Leslie Lawton
and Tim Albery; December 1976

❛ My friend Franny Scully was "born" when I first started teaching on a
housing estate in my home town of Huyton in 1967. He is made up of
three or four boys in the school, and none of them were called Scully.
Originally, I was going to christen him "Scally" as in "scallywag" but
that sounded too cockney, so I replaced the "a" with a Liverpool "u".
He has been called a "juvenile delinquent Just William", and a lot more
unrepeatable names as well, because there are aspects of his character that
appear to be unpleasant and anti-social.

However, before anyone leaves the theatre or wonders what kind of a
delinquent pantomime they've come to see this afternoon, there is always
another side to Scully's story, and in this case, it's the funny side of the
story. Many of the children I knew and taught had a remarkably quick
sense of humour and an ability to tell a good story – usually a lie, but a
good story nevertheless! ❜

ALAN BLEASDALE, PROGRAMME NOTE

Down the Dock Road by Alan Bleasdale,
directed by Brian Howard; March 1976.
(Colin Thorpe) The cast included David
Browning, Christopher Neil, David Jackson,
Antony Webb, Anthony Haygarth,
Alan Hunter, Geoffrey Hughes, Richard Henry,
John Challis, Mickey Finn, Robert Hamilton,
David Browning and John Peel

Franny Scully's Christmas Stones by Alan
Bleasdale, directed by Leslie Lawton and
Tim Albery; billed as a new scouse panto,
December 1976

142

Macbeth by Shakespeare, directed by Leslie Lawton; John Barcroft (foreground) as Banquo, Michael Elwyn (centre) as Macbeth, Jane Lowe (right) as Lady Macbeth, November 1976 (Colin Thorpe). This was the theatre's 65th birthday production

❛ I find it hard to comment on the children's show *Scully* as I seem to be alone in thinking it witty and entertaining. My own children loved it. But then as one irate patron said when I told him this, "Well, of course, your children are bound to be peculiar." Maybe Bleasdale and I misjudged our audience – but I think it more likely that we overestimated their parents. ❜

Leslie Lawton, Annual Statement to the Board, July 1977

Some shows from 1975–76 season

❛ There is no permanent answer to the question: "What fills theatres?" The answer in 1976 is very different to that in Maud Carpenter's time and such is the speed at which public taste changes the answer will no doubt be different again in twelve months from now. Faced with the all too simple facts of the theatre's economy – never unrelated to that of the rest of the world – and knowing that over the years the Liverpool public has been unpredictable to say the least – the varied and wide-ranging programme presented over the last year required courage and determination from the Board and the new Artistic Director … My own Liverpool debut as director was a "curate's egg" production of Pinero's delightful comedy of theatrical life *Trelawney of the 'Wells'* …

My own heart came in for a bit of a battering with the next production. I had complete faith in Hugh Leonard's autobiographical play *Da* and from the moment I started rehearsing … I felt sure we were finally to set Liverpool alight with a theatregoing highlight of the century.

143

Privates on Parade by
Peter Nichols, directed
by Brian Howard; Leslie
Lawton as Acting Captain
Terri Dennis, April 1979

The indifference with which the majority of the press and public greeted what is in my opinion a truly great play was shattering ... I would prefer to draw a veil over the next production. Willis Hall, an old friend of mine, was persuaded to write a play for Liverpool which the people of Liverpool would find pertinent in 1975. The result was *Walk On Walk On* – a football comedy with a brilliant set by Billy Meall ... The "people of Liverpool" might have found it pertinent, hilarious, moving, amusing or just plain boring. Unfortunately we shall never know as they chose to stay away in their thousands and I spent three weeks trying to jolly along the flagging spirits of a disillusioned cast ... Things were not likely to get any brighter either as I had in a foolish moment of bravado announced that I would play the horribly exacting all singing-dancing role of the M.C. in the Christmas musical *Cabaret* – the part for which Joel Grey got an Oscar in the movie version – as no-one ever tired of reminding me.

LESLIE LAWTON, ARTISTIC DIRECTOR'S ANNUAL REPORT, 1976

Cabaret, although described by Lawton as one of the biggest gambles in the history of the theatre went on to be a success and restored the confidence of the company. The theatre also scored financial (and critical success) in that season with Peggy Mount's performance in *The Anniversary*.

Streamers by David Rabe, directed by Leslie Lawton, February 1978

**New York to
London via
Liverpool**

I went to New York, saw the play *Streamers*, and bought it for the studio. Then quite suddenly one day I thought: come on, you've been talking about this for ages. Why don't you really do a studio play in the main auditorium?

LESLIE LAWTON; QUOTED IN VOAKE

‘ On a visit to New York in 1977 I had a deeply moving experience at the
Lincoln Center where I saw *Streamers* by David Rabe. The play was set in
an army barracks and most of the characters were young men waiting to
be shipped out to fight in the Vietnam War. It was an angry, visceral piece
with a shocking climax of such impact that the audience left the theatre in
a near traumatic state. I had never seen anything like it and, although I
knew it would be a risky piece to stage at the Playhouse, I was determined
to do it.

I discovered that the London Royal Court and National Theatre had
both expressed strong interest but neither had a definite production date.
I did a quick mental reshuffle of my next season and, going directly to
Rabe himself, gave a firm commitment to produce the play in February
1978 and to transfer it to London in March. I had no idea if the Board
would agree and no immediate thoughts on where we would do it in
London or how we would finance it. But I knew we had to take a chance.
My first two seasons had been commercially and artistically successful
but now we had to expand our work and be recognised away from our
home base.

The Board backed me all the way and I contacted the brilliant
independent producer Thelma Holt who was running the Roundhouse in
London at that time. I told her about the play and we shook hands on a
rental deal in the back of a London taxi. But where to find the cash?

Carl Hawkins, a Board member and my best friend, knew a man.
As simple as that. He softened up a local businessman and between
us we somehow convinced him that this disturbing, explosive piece of
modern theatre would bring great glory to his business on Merseyside. I
offered him the Roundhouse’s catering facilities in which to entertain his

Streamers by David
Rabe, directed
by Leslie Lawton;
February 1978
(Colin Thorpe)
Below: Trevor Jones
as Billy, James
Aubrey as Richie, Don
Warrington as Carlyle
Below right: Don
Warrington as Carlyle
and Jeffrey Kissoon
as Roger

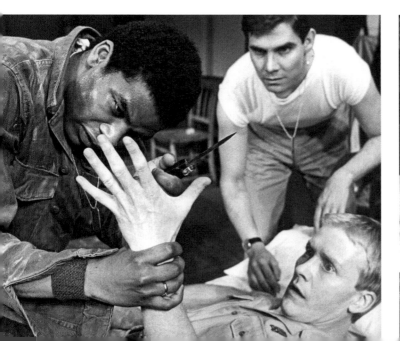

corporate clients and prominent billing in the programme, all over both theatres and on all advertising matter. It was the first time I had ever gone after sponsorship and it was never as easy again. All it took was one boozy dinner with me waxing lyrical and Carl enthusiastically reacting in the background. By the time the coffee came round I had a cheque to cover all the costs of a London transfer.

The production made a terrific impact on Merseyside and, if possible, the reviews were even better in London. Joe Riley covered the whole process in a series of articles for the *Echo* and after the triumphant opening night at the Roundhouse he wrote, "the Great Liverpool Playhouse Experiment is complete. With the British Premiere of *Streamers* the theatre can claim to have shed the last vestige of its maiden-aunt image. Leslie Lawton has snuffed out the candle of provincialism to put the Playhouse in the mainstream of dramatic creative potential."

Mission accomplished! '

LESLIE LAWTON, ARTISTIC DIRECTOR

Comedians by Trevor Griffiths, directed by Brian Howard; March 1978

Shocking the audience

The Anniversary by Bill McIlwraith, directed by Malcolm Farquhar; Peggy Mount as Mum, March 1976 (Colin Thorpe)

' The last main auditorium play of the financial year, Trevor Griffith's *Comedians*, brought dozens of letters of abuse and protest from shocked members of the public and I diligently answered each one with my firmly held belief that this is one of the most important plays to be written in the past decade, that in years to come it will be regarded as a classic, that Brian Howard's production was superb and that it should have been an ideal choice for a regional theatre with a forward-thinking policy and an eye on the audience of tomorrow. My somewhat unflinching stance in the face of much personal abuse (for having "brought pornography to Liverpool") was due to a lesson I was taught early in my career – in my first directing job for Arthur Brough ... he had been successfully running the rep. at Folkestone for 30 years on an undiluted diet of Agatha Christies and drawing room comedies when he boldly went "experimental" and dared to present in one season *Roots, Look Back in Anger* and *A Taste of Honey*. He had many abusive letters and was finally physically attacked on the sea front by two elderly ladies brandishing umbrellas. They said words to the effect, "You must realise that we are your regular supporters, Mr Brough and we don't like these plays." To which he calmly replied: "I know but what do I do when you're dead?" '

LESLIE LAWTON, ARTISTIC DIRECTOR'S ANNUAL STATEMENT TO THE AGM,
1977–78 SEASON

Walk On Walk On by Willis Hall, directed by Leslie Lawton; November 1975 (Colin Thorpe) The *Walk On Walk On* team: back row (l–r): Leslie Lawton, Philip Guard, Robin Wentworth, Willis Hall, Glyn Owen. Front row: Anne Stallybrass, David Beckett, Michael Cotterill, Alan Rothwell, Pamela Blackwood. Kneeling: Billy Meall (designer)

6 It may interest regular patrons to see the list below in which we show the past season's productions in order of audience attendance percentages … It is an interesting "sign of the times" that the progressive choices such as *Jumpers* and even *Streamers* did better business than the more traditional Playhouse plays.

Top of the pops

1. *The Adventures of a Bear Called Paddington*
2. *Hamlet*
3. *A Man For All Seasons*
4. *Confusions*
5. *Jumpers*
6. *The Norman Conquests*
7. *A Funny Thing Happened on the Way to the Forum*
8. *Private Lives*
9. *The Sunshine Boys*
10. *Double Edge*
11. *Streamers*
12. *A Touch of Spring*
13. *Comedians*
14. *The Miracle Worker* 9

LESLIE LAWTON, IN THE PROGRAMME FOR *MURDERER*, JULY 1978

Leslie Lawton leaves

6 What an exciting four years they have been! What a tremendous contribution Leslie has made to the Playhouse. We thank him for putting Liverpool Playhouse back on the theatrical map. We shall long remember those memorable productions of *Trelawney*, *Da*, *Inspector Calls*, *Front Page*, *Saturday, Sunday, Monday*, *Bedroom Farce*, *Royal Hunt of the Sun*, *King Lear* and, of course, *Streamers*, which transferred to London. Not only have his productions been widely acclaimed but so have his performances in *Cabaret*, *Butley*, *Ashes*, *Boys in the Band*, *Privates on Parade*, *Absurd Person Singular*, *Confusions* and *A Touch of Spring*. 9

HENRY COTTON, PROGRAMME NOTE, JULY 1979

William Gaunt, 1979–1981

❝ I think it's important that the director should have an identity with the public ... I shall establish a nucleus of people here, but will be asking actors and directors to pay guest visits. I shall also encourage new work as a theatre exists for authors as well as performers.❞

WILLIAM GAUNT, QUOTED IN *LIVERPOOL ECHO*, 23 MARCH 1979

❝ We were already into a difficult time in my last year. The theatre had either to go back and make up its mind to be a sort of glamorous respectable sort of Willard Stoker/Maud Carpenter emporium, or go really forward. People say that Bill Gaunt's programme was different from mine; and if I have any criticism it is that it was not different enough.❞

LESLIE LAWTON, QUOTED IN *VOAKE*

❝ Bill was very thoughtful about the plays he chose. I think the level of direction grew under his regime in a way that sowed the seeds that made it possible for Chris Bond, Willy Russell, Alan Bleasdale and Bill Morrison.❞

PETER LICHTENFELS, QUOTED IN *VOAKE*

An artistic director's view

❝ I was directing *Candida* at the Playhouse, towards the end of Leslie Lawton's tenure, and we were living in a flat in Huskisson Street. My wife Carolyn was due to have a baby in the February but went into labour in the middle of a November night and was rushed into the hospital where our son Albie was born, weighing just over 2lbs. So when Henry Cotton offered me the job, I took it. It was a chance for us all to be together, for me to stay in one place and I even bought a house in Mount Street. And then I plunged into the work without realising quite how demanding it would be with three week changes in two spaces and running for 40 weeks of the year. It was a very steep learning curve to step into that position at Liverpool Playhouse at that time and with such a small staff – five of us ran the entire theatre.

Educating Rita by Willy Russell, directed by Willy Russell and Pip Broughton (on special release from the West End); William Gaunt and Kate Fitzgerald, February 1981. This was the first Liverpool performance for the show which started life at the Royal Shakespeare Company

I ran the Playhouse in a series of seasons doing a lot of very serious and challenging plays. We did the first regional production of David Hare's *Plenty* and took two shows to the Edinburgh Festival – Barry Collins' one man show *Judgement*, which won a Fringe First and *Here's a Funny Thing*, an entertainment with music based on the life and performances of Max Miller. I made some bad decisions, one of which was to put on *The*

Set for *Betrayal* by Harold Pinter, directed by William Gaunt; set designed by Andy Greenfield, April 1981 (Colette Rawlinson)

Fantasticks, a notorious theatre emptier although I did not know it at the time, for my second Christmas. Luckily, I had commissioned a play from David Woods for the afternoons, *Chish and Fips* (originally called *The Ideal Gnome Experiment* but we didn't think the children would get the joke) which ensured it was a successful Christmas. But, overall, I discovered people in Liverpool did not come to see plays that they did in other places. So we struggled on from season to season, although I did do Willy Russell's *One for the Road* which went on to the West End with Russ Abbott.

When I came towards the end of my time at the Playhouse, I asked Willy if I could do *Educating Rita* which had never been done in Liverpool. Because Willy always looked glum in rehearsals (not that he necessarily was), I asked him to co-direct it with Pip Broughton and this became his directorial debut. I'd left the end of the season open, hoping that *Rita* would help us to make up some of the seasons losses and it ran for eleven weeks to full capacity meaning I could leave the theatre in the black.

WILLIAM GAUNT, ARTISTIC DIRECTOR

A left-over piece of set

It is a third of a century since I first started work for Liverpool Repertory Theatre. There are only three out of the thirty-three intervening years when I did no work at the Playhouse, so there are many productions, many memories and many emotions as I look back. To try and pick a single production as the best, or worst, or most memorable out of the hundreds, I find impossible. It is no mere cliché to say the Playhouse has extracted blood, sweat and tears but there have also been hilarious moments – usually at 4.00am on an all-nighter when everything is hysterically funny. Whilst I still bear the scars of many productions, the buildings have faded, as time, refurbishment and the latest production wear away the old. The building gains patina, whilst I just get worn down and only gain grey hairs.

However, in the basement, under the stage, a glimpse of a production from thirty years ago can still be seen. It is a piece of set that has, for nearly three decades, been employed as a screen, stopping detritus from the stage falling into what, until the 1960s building works, was the theatre boiler room. I have always known it as the gas meter room and an electrics store, at various times filled with spare lamps, light fittings from sets or a motley array of old radios, phones and various plug-inable objects. The piece of set is some hardboard that formed part of Andy Greenfield's design for William Gaunt's April 1981 production of *Betrayal*. The production was part of Bill's triumphant final season as Artistic Director and came between the first out-of-London production of *Educating Rita* and the play's revival, that closed Bill's tenure and compensated for the financial failure of the previous autumn and Christmas season, which although of exceptional artistic quality had not proved alluring to the people of Liverpool, who were gripped by recession and discontent that was soon to spill over in the riots of July 1981.

Betrayal, we now all know, was inspired by the affair of its writer, Harold Pinter, with television presenter Joan, now Baroness Bakewell. The play is a wonderfully spare piece of writing, as you would expect with Pinter, with just four characters. Jerry and Emma who are having the affair, Robert, Jerry's close friend and Emma's husband and a waiter, who has no name. The play is as telling by what is not said, as by what is. It also uses the device of reverse chronology for the main part, opening in spring 1977, two years after the affair ended and closing in the winter of 1968 as the affair begins. The Playhouse production was Bill Gaunt at his directorial best, tightly focused, played at a brisk pace without being rushed and with great performances from Christopher Saul as Jerry, Gay Hamilton as Emma and David Quilter as Robert. The staging was equally tight and focused, with the three tall walls enclosing a shallow, rectangular, black carpeted playing area. A section of back wall moved to allow the furniture for the next scene to be quickly set, whilst the three protagonists stood downstage in three tightly focused spotlights, staring out at the audience to the accompaniment of a pounding rock instrumental, reflecting the three blow-up faces in black and white that were repeated all over the walls.

The waiter was played by Wayne Morris, an acting-ASM (an assistant stage manager who plays small parts and usually just gets under the feet of the real stage management team when not on stage) who was killing time before going to drama school. Also now known as Adam Morris, he fondly recalls on his website his nightly battle with wine bottle and waiter's friend.

By my recollection he proved time and again that in a battle between an actor and an inanimate object, the actor is rarely victorious.

ROBERT LONGTHORNE, BUILDING MANAGER

Mathew Street

Mathew Street is my favourite street in Liverpool. Well, it isn't really a street, more of a backstreet, but I loved it. The backs of nineteenth century warehouses, a parking lot covering the remains of a demolished Cavern, a vegetarian restaurant, and the Playhouse's rehearsal rooms. There, embedded on the outside wall of the restaurant was a plaque "Liverpool is the pool of life – Carl Jung". It stayed with me. My first thoughts turned to visionary prankster Ken Campbell, he of the Everyman, who must've put it up. Only later did I find out that it was Carl Jung who said it while visiting and dreaming the city. That was about ninety years ago. I thought then that anything and everything was possible. "Liver" is the seat of passion in the body, a "liver" is someone who hungers to live, "the pool of life" a place where you begin and end journeys. That's how I thought of Liverpool: passionate, proud, a hard humour (perhaps because of the poverty), pitiless, sometimes forgiving. The ships were gone. The Mersey Sound had come and gone. No more Beatles. When I was there in 1980 I walked along abandoned quaysides, there was the odd old poster now and then, one advertised a Beatles gig.

Liverpool Playhouse was a challenge to fill. It was open in a pedestrianised concrete wasteland of shops. Nobody lived or played there. Except us. We were constantly trying to figure out how to reconnect this theatre to Liverpool. Nobody was interested in coming to Williamson Square at night. William Gaunt was Artistic Director and a gifted actor, caring and kind with a good sense of humour. He took me on as Associate. Bill began to feel his way to how best the theatre might work. He started commissioning young Liverpool playwrights like Catherine Hayes. And then he started enticing writers from the Everyman who had lost a home. I worked with Catherine on *Skirmishes*, and Willy Russell on a re-write of *One for the Road*. Gaunt did the first production of *Educating Rita*, as well as Bill Morrison's *Flying Blind*. Alan Bleasdale and Chris Bond started coming around. At first they had misgivings, from an Everyman perspective the Playhouse represented all that they found difficult in theatre. It was the old enemy. And yet keeping to the Everyman pigeon-holed them. Their plays could fill big theatres. And so it proved. Houses were getting fuller, and the national press, meaning the London press, was coming to Liverpool regularly. Not only for Scouse plays, but others such as my productions of Tom Stoppard's *Travesties* and *The Revenger's Tragedy* by Cyril Tourneur, then rarely done.

The Revengers Tragedie by Tourneur, directed by Peter Lichtenfels; November 1980 (Nobby Clark)

We did workshops in schools to connect with a new community. One such was *The Revenger's Tragedy*. We rehearsed in Mathew Street, played it on the main stage, and back to Mathew Street to prepare for Quarry High School. It was Dec 9, 1980. I woke up to the news that John Lennon had been murdered in New York. So many of the ships that left Liverpool arrived in New York. Liverpool was in shock, mourning was still to come. People started hanging out in the parking lot. First a few, then a trickle, then as the news began to sink in there was a crowd – in turn quiet, in turn singing. I watched from our third floor space trying to concentrate, feeling numb. In 1964 I stopped going to confirmation classes, and listened to Beatles songs instead. John Lennon meant a great deal to me. We arrived at Quarry Bank and I was greeted by two teachers who had taught him. There was real sorrow that he had died; there was admiration for what he had achieved in life. But there was no nostalgia. They remembered a difficult and unruly student. Someone who had made their life miserable. I don't really remember how well the workshop went. I thought about "unflinching compassion", the "beginnings and endings of journeys", and "Liver-pool". What a wonderful people to play for. Later, walking across Williamson Square, I was on my way to *The Revenger's Tragedy*. An eleven year old kid not particularly in the know asked "where's the Lennon thing?" "Mathew Street, over on Mathew ..."

PETER LICHTENFELS, ASSOCIATE DIRECTOR, 1979–81

William Gaunt leaves

Bill Gaunt ... is leaving Liverpool after two very exciting and distinguished years. The hallmark of everything Bill has done has been quality, exceptional quality ... His play choice has always been challenging and exciting and we have been fortunate to see a number of rarely performed plays.

Fortunately it is not only as a director that he will be remembered by us, but as an exceptionally talented actor. The part of Ken Harrison in Brian Clark's *Whose Life is it Anyway?* is one of the toughest in every sense and Bill was quite simply very, very good in this most demanding part. The whole production was a "first" for the Playhouse because we worked jointly with George Romain and Theatr Clywd and the production was seen not only here but in North Wales.

Records are always there to be broken, but who could have anticipated the financial and artistic success of this current production of *Educating Rita*? The whole concept was Bill's; his inspiration and successful negotiation (it's still playing in London), and tonight you will see his superb performance as Frank. By the end of the run on 6th June, about 40,000 people will have seen this Playhouse production, and what a high point it will be both in Bill's career and the history of the Playhouse. No production here in the last 70 years has been seen by more people.

HENRY COTTON, PROGRAMME NOTE, MAY 1981

6 I can do no better than repeat the words of Robin Thornber, the *Guardian* critic, who has written: "He has given us a lot of intelligent drama and his casting and production standards have been consistently sound. The Playhouse has been a better place since he came." We'll miss him. Not the least of his achievements has been a stunning quality of programmes in Playhouse Upstairs.

HENRY COTTON, CHAIRMAN'S STATEMENT, 27 JULY 1981

Whose Life Is It Anyway? by Brian Clark, directed by George Roman; with William Gaunt, April 1980

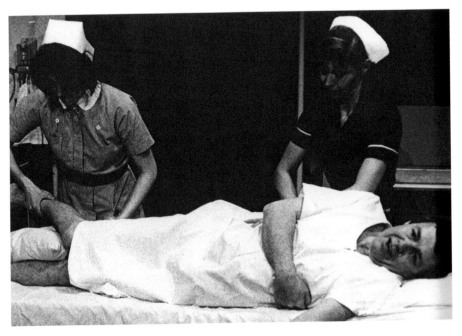

> ❛ The new work I never managed to generate sufficiently, mainly because of lack of time. It takes about 18 months to get a play from conception to staging. If Peter Lichtenfels and I had stayed we would have moved into the sort of area Bill Morrison and Chris Bond are going to move into in the Studio presenting virtually all new work. ❜
>
> WILLIAM GAUNT, QUOTED IN VOAKE

1981

19/1	*The Fantasticks*, Harvey Schmidt, directed by Bill Gaunt and Peter Lichtenfels
5/2	*Educating Rita*, Willy Russell, directed by Willy Russell and Pip Broughton
19/3	*Last of the Red Hot Lovers*, Neil Simon, directed by David Tucker
16/4	*Betrayal*, Harold Pinter, directed by William Gaunt
13/5	*Educating Rita*, Willy Russell (return)
24/9	*Having a Ball*, Alan Bleasdale, directed by Chris Bond
5/11	*A Tale of Two Cities*, Charles Dickens (adapted by Chris Bond and the Company), directed by Chris Bond and Pip Broughton
17/12	*Dracula*, adapted by Chris Bond, directed by Susan Todd

Studio

18/2	*Laurel and Hardy*, Tom McGrath, directed by Peter Lichtenfels
18/3	*Writers Cramp*, John Byrne, directed by Janet Goddard
15/4	*Skirmishes*, Catherine Hayes, directed by Tim Fywell
23/9	*Blood on the Dole*, Jim Morris, directed by Pip Broughton
14/10	*The Circus*, Sean Walsh, directed by Janet Goddard
4/11	*A Doll's House*, Ibsen (version by Christopher Hampton), directed by Bill Morrison
25/11	*Delusions of Sunset*, Kenny Murray, directed by Pip Broughton
16/12	*The April the First Show*: A night of music and mayhem by local writers, directed by George Costigan, Janet Goddard and Willy Russell

On 3 July the arrest of Leroy Cooper on Selbourne Street led to nine days of rioting in Toxteth. Over 500 people were arrested and 70 buildings destroyed including the Rialto Ballroom. Police used CS Gas for the first time in mainland Britain. In the wake of the riots, Michael Heseltine became known as the Minister for Merseyside, creating the Merseyside Development Corporation, the first urban development corporation in the country.

The Gang of Four: Chris Bond, Alan Bleasdale, Willy Russell, Bill Morrison, 1981–84

> ❝ They are a calculated risk. We either played safe or tried to move up a division. Financially it's a bit hairy but we're playing for high stakes. ❞
>
> BOARD MEMBER, QUOTED IN *GUARDIAN*, 25 SEPTEMBER 1981

New artistic team

> ❝ The air of excitement and anticipation is ... intense because, since the beginning of July, we have been seeing the new Artistic Team develop their plans and expand their ideas to bring to you and all Merseyside a unique season of theatrical enterprise ... They will both uphold the traditions and standards of the Playhouse and develop a new policy, with added emphasis in the development of new playwrights – not just local ones, as some people have mistakenly thought.
>
> The great strength of their appointments is not only their wealth of experience as directors and writers, but their devotion to Merseyside ... No wonder *The Stage* newspaper was so enthusiastic about their appointment: "The news that a quartet of writers is to take over the artistic direction of the Liverpool Playhouse could well be one of the most significant moves in the theatre this year ... it proves the regions can lead the way with innovation and experiment on a major scale – and the West End will share in the benefit." ❞
>
> HENRY COTTON, CHAIR OF THE BOARD, PROGRAMME NOTE, SEPTEMBER 1981

Above: The Gang of Four – plus one l–r (standing): Chris Bullock, the administrator, Bill Morrison, Willy Russell; (sitting) Chris Bond, Alan Bleasdale

They were offered a two-year contract with Chris Bond as Artistic Director; Bill Morrison was an associate director with responsibility for the studio, and Bleasdale and Russell were associate writers. At the time of their appointment, the Everyman, with which all four had been strongly associated, was being run by Ken Campbell, reducing the possibility for new writing of the kind associated with the Gang of Four in the city.

An artistic director's view

‘One of the things I like most about working in the theatre is that you are writing in sand. By that I mean that the shows you do only really exist during the time you are doing them; and occasionally in the partial and selective memory of those who were part of them, either on the stage or in the audience. Photographs and recordings can only give a faint echo of what they were actually like, (good or bad!) and as with all, "unrepeatable offers", once they're gone, they're gone. Their only legacy is what everyone has learnt, and can carry forward to the next show, job, career, stage of the journey, rest of the night out, whatever … And the possibilities that are left behind for others to build on.

So, 30 years on from the time I spent at the Playhouse with Alan, Willy, and Bill, what do I think we achieved? We blew away some cobwebs; we encouraged some new writers and directors; helped some good actors, designers and technicians; and did some shows that worked. We broke box office records – both high and low! – and with Alan and Willy's shows at any rate, we brought a new audience into the building; although sadly we didn't manage to carry them with us to too many of the other shows. We left the theatre in a marginally better financial state than we found it in, and with a higher national profile.

Given the hype that surrounded our appointment to run the Playhouse, if those achievements seem relatively modest, well, that's the nature of hype, and I'll take most of the responsibility. I enjoyed, and felt comfortable, directing shows in the rehearsal room, or running technicals, but my forward planning was hopeless, the mountains of paperwork bored me rigid, and I, "lacked the requisite personality skills", to deal with the pressure that built up as a result, (i.e. I got drunk and behaved badly.) Hardly surprisingly, these shortcomings led to a bumpy ride for all concerned …

… that was the downside of my time at the Playhouse, but it wasn't all chaos and booze; on the contrary, it was a real pleasure to work with a Chairman, Henry Cotton, who brought such passion and selfless commitment to the theatre, and to whom the Playhouse owes an enormous debt. I also remember, amongst others, Pip Broughton's dazzling studio production of Zola's *Therese Raquin*, with Val Lilley and Joanna Whalley; and my productions of *Blood Brothers* and *Sweeney Todd*, were as good as anything I've ever directed, and I've carried through aspects of what I learnt from those shows to all the work I've done subsequently.’

CHRIS BOND, ARTISTIC DIRECTOR, 1980–82

157

Sweeney Todd by Stephen Sondheim (adapted by Chris Bond), directed by Chris Bond, September 1982 Leon Greene and Gillian Hanna; Sept 1982 (Kevin Cummins) 'Business was disappointing and it is interesting to compare the Box Office returns In Liverpool and in Watford, with whom we co-produced the show: Liverpool: 36% Watford: 86%' (Chris Bond)

At the end of the 1981–82 season, Chris Bond handed over to Bill Morrison as Artistic Director, remaining at the Playhouse as principal director until he left to go to The Half Moon in London in 1984. The response to the Playhouse taking on a gamble with the 'fab four horsemen of the Apocalypse' as they became known had not been rewarded with a faithful audience, as Robin Thornber pointed out. 'The 100-seat studio thrives adventurously but in the main house ... they stay away in droves ...' (*Guardian*, 7 January 1983)

Blood Brothers by Willy Russell, directed by Chris Bond; January 1983

Barbara Dickson in *Blood Brothers*

❛ I had never set foot in the Liverpool Playhouse until I went to work there at the end of 1982, beginning of 1983. My late mother, a proud Scouser to her fingertips, recalled sitting in the "gods" there watching *The Anatomist* as a teenager. But I had never been inside. I think I thought of it as being the "posh" theatre, in that the Everyman was a modern institution and had been an old assembly room converted into a theatre. In that regard it wasn't viewed by many as a "proper playhouse" like the proper Playhouse!

Many fabulous things happened to me immediately I was within the walls of that theatre. I did loads of interviews for the new and up and coming production of *Blood Brothers* by the, at that time, legendary Willy Russell. What was it about? What would I be doing in it? I was a singer, after all. I didn't act. Was it really a musical? All these questions seemed to be asked in the "new" part of the theatre, the café/bar and numerous photos of me were taken there and outside where I was seen "jumping for joy" at the prospect of being in another hit in the making.

So we opened in January 1983. I was pretty pooped at the start as I'd come right off two concert tours the previous year and I found the show both exhilarating because of the amazing response from the press and public but also very tiring. Eight shows a week on the rack, emotionally, were new to me. We played for 3 months at the Playhouse. By the time I left there, I knew every brick. I had to do a big run from the back of the stalls every night during the last scene and so I had to lurk just out of sight of the audience. The theatre usherettes were always keen to involve me in conversation there, while I tried desperately to keep in character, both hopping from leg to leg to encourage energy and immersing myself in sad thoughts to reveal the whole hideous tragedy to the twins on stage. What a job that was.

I returned after the London run of *Blood Brothers* to do a fortnight stint in concert directed by Chris Bond. It was a sell out and probably one of the few times that the Playhouse staged a season of concerts as opposed to a season of drama.

Blood Brothers by Willy Russell, directed by Chris Bond (in association with Bob Swash Ltd); January 1983 Barbara Dickson as Mrs Johnstone; l–r: George Costigan as Mickey, Barbara Dickson as Mrs Johnstone, Peter Christian as Sammy, Hazel Ellerby in the chorus

I met many friends within the Playhouse's old walls. Reacquainting myself with Willy Russell, the magnificent. Hearing his laugh in the dark auditorium during a technical rehearsal. My mum and dad coming to *Blood Brothers*' first night and my mum saying that she was so immersed in the show, she didn't keep thinking that "there was her daughter". That was a huge compliment from her. Wendy Murray, the godmother to my middle son, Gabriel, was my Mrs Lyons. She was fantastic. We were always approached out in the town with people saying to me, "How can you speak to that woman, after what she's done?" … great fun for us both. But best of all, I met my husband Oliver while working at the Playhouse. We've just celebrated our 26th wedding anniversary in August … good old Liverpool, matchmaking like that!

BARBARA DICKSON, SINGER AND ACTOR

**An associate
director's
thoughts**

6 Why the concept of a writers' theatre? Because it is its reality and
tradition. When Harold Clurman founded The Group in the back room of
the Algonquin Hotel he called it, in his biographical work, The Fervent
Years. In his time it encouraged Dorothy Parker and Lillian Hellman,
herself long-time companion of Dashiell Hammett. Shakespeare had Ben
Jonson, Farquhar had Congreve and in my time Willy Russell had Alan
Bleasdale, or the other way round – take your pick on that one. All
theatre is a collaboration.

Its distinguishing feature is the present tense. It may deal with the
past but it is the two hour traffic here and now before your eyes. Time
stretches to seeming infinity with a bad play. There you are trapped in
the dark, can't move, can't smoke, can't drink. It is not the cinema – no
groping on the back row!

If you run a theatre you must understand that the most important
people in the building is the person who answers the telephone and the
ticket seller and then the bar staff.

So why is it such a vibrant art form with such a long tradition?
Because an audience know they are the most important part of the
collective experience. They are the indispensable element – from the
groundlings to the executive side boxes, which always have a lousy view.
But that is because the point of them is to be seen as privileged.

As long as you bring the curtain down before the pubs close.9

BILL MORRISON

Adrian Henri   *I Want: the Story of a Lifetime* by Nell Dunn and Adrian Henri, directed by
Bill Morrison; August 1983

6 *I Want* was born out of a chance meeting of Nell Dunn and I on an Arts
Council Writers' Tour of Merseyside. I felt an immediate affinity both as a
person and as a writer, despite the differences of background and life-style
(which became very much the theme of the resultant work); one late night
in a Liverpool club we decided to try writing something together and see
what happened.

The next day she appeared with the flyleaf of an old book she'd
found in a second-hand shop: there was a circular sepia photograph of an
old couple sitting on a bench in a formal garden, and the caption "The
Authors in Their Garden". She said, "Let's be them", and so for the next
six months or so we exchanged letters, postcards, pieces of writing in the
personae of these two old people.

Over a week at Nell's farmhouse in Somerset we read through it all,
and a storyline gradually emerged. Having established our two characters

I Want by Adrian Henri and Nell Dunn, directed by Bill Morrison; Linda Marlowe and Philip Whitchurch, August 1983 (Kevin Cummins)

– by and large I wrote the man's part, she the woman's – we had another spell apart, sending each other letters signed "Albert" and "Dolly". Conversations were written in alternate sentences on sheets of paper, rather like a couple not speaking over breakfast. Notebooks, letters, diaries were plundered, memories and dreams recalled. The result was initially dismissed by our publishers as "too short". Even then, we thought of it as perhaps a radio play, or some sort of performance-piece. Certainly we never consciously thought of it as a "novel": perhaps because it was too close, too personal to both of us. It was published in 1972 by Jonathan Cape, and a year later by Pan in paperback.

Though never a best-seller (and long out of print) the book has acquired a devoted "cult" following: I find it strange that so many people attached so much significance to the most enjoyable piece of writing I've ever done, a real labour of love, a sort of literary courtship-by-correspondence ...

Watching the characters grow was fascinating, to suddenly know "Albert wouldn't say that" or "Dolly wouldn't do that". Now the process is being repeated, trying to re-think their lives in physical terms, not just on the page, watching actors putting flesh on the bones of the words. I can't say how much I enjoyed meeting Albert and Dolly. ❯

ADRIAN HENRI, PROGRAMME NOTE

161

Adam Faith

Alfie by Bill Naughton, directed by Alan Parker; October 1983
(revived April 1984)

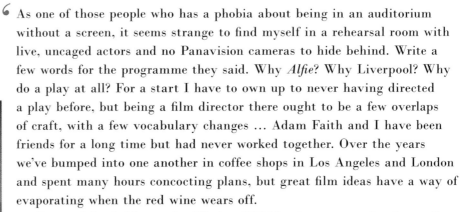

❛ As one of those people who has a phobia about being in an auditorium without a screen, it seems strange to find myself in a rehearsal room with live, uncaged actors and no Panavision cameras to hide behind. Write a few words for the programme they said. Why *Alfie*? Why Liverpool? Why do a play at all? For a start I have to own up to never having directed a play before, but being a film director there ought to be a few overlaps of craft, with a few vocabulary changes ... Adam Faith and I have been friends for a long time but had never worked together. Over the years we've bumped into one another in coffee shops in Los Angeles and London and spent many hours concocting plans, but great film ideas have a way of evaporating when the red wine wears off.

Alfie by Bill Naughton, directed by Alan Parker with Adam Faith as Alfie; October 1983

It was Adam's idea to do *Alfie* but Bill Morrison must take the credit for being daft enough to invite us up to Liverpool. I'd been a great admirer of the work done here and the thought of doing a London play at such a prestigious theatre as the Playhouse is a little daunting for myself ... So why *Alfie*? Could a play set so firmly in the early sixties (and conceived by Bill Naughton probably a few years before that) be relevant to an enlightened 1983? Twenty years doesn't seem so long ago but remember before 1963? When the closets were full, gay meant happy ... Some things have undoubtedly changed. The attitudes expressed in *Alfie* will hopefully make you laugh, make you think and doubtless make you angry. *Alfie* is part of a generation that had been told for a decade that they'd "Never had it so good", only to discover that we'd never really had it. ❜

ALAN PARKER, PROGRAMME NOTE

Shakespeare revamped

Macbeth by Shakespeare, directed by Chris Bond; November 1983

❛ What joy to be at The Playhouse under the reign of Alan Bleasdale, Willy Russell, Bill Morrison and Chris Bond. If these were poachers turned gamekeepers then give me the poachers any day!

I've been lucky enough to work with Chris Bond quite a few times and he directed one of the most exciting productions I've ever been involved in ... his production of *Macbeth*. I've never witnessed people arguing in an auditorium while a play is actually on. The concept showing the chaos surrounding the Macbeths was the talking point. I thought Chris's staging really reflected the themes of the play ... that appearances do not always reflect reality, great love, reason subjugated by ambition, greed and guilt all shown with great clarity yet argued about nearly every day of the production. Duncan arrived on a wheelbarrow. The guests at the banquet were household appliances. On the night of the murders when the alarm was sounded ... all the cast came on stage through a shower of blood ... hiding the real murderers. And as for the witches ... they were based on The Marx Brothers. Audiences left talking and arguing about the *Macbeth* that they had just seen. We had done our job.'

NOREEN KERSHAW, ACTOR

Working with Willy Russell

Breezeblock Park by Willy Russell, directed by Bill Morrison; January 1984

'I have never directed a play by Willy before. I have always until now been a reader of an early draft or in the audience of the finished show. I had not expected to be so surprised at the difference. To direct a play by Willy is to become a musician, or at least a conductor. There is an intense musicality, a rhythm to the writing which has been exhilarating for me.

Breezeblock Park by Willy Russell, directed by Bill Morrison; January and May 1984. L–r: Richard Tate, Val Lilley, Gil Brailey, Barry Gunner, Ian Hart, Noreen Kershaw

The rehearsal period has been a continual journey of discovery, finding a new cross-rhythm, another hidden harmony, a subtle shift of tempo. Willy has that skill to make things appear effortless, logical and simple as if the lines just fell onto the page. It is only in mining that text deeply that one discovers the art concealed by the art.'

BILL MORRISON, PROGRAMME NOTE

'I acted in the popular plays by Willy Russell: *Breezeblock Park* and *Stags and Hens* at The Playhouse. Funny plays that reflected the way we live our lives. Is good writing fuelled by great observation? It must be. Everyone recognised and laughed at themselves and the Playhouse was packed. There's nothing like being in a popular play in a full theatre. Friends made in theatre dressing rooms are often friends for life … and the Playhouse sealed my friendship with Val Lilley and Mary Cunningham.'

NOREEN KERSHAW, ACTOR

New work   *Cavern of Dreams*, a musical play by Carol Ann Duffy; scenario by Bill Morrison with Spencer Leigh based on his book *Let's Go Down the Cavern*, directed by Bill Morrison; August 1984.

'I am not a fan of the past. I am not sentimental about it. I don't see my own slow motion flash backs tinged with gold. Yet history makes us. And the spirit of one generation can revive another. Official histories celebrate the doings of the great which are usually the spreading of war and mass destruction. The unofficial histories celebrate the anarchic spirit and survival of ordinary people. I was born in 1940 in the blackest nights of war. By 1946 the mushroom cloud had risen to haze the sun for all the young. The Fifties were grey, censored, repressive, ugly with the threat of war.

City Echoes by Jimmy McGovern, directed by Andy Jordan; Annette Ekblock and Gillian Hanna, April 1983 'An angry controversial saga of Liverpool family which though not a popular success brought a new committed audience to the theatre.' (Bill Morrison)

The Holiday by Jim Morris, directed by Pip Broughton; four girls from Wallasey swotting for their 'O' levels on a hill in Wales meet up with four boys from Birkenhead who are up to no good; Francis Iwediebo and Vicki Chambers, December 1983 (Kevin Cummins)

For Aldermarston read Greenham Common – the Eighties begin to feel the same. A rootless generation, born in war, fired by rebellion, stirred by existentialism and the beat generation, found a common language – rock 'n' roll. The first 78 I ever bought was "Heartbreak Hotel". In *The Wild One* Brando was asked – "What are you rebelling against?" – and memorably replied – "What have you got?" I hope this show isn't just nostalgia, although nostalgia is fun. I hope it celebrates the spirit of defiance of convention, of refusing to let being young be snatched away, of making it all up as you went along, identities, styles, music, fun … I hope this show is a celebration of all the people who made the music and danced to it, of a club that was a dirty hole in the ground, of a city patching up the wounds of war, of a spirit that eventually hit the world like a fist. "Don't let the bastards grind you down," said Arthur in *Saturday Night, Sunday Morning*. "Roll over Beethoven," said Chuck Berry. The worst of the past doesn't have to be the future.

BILL MORRISON, PROGRAMME NOTE.

Carol Ann Duffy was the Thames Television writer in residence at the Playhouse and her first play, *Take My Husband*, was premiered in the studio in 1982. The cast included Ian Hart as Billy and Michael Starke, Paul Codman, Andrew Schofield and John Wild as the Dingles.

Other new work on the main stage included:

Chris Bond's version of *Dracula* in which Van Helsing was a woman (December 1981)
Bill Morrison's play about Northern Ireland *Scrap* (January 1982)
A musical version of Orton's *Erpingham Camp* (February 1982)
Michael Beckham's *The Joke Collector* based on his Granada TV play, *Tiny Revolutions* about Czechoslovakia (April 1982)
Jimmy McGovern: *City Echoes* (April 1983)
Claire Luckham: *Walking on Walter* (May 1983)
Jim Morris: *The Holiday* (December 1983)
In their first 3 seasons, the gang of four offered 12 world premieres on the main stage of the Playhouse.

Starting out at the youth theatre: Colin Tierney

The Liverpool Playhouse is a special place to me. I attended the Playhouse Youth theatre from 1982 to 1984. I had done a few school plays and acting was beginning to fascinate and absorb me. We'd spend our evening sessions improvising and devising work and rehearsing new plays, which we would put on in the Playhouse studio, now the theatre's rehearsal room. Plays like *Making Hay, The Innocent Mistress, The Wall* and *Yer Dancin'*.

165

We'd build and paint the sets, make the costumes and create the lighting. It meant that I was constantly in and around the building. As a fourteen-year-old, hopeful actor, the place was as important as Anfield!

I'd wander backstage and see the dressing rooms with the mirrors surrounded by light bulbs, the lighting rigs and the paint dock. I'd walk on the stage and be fascinated by the still, somewhat forbidding empty auditorium. Waiting to see a ghost.

Whilst at the youth theatre I auditioned for and got the part of the young Nazi in Pip Broughton's production of *The Blue Angel*. It was 1983 and my first professional acting job. I was paid £2 a show. Pauline Black played Lola Lola. She would make fun of my dimpled knees. I'd watch from the wings as she'd sing "Falling in love again, never wanted to ..." my heart thumping. In that same season I was Fleance in Chris Bond's production of *Macbeth*. Alfred Molina was Macbeth. The play opened with Talking Heads' "Once in a Lifetime", "And you may find yourself living in a shotgun shack". The Witches operated the lights and the sound from onstage.

Then I saw *Blood Brothers* and had a sudden intuitive understanding of what I wanted to do with my life. I left Liverpool to go to Drama school in London, where I have lived ever since, but I relish every opportunity I get to work back home and especially at the Playhouse. In 2006 I appeared in Hubert Henry Davies *The Lady of Leisure* directed by Gemma Bodinetz, one of the happiest jobs of my life and in 2007, *Our Country's Good*, where I had the opportunity to work with Andrew Schofield, one of the greats. I started out at the Playhouse 28 years ago, saw plays by Shakespeare and Russell, Chekhov and Bleasdale. It's a beautiful building, a mysterious and mighty theatre with fantastic acoustics. It's an amazing space to act in, epic and intimate and I'd work there again in a heartbeat.

COLIN TIERNEY, ACTOR

Stags and Hens by Willy Russell, directed by Pip Broughton; May 1982
l–r: Bill Leadbitter, Angela Walsh, Nick Maloney, Andrew Schofield, Brian Regan, Judy Holt, Noreen Kershaw (Kevin Cummins)

Studio 2

A 1980s
programme
for the studio

❛ *Blood on the Dole* by Jim Morris: A first full length play by a local 27-year-old writer. He is our choice as resident playwright. On the basis of the script alone the production is booked for a London run at the Tricycle Theatre, has been bought by BBC radio and he has been taken on by a leading agent

Delusions of Sunset by Kenny Murray: The writer is a Scot who has lived for a number of years in Liverpool. He had early success as writer in Scotland with plays on radio and television. He is a very original talent and has been struggling with stage form. He has come through that struggle partly with the help of Ken Campbell who put him to work on *War with the Newts* which has proved a highly successful adaptation. The play is a 3-hander, set in the USA in 1941 and based on the true story of a Russian defector called Krivitsky.

The April the First Show: This will be a collection of tales for Christmas which is designed as a showcase for local writing ... I think it very important to offer writers opportunities to write short pieces where the main aim is entertainment so there's not too much pressure.

Finishing School by Claire Luckham: Claire is now well known as the author of *Trafford Tanzi*. She has had several plays performed at the Everyman and by Monstrous Regiment, including *Scum*. Her new play ... tells the story of three girls in their first few years of leaving school. It will be part of our season of stories about women.

Ladies in Waiting by Ellen Fox: Ellen is the Thames Resident Writer at Hampstead Theatre Club. She is a young Canadian writer. This is her first play which has attracted a lot of favourable reaction from managements but has not, so far, been performed. It is set in Canada in 1916 and concerns the women waiting for their husbands to come home from war. It will be another in the season of stories about women.

The Reunion by David Evans: Dave is a South African who, after serving a prison sentence for protesting against apartheid, has had to settle in England. He lectures at Liverpool University. I have worked

Above: Take My Husband by Carol Ann Duffy, directed by Bill Morrison; Maggie Ford as Clare, the agent behind comedienne Terri, who has found success by upending jokes like 'Take my wife – please'; November 1982

on this play with him since its inception. A short version of it is being recorded this month by Yorkshire Television.

There are also plans for lunch time shows in the Spring.

I have aimed for a policy which mixes local plays with international plays and fortunately that range of writing presently exists on Merseyside. In most cases we are backing established talent, in other cases we are backing hunches.'

BILL MORRISON, ASSOCIATE DIRECTOR, APPLICATION TO THE ARTS COUNCIL, 2 SEPTEMBER 1981

Blood on the Dole by Jim Morris, directed by Pip Broughton; September 1981

Starting out: Jim Morris

'I wanted to record the simple fact that a person can go out to work and be killed while he is at work – that's for personal reasons that I don't want to go into.'

JIM MORRIS, QUOTED IN *GUARDIAN*, 11 SEPTEMBER 1982

'In the sixties it was poets and musicians. Now it's playwrights as well. Merseyside has always been a pool of talent. To my knowledge there are over 30 playwrights living and working here who have had plays professionally produced. Jim Morris is the latest. It is our intention at the Playhouse to bring you the best of their work together with classic and international plays. It's an exciting time. We want to encourage new

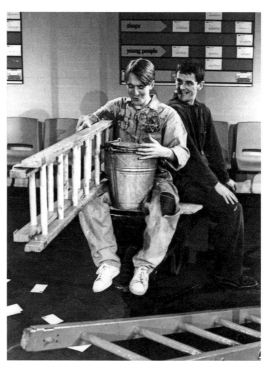

Blood on the Dole by Jim Morris, director Pip Broughton; September 1981 and January 1982 John Wild as Ricky and Andrew Schofield as Joey

The April the First Show: A night of music and mayhem by local writers, directed by George Costigan, Janet Goddard and Willy Russell; December 1981

Red Devils by Debbie
Horsfield, directed by
George Costigan; Judy
Holt as Alice, Angela
Catherall as Beth,
Anna Lindup as Phil,
Ishia Bennison as Nita
March 1983

talent, help it to grow. We hope you will join us in supporting them. For
the first time we have introduced a Subscription Scheme for the Playhouse
Upstairs which offers a big discount. In the spring there will be more new
plays with the emphasis on stories about women. We see our job as giving
you value for your money. '

BILL MORRISON, PROGRAMME NOTE.

The play transferred to the Tricycle Theatre and returned to the studio in
January 1982.

Starting out: Carol Ann Duffy

Take My Husband by Carol Ann Duffy, directed by Bill Morrison; November
1982

' It was a dark winter's night in 1981 and I was driving down Edge Lane in
a battered Morris Traveller aiming for my digs in Huskisson Street. It was
my first time in Liverpool and I was about to start rehearsals for Carol
Ann Duffy's theatre play *Take my Husband*. As I recall, the play was a
"first" for her as well. That was the beginning of a long love affair with
Liverpool. So what are my memories from that time?

We had a very relaxed enjoyable rehearsal period and sharing the

169

house in Huskisson street with fellow actor Gaye Brown guaranteed lots of laughs. Gaye and I had toured Europe together in *Oh What a Lovely War* so quickly settled in to sharing a house as opposed to long train journeys. We soon struck up a good friendship with Carol Ann and Adrian Henri, often eating together at Zorbas. It was from Adrian that I learned about Liverpool's dark history and its involvement with the slave trade. He pointed out the old sheds that had been used to keep the captive slaves. Chilling. I still think of that whenever I am back in Liverpool. The play was very well received and to celebrate we would often go for drinks after the show to the "Cazza" in Hope Street.

MAGGIE FORD, ACTOR

Starting out: Debbie Horsfield

Red Devils by Debbie Horsfield, directed by George Costigan; March 1983

Debbie's first play, *Red Devils* was commissioned by Bill Morrison in 1982 and subsequently submitted for, and awarded, a Thames Television Writers' Award which carried with it an attachment to the theatre for a year.

Following the final performances of *Red Devils* in May 1983, Bill Morrison floated the suggestion that Phil, Beth, Alice and Nita, on the threshold of adulthood, should not be consigned to oblivion in the backstreets of Manchester, but could each be the subject of four separate plays which would continue their lives up to the then present, 1983. Financial constraints inevitably intervened: four short plays became two longer plays, each half concentrating on one girl ... As an added "incentive", the plays were to commence rehearsal at the end of September, allowing the princely period of four and a half months in which to produce five hours of drama. For a companion-cum-supporter on this odyssey, I was assigned the Playhouse's new trainee director, Richard Brandon: my first work as a full-time professional writer were to be his first productions as a professional director. Bill Morrison is a great exponent of the "in-at-the-deep-end" philosophy.

In retrospect, it seems an act of near-lunacy to undertake such a mammoth enterprise in so short a period, but at the time we were obliged to call it "daring". Bill Morrison challenged us to take risks, experiment with form and content ...

DEBBIE HORSFIELD, INTRODUCTION TO THE RED DEVILS TRILOGY (METHUEN, 1984).

Her subsequent plays, *True Dare Kiss* and *Command or Promise* both moved to the Cottesloe Theatre, London in 1985.

Jules Wright, 1985–1986

❝ I think it is a particularly exciting season though it might be controversial. We feel it is experimental to a certain extent because there is some concentration on new work and we have a lot of new faces here, many of whom have worked in London. But we are not ignoring popular theatre.❞

DAVID FISHEL, ADMINISTRATOR, QUOTED IN *STAGE*, 10 OCTOBER 1985

❝ We've got our backs to the wall.❞

JULES WRIGHT, QUOTED IN *GUARDIAN*, 23 APRIL 1986

❝ I wish ... to pay a particular debt of thanks to my predecessors ... They refocused the nation's attention on the Playhouse, reminded those of us who knew little of Liverpool that the city produced some of the best playwrights presently working in this country.❞

JULES WRIGHT, REPORT TO AGM, 22 JULY 1985

Are You Lonesome Tonight? By Alan Bleasdale, directed by Robin Lefevre; May 1985 (in association with Bill Kenwright)

Staging a myth

❝ This play is about the most loved, famous and finally grotesquely abused man of our times. It is also meant to be a fable about a truly fabulous man, a myth about a myth, and an *impression* of what I believe to be the causes of the last painful and traumatic years in the life of Elvis Presley.

There's far more I could write but programme notes can sometimes become a playwright's first and last line of defence or explanation ... So, instead, some images of Elvis Presley that forced me to the typewriter – the totally revolutionary early music; that voice like no other; his secret sideways smile that always made me laugh out loud; the stunning sexuality that managed to be even more warm and humorous than erotic, as if he was telling a whole generation that carnal knowledge was a situation comedy as well ... *a boy who dared to be different*, hurtled to fame

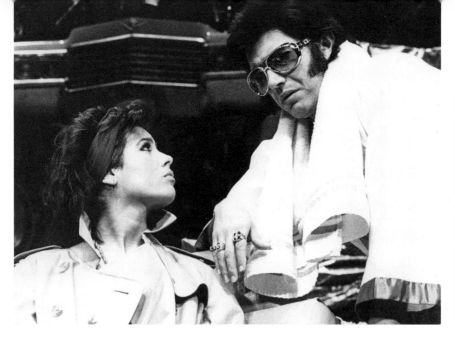

and success and staying there, despite the banality of much of his later music and the wretchedness of most of his movies, for well over twenty years; a man who must have thought at first that he might have become a prisoner but it was a wonderful prison … until he realised it was a life sentence; the shock and sadness that I felt on the day of his abjectly early death, to be swept away with a sense of sickened rage by the books and stories and slurs that followed, smelling of the sewer and the sweat of dollar bills.

Then there was the writing of the play. I didn't expect *that much* pain or all those tears. I was just trying to redress the balance. That's all. I never expected to love the man to such a degree, but that often happens to prison visitors.

ALAN BLEASDALE, PROGRAMME NOTE

This play is dedicated to Bill Morrison and Timothy Bleasdale. They both know why.

Jules Wright's first production

Not Quite Jerusalem by Paul Kember, directed by Jules Wright; June 1985

I was at the Royal Court when Paul Kember's play was first performed and at that time I wondered why it was not being given its premiere in its national home – Liverpool. It was not difficult for me to decide that my first play here should be a production of *Not Quite Jerusalem*. Paul writes with the wit and intelligence of all the best writers to have emerged from this city, and his humour has incisiveness that only Liverpool writers seem able to achieve.

In recent weeks many people have talked about the merits of this city and wondered what we have left. I believe that there is something which Liverpool has that is unique in Britain – the greatest concentration of fine writers presently working in the U.K. The presence of artists of their calibre is to be found nowhere else. There is a creative urgency in Merseyside unequalled in England, and yet the city still has to recognise this. This is a time when Merseyside has to reassert its pride, and luckily it has something on which to focus this regeneration – the theatre.

Perhaps being a newcomer to the city I am more acutely aware of the wealth of talent here, and more bemused by the lack of celebration which surrounds it. To survive in Williamson Square we need this acknowledgement. We need our audiences to be regular, committed and big. We need your affection and your loyalty. Loyalty is important. Like a concert, or a gig, or a football team, a play isn't always a winner, but a sense of loyalty will override occasional disappointments …

A society may be measured by the quality of the artists it produces. In this, Liverpool is a leader. But more importantly, the quality of the society may be measured by the extent to which it values those artists. In 1985 I hope that we can surpass the people of Glasgow whose commitment to the Glasgow Citizens Theatre remains unequalled.

JULES WRIGHT, PROGRAMME NOTE

An artistic vision

To maintain this theatre's livelihood we must draw on a young audience but we won't survive by appealing to one sector only. It must be a "broad church". This does not mean a soft and unfocused Artistic Policy which is crudely "repy", striving to meet all needs and actually assuaging none but rather the pursuit of a strongly held vision and a desire to put specific plays on the stage. It means that not all of our audience will like all of our work all of the time but they will be and must be gratified by its quality, recognizing that the standards we set are amongst the finest to be found. This is also a way to develop loyalty, pride and commitment from our audience. We have plenty of examples to substantiate such an approach – the obscure classics played at the Glasgow Citz to full houses in the Gorbals, the new and popular work of Joan Littlewood in the theatre I

Not Quite Jerusalem by Paul Kember, directed by Jules Wright; Neil Pearson and Sam Dale, June 1984 (Phil Cutts)

173

began in, Stratford East, the determination of the board of the Stratford Memorial Theatre who passionately argued that there was an audience for a company which played only Shakespeare – undoubtedly those theatres which have made their mark and sustained and built faithful audiences have pursued a firm vision with real resolution. There is work that I want to put on this magnificent stage. It includes modern, raw writers, the classics of Chekhov, Strindberg and Ibsen as well as Shakespeare, the Jacobean and Restoration writers and work commissioned from the best of our local and national writing talents. I know that as a Director if you haven't wanted to do a play your audience smells it. 9

JULES WRIGHT, REPORT TO AGM, 22 JULY 1985

Winning an audience

6 And now to you, the audience whom I seek to woo and win as permanent and committed backers of our work. Many have wondered first why I should begin my directing career here with a production of the controversial, though very successful, *Not Quite Jerusalem*. Others wonder why the first play of the Autumn season should be a production of a classic. Liverpool audiences don't like classics many have claimed. Until proven wrong, I have had to prepare a season of work which I think has style, impact and quality. Work which has a contemporary voice and which speaks primarily to a younger audience. I'm putting my money on quality, and the hunch that my audiences want that too ... Going to the Playhouse must become part of the everyday life of Liverpudlians. I shan't be satisfied with anything less. The job is just beginning. 9

JULES WRIGHT, PROGRAMME NOTE, *MISS JULIE*, SEPTEMBER 1985

Miss Julie, the classic that opened the Autumn season, marked the stage debut of Joely Richardson, grand-daughter of Michael Redgrave and Rachel Kempson.

The Divvies Are Coming by Eddie Braben, directed by Bill Morrison; December 1985

Miss Julie by Strindberg, directed 6 by Jules Wright; September 1985. The production was set in Ireland in 1900 and starred Joely Richardson; Michael Feast as John and Veronica Quilligan as Christine (Phil Cutts)

Did your parents ever tell you fairy stories when you were a child? Can you remember how you listened wide eyed at tales of wonderful enchanting places? Did you know that you, the adult, still have the small child hidden deep down inside you? I know that I have, a small boy who won't let me forget that life is fun. I look around at the city and the people I love and feel very sad, then the child inside me pops up again and helps me to forget the misery and unhappiness I see about me ... It was a small part of me that never grew up that was the inspiration behind *The Divvies Are Coming.*

It happened one day as I was walking around the city following a horrific event which needs no further elaboration from me. People of all ages were walking around with faces etched in shame, eyes downcast, the sparkle had gone along with that God given gift for laughter and humour. I watched and I was deeply saddened that the warm and wonderful people I had lived with and grown up with, the same people who had unknowingly given me so much should be suffering for something not at all of their making. They had all been branded as "baddies". They had heard it and read it so often they were beginning to believe it. They had been condemned along with the minority of real villains and they didn't deserve it.

That little boy inside me popped up again – make them laugh. Could I? I looked across Williamson Square at the Liverpool Playhouse. I was just an ordinary comedy writer. I couldn't write a proper play that would make people laugh. That little devil inside me would not relent – "You can write jokes, write a lot of funny things and make people laugh again." It was a very simple childish philosophy. I couldn't do it. I'd only written for Morecambe and Wise and they weren't proper plays what I wrote! ... It's the most important, most personal work I've ever done. It's not personal vanity on my part when I say that I want you to laugh as you have never laughed. That small child inside all of you, take it by the hand and let it lead you on a romp through the fields of "Funtasy Land". You deserve it. For the next couple of hours we are once again wide-eyed children.

EDDIE BRABEN, PROGRAMME NOTE

WCPC by Nigel Williams, directed by Pam Brighton; February 1985

Taking a chance

It is time to be brave. This is a liberating play which can alter people's perceptions. We are not like other provincial cities. We are not Chester nor Oldham. I think Liverpool can face up to this kind of debate. We are far more sophisticated than most in our mental approach to things.

JULES WRIGHT, QUOTED IN *LIVERPOOL ECHO*, 17 FEBRUARY 1986

What I'm after is a mixture of laughter and thought. The play is about a policeman who sees himself as a man with a mission to clean up corruption. But in presenting this, we are forced to ask questions about puritanism ... And because sexuality is common to us all, I don't actually think it is any degree offensive. Yet the whole mainstay of the play does question double standards so far as sexual morality is concerned ... What *WCPC* does require on the part of its audience is an act of surrender, to give it a proper chance of saying different things.

NIGEL WILLIAMS, QUOTED IN *LIVERPOOL ECHO*, 17 FEBRUARY 1986

' This year the Playhouse has achieved a remarkable first, transferring more plays from its home base than any other regional theatre. The work has been widely praised nationally and we have been acknowledged as an adventurous, bold company forging work in the regions which is most often the product of well-funded national companies or London based houses ...

Are You Lonesome Tonight? ... was co-produced with Bill Kenwright Productions. It won best musical in the *Evening Standard* Awards and is still enjoying a highly successful run at the Phoenix Theatre in the West End.

Beauty and the Beast by Louise Page was co-produced with the prestigious Women's Playhouse Trust and transferred for six weeks to the

Gimme Shelter, Barrie Keefe, directed by David Leveaux; March 1986

David Morrissey as P.C. Simon under the watchful lens of a colleague in *WCPC* by Nigel Williams, directed by Pam Brighton; February 1986. Billed in some quarters as the most controversial play in the 75 year history of the Playhouse, this was only its second staging, having started life at the Half Moon Theatre in 1982 (Phil Cutts)

Old Vic in London's West End where it received wonderful notices ...

Ourselves Alone by Anne Devlin was co-produced with the Royal Court Theatre, where it subsequently transferred. It has just been brought back in London for a second sell-out run ... Again the critics were ecstatic ... .

Short Change by Terry Heaton, presently running in our studio, is to transfer to the Royal Court following its run here. This, too, is a new play and produced, as was *Ourselves Alone*, in our Granada season.

What is extraordinary is that each of these plays is new. New work takes a particular commitment from the theatre involved in creating it. Few theatres take such risks. Ours have paid off in re-establishing the Playhouse as a unique creative force in British theatre.

The national response to the work of the Playhouse has been of an entirely different order to that experience within Liverpool. Of the twelve plays produced since April, five have been new and three regional firsts. Why is it that the national response has contrasted so markedly with the local response? In making choices for the Spring season, I have sustained the policy operating here for last year. Both *WCPC* and *Gimme Shelter* are regional firsts. Both will prove controversial with a proportion of our audience. Both are directed by remarkable directors – Pam Brighton who did the first production of *WCPC* has been persuaded to re-direct the play here. David Leveaux ... directs the *Gimme Shelter* trilogy ... National praise, status and admiration will not keep the Playhouse, but your commitment will. ⁹

JULES WRIGHT, PROGRAMME NOTE, FEBRUARY 1986

Hard times

⁶ Many of you will know that the consequences of the abolition of the Merseyside County Council is having a serious effect on the arts in Merseyside. The present impasse between the successor authorities in Merseyside and organisations such as the Playhouse are making it nearly impossible to effect any long term planning ...

The Hard Facts

Liverpool Playhouse is one of the seven major repertory companies in England. It is the most poorly funded:

Royal Exchange Manchester	£1,198,500
Birmingham Repertory	£882,500
Sheffield Crucible	£882,000
Leicester Haymarket	£872,330
Nottingham Playhouse	£728,330
Bristol	£674,000
Liverpool Playhouse	£572,000

The Divvies Are Coming by Eddie Braben, directed by Bill Morrison; Alison Steadman, Jim Casey and Eli Woods, December 1985 (Phil Cutts)

Despite the differentials in funding and size, the Playhouse has transferred more plays this year than any of the other "Big Seven". We will have produced a total of 13 home based plays (more than Manchester – 8, Leicester – 12, and the same as Nottingham), seven of which are new plays (more than any other regional theatre) ...'

JULES WRIGHT, PROGRAMME NOTE, GIMME SHELTER, MARCH 1986

Jules Wright leaves

'A new mentality has emerged over the last five or six years. Afraid not to play it safe with those who hold the purse strings, it denies the strength of the artist's vision. It lacks heart, spirit and soul. Theatre doesn't work without those qualities, but instead we are seeing a new breed of career administrator who is valued far more highly than the artistic director he or she is supposed to serve. I have found it impossible to work with this arrangement. In the past the Liverpool Playhouse has been a safe middle-of-the-road rep. The pressures are building up to force it in that direction once again.'

JULES WRIGHT, QUOTED IN HELEN CHAPPELL: IT LACKS HEART, SPIRIT AND SOUL,
GUARDIAN, 23 APRIL 1986

Ian Kellgren, 1986–1991

**Starting out:
Ian Kellgren**

❝ When I started as Artistic Director, in May 1986, although I had run a theatre company and even started my directing career at the Royal Court Theatre in London, I had never actually run a building based company. I therefore decided to take advice and turned to a friend, who was successfully running the Sheffield Crucible at the time, Clare Venables.

There are two things that she said that I still recall. Firstly, identify a friend or friends. She warned that this may not be an obvious person that you work closely with, such as the administrator or an associate director. It could be the person on the stage door or a junior in the workshop. What was important was that you could talk to them, ask their opinion and get a true sense of what was happening. I won't specify whom I found, although I always had a soft spot for Sam the maintenance man, whose wife led her vibrant gang of cleaners.

Clare's second piece of advice was to remember how the theatre looked the first time I saw it because she said I would soon forget. My first impressions were not altogether favourable. The 60s concrete entrance area was unwelcoming; the toilets were primitive; the stairs to upper levels seemed chilly; and the seats in the auditorium were cramped and shabby. As the theatre had been originally a Victorian music hall, with well over a thousand seats as against the 758 by 1986, the best place on stage to be seen by all the audience was in the middle at the front. Otherwise those in side seats or up in the "gods" could never see the entire stage; a constant challenge for the modern director and designer.

The backstage areas were not particularly inviting either but most troubling was the stalls bar. This had a slightly unpleasant smell that never quite went away. I was to discover that it was below the water table. Just after a refurbishment, a combination of tide and weather conditions left our prized, newly designed carpet at the bottom of a swimming pool of sewage water.

All this I did remember but I also remember, in 1986, the 75th anniversary of the opening. After the cast of *Chicago* had taken their bows

Ian Kellgren (right)
in *Loot* by Joe Orton
directed by Joanna
Hole, January 1991
(Phil Cutts)

to a full house, in the first production I directed at the Playhouse, I came on stage, gave a speech and supervised the cutting of the birthday cake. I will never forget the sheer energy and warmth coming from the audience and the knowledge that so many great actors had come onto that stage in the previous 75 years. The heart of the Playhouse was and always will be the magical exchange between audience and cast in a special place where individuals come through not always inviting circumstances, but leave part of a group having witnessed and contributed to something unique.'

IAN KELLGREN, ARTISTIC DIRECTOR

Soaplights by Phil Redmond, directed by Phil Redmond; May 1987

New work

'*Soaplights* was a unique collaboration between Mersey Television based in Liverpool and the Liverpool Playhouse Theatre. It was the first television "soap opera" to hit the stage and to date still is. Using actors from the hit Channel Four on-going, twice weekly (then), drama television series *Brookside*, it is a play that was to parody the often crazy world of television "soaps" and the people who worked on their creation, both in front as well as behind the camera.

Phil Redmond had written a script about the making of a "Euro soap" that intended to poke merciless fun at the world of soap operas, and give an insider's view of the making of a popular television series. The idea for the project came about from a meeting Redmond had with the artistic director of the theatre, in which they talked about mounting a production that combined the skills of television and the theatre, in a way that had not been seen on stage before. The script drew heavily on the perceived problems with temperamental stars and their egos, problems over contracts and the general mayhem surrounding the making of television soap – although Redmond did point out that the stage show did not reflect real life at *Brookside*.

Soaplights is about a wily executive producer who persuades a feminist writer to abandon her ideals and develop her play and ideas into a glossy soap opera, and who then goes on to cajole an over ambitious director to rein in his over-the-top production values to fit with his own definite ideas of how the show should look. Forward two years. The soap is a huge success with the actors demanding huge salary rises and their cut of the lucrative profits. As the play progresses, so too does the size of the executive-producers' house, as evidenced with each new framed photo of the new property brought on-stage. The play ends with the screening of the final episode of the television show.

What made the production unique was that a huge screen, upstage,

Blues in the Night written and directed by Sheldon Epps (co-production in association with Exacalibur Productions); Stephanie Lawrence as The Woman of the World with Miquel Brown and Precious Wilson; March 1990

was used as part of the set onto which were projected scenes from the fictional television series, which were actually filmed on sets at Mersey Television – the action thereby shifting between the scene on stage and the on-screen scene of the fictional soap, as well as behind-the-scene scenes!

I played the central, lead character of the play and executive producer of the soap, Freddie Hertzog; other regular members of the cast from *Brookside* included in the production were Marji Campi, Annie Miles, Stifyn Parri, Stephen Pinner, Jason Hope and Brian Reagan, as well as an actress from *Grange Hill*, another of Redmond's devised TV productions.

The play ran to over three hours but was cut after the preview performance, adding to the already enormous pressure on the cast on opening night. It had mixed reviews but was well received by appreciative and "sold-out" audiences.

DEAN SULLIVAN, ACTOR

6 Theatre is more than buildings. Too often we lose sight of this simple truth, just as we lose sight of the idea that culture itself is more than the performing arts. It is in everything we do. Arts and literature play a great part but culture is really embedded within the shared lifestyles we all experience, sometimes explore, as we come together as a collective of differing communities.

Often separated by differences but equally often drawn together, perhaps overlapping, through common interests which could range from drama, sport, politics, bee-keeping or town-planning and, of course, the dramas within them all. We all arrive at common points from differing pasts to share a common present that helps shape a collective future and theatre is a place in which to do it all.

My own shared moment with the Playhouse came in the 1980s in a production I wrote and directed partly, I admit, as a break from the relentless treadmill that serial television production can become, but also to experience that great difference that theatre brings. The direct link to a live rather than statistically analysed audience represented on a database of viewing habits. If only the market researchers and focus group facilitators could sit and sense the different nuances of each individual audience they would appreciate that every line in every production is appreciated by someone. The quest for the homogenous all is not everything. We do not need to appeal to everyone at all times.

I learnt a lot about theatre, but little I could take back to TV. They are different storytelling forms and no one should try and confuse the two. While my instinct is naturally for the fast and furious nature of single camera production, the challenges of mega-stunts and big action sequences set against the calm and quite of the resuscitation unit we called post-production; there is a different adrenalin rush on seeing the curtain go up and action being called without the corresponding capacity to call "cut, let's go again".

So when we stand in Liverpool's much-changed Williamson Square, itself a metaphor for changing times, fortunes and fashions we can stare at the Playhouse and sense many shared moments past. Its own past starkly represented in its counter-pointed architectural provenance, reminders in themselves of the fact that all communities want and need their storytelling emporiums.

Theatres can act as great focal points, but we should never forget that theatre is not about buildings. It is not about stages. But about people and how they use those stages as platforms. For their ideas, energy, enthusiasm and their talent and what they do with it all. It is about ideas

Soaplights written and directed by Phil Redmond; Dean Sullivan as Freddie, May 1987 (Phil Cutts)

and how people interpret, test or challenge old ideas and introduce the shock of the new.

Long may the Playhouse, in whatever shape or form, remain both the platform and the metaphor for different ideas from differing pasts coming to a common present, leading to a shared collective future.'

PHIL REDMOND, WRITER AND DIRECTOR

Journeyman Jack by Phil Woods, directed by Graham Devlin; April 1989

Heritage city

'As manufacturing industry declined under the Conservative Government of the 1980s, new museums were opening at the rate of one a fortnight. Each new cotton museum would be in competition not merely with other museums but with other cotton museums. Manufacturing industry was coming to terms with the fact that there would be no more state intervention to rescue "lame ducks". Now the spotlight was being turned to the world of the Arts.

Unemployment had more than doubled in the early years of the Thatcher administration and the "leisure industry" was being promoted as a way of mopping up some of the surplus labour. As Robert Hewison remarked in *The Heritage Industry*, "The past has been summoned to rescue the present". Museums, galleries and theatres would be treated no differently to the docks, pits or railways. If they couldn't justify their grants under strict business criteria then they too would go to the wall. The Government aimed to reduce state subsidy and make up the deficit by encouraging business sponsorship and patronage.

The largest example of this was the Royal Insurance's involvement with the RSC, and it is easy to see why it was such an attractive proposition. The brand could reach a specific demographic. The associated product was comparatively uncontroversial and the size of the logo on all publicity material gave the impression that it was Royal Insurance (rather than us taxpayers) who were putting up the lion's share. Even this deal eventually bit the dust when Royal Insurance's own problems increased during the recession of the early 90s.

So it's not hard to imagine how difficult it was to attract sponsors for the Museum of Sewerage (or "Underground Manchester" as it was more delicately titled) "authentically reconstructed with smells, rodents and gurgling sounds" and its "harrowing graveyard scene of the 1840s with sound track and life-size models depicting the shocking scale of child mortality due to poor sanitation". The degree of sponsored income was usually in direct proportion to the type and size of the target audience.

This then was the background to *Journeyman Jack*. The Albert Dock development was a typical example of what was happening elsewhere. The Adelphi no longer playing host to transatlantic passengers but instead to tourists from home and abroad who had come to sample the Liverpool Experience. The play was set in a recently closed family-run cotton mill in rural Lancashire. The young couple who have inherited the business can take the easy route by selling out to a hotel group and returning to their home in Chelsea. Or … they could embrace their ancestors' philosophy of paternalistic responsibility to the workforce by creating a "cotton experience".

A young student, who has been researching (for reasons which he does not immediately divulge) the history of the family firm, appears on the scene and makes himself indispensable by offering to create a historical pageant for a fundraising sponsors' night. However, the more he reveals the more we realise the true nature of the founder's business methods. And how it was that the firm had flourished during the American Civil War while the rest of Lancashire suffered. And why the Victorian cotton hands felt they had no need of a union. Agitation was nipped in the bud, as in the case of Jack, a journeyman mechanic, who discovered more about the mill owner than was good for him.

The young couple see no reason why the pageant should reveal the unsavoury truth about their hitherto respected ancestor. The point of the evening is to raise money from sponsors not to hear unfounded accusations that Sir Samuel Clayton M.P. had exercised droit de seigneur with a millgirl or been responsible for the murder of Journeyman Jack to prevent the spread of radicalism amongst the workforce. At this point the evening takes an unwelcome turn.

Does any of this matter? Only to the extent that we owe to future generations an objective view of the past and present. Patronage of the arts often requires something in return. Which is probably why Reynolds received more commissions than Hogarth. And why we should never forget that Hogarth's view of Georgian England was just as valid (if not quite as photogenic).

Journeyman Jack opened at the Playhouse on Thursday April 13th 1989. On the Saturday of that week a tragedy took place in Sheffield in full view of the country's media. Despite that fact, there remain different versions of what happened. Life can be interpreted in so many ways that those who earn their living in the Arts should always be wary of who it is that pays the piper.

PHIL WOODS, WRITER

Chicago by Kander and Ebb, directed by Ian Kellgren; Jacquie Toye as Roxie Hart, October 1986 (Phil Cutts)

Starting out: Ramin Gray

I remember running down to Mathew Street and bounding breathlessly – and late – up the rickety stairs to the big, long rehearsal room on the top

Ian Kellgren (left) and Gabrielle Drake as Fay in *Loot* by Joe Orton, directed by Joanna Hole; January 1991 (Phil Cutts)

floor. It was great being an Assistant Director at last and so romantic to be working, yes working, not being a scuzzy tourist, in the street where the Beatles kicked off. But Liverpool had had the stuffing kicked out of it since then.

I'd arrived at the Playhouse in June 1990 as the new boy from down South, the latest recruit on the Regional Theatre Young Director Scheme. My accent, glasses, everything, gave me away: I was clearly a tosser and Scousers made sure I knew who I was at every turn, sometimes gently, sometimes harshly. It was, as they now euphemistically say, a huge learning curve. And as the Playhouse staff and crew would snuggle up in Sloane's, the totally un-Sloaney pub across Williamson Square and struggle collectively through the *Echo* quiz, I started to see the world through new eyes.

Liverpool had suffered hugely through the 1980s and arriving when I did, all I could see were the scars. The rhetoric was all about moving forward and shiny new futures but the reality gap was devastating. With the inaugural Brouhaha Festival of youth theatre from Eastern Europe, it was surreal comparing notes with young people just out of Mostar. They were experiencing the joyous wealth of the free West for the first time while I was noting the scandalous neglect and decay of a world that seemed reminiscent of the worst of Eastern Europe.

I tried making my way: *Spring Awakening* with the Youth Theatre in an abandoned church in Toxteth. What was I thinking? I got beaten up, locals tried to nick all our kit and it ended up with me and the designer camping overnight in the damp, cold church protecting the gear while the Board asked questions about the advisability of getting teenagers to group wank, as called for in the script. But we got away with it.

Eventually Ian Kellgren, then Artistic Director, suggested I direct *A View from the Bridge* on the Main Stage. He was short of cash and I must have seemed like a cheap option. It was my first professional production and on press night the theatre went into receivership and twenty-five staff were made redundant. They all dutifully trooped on stage at the curtain call and somebody, probably Billy Meall, made a speech. It seemed like the end of the world.

But back to Mathew Street and as I bounded up those stairs, I knew exactly what it felt like to be the Messenger in a great classical play. I was the lowliest person, a mere Assistant. And as I burst, late for rehearsal, through the door I saw the actors away down the end of the room, all turning to look at me in surprise at my unseemly haste and breathlessness. I held the moment. Milked it, even. Then: "Thatcher's resigned"' The room erupted.*

RAMIN GRAY, DIRECTOR

Starting out: Pauline Daniels

*It has been my favourite theatre since I first walked through the doors 25 years ago to play Mama Morton in *Chicago* – my first ever venture into "legitimate" theatre. I had been up till then a stand-up comedian and club singer and had a bit of a break on telly when I did a mini musical on a Central TV show which happily was seen by Ian Kellgren who was casting *Chicago* to celebrate 75 years of the Playhouse. I arrived at rehearsals three flights up in the rehearsal room in Mathew Street and met the rest of the cast, when I was introduced as a "club act". Unsurprisingly, they did their fair share of looking down their noses at me, which if I'm honest only led to me being more determined about making this venture in to acting a great success. I was then to go on and make firm friends with the cast and to gain their respect but for a while I had never felt so alone. My family had all gone to Greece for a holiday which I gladly cancelled to

Fences by August Wilson, directed by Alby James (in association with Bill Kenwright); Yaphet Kotto as Troy and, in the background, Adrian Lester; August 1990

take this opportunity. I remember taking flyers to all the gigs I was still doing during rehearsals and putting them on tables and I know it worked. I still meet people today who say that it was the first time they had ever been to the theatre and – this is the best bit – they are still going. On the actual 75th birthday night I lit the candles on the cake and the lovely Carl Hawkins delivered his speech, which went on just a bit too long and the cake nearly caught fire.

I went on to enjoy playing many roles at the Playhouse including Mama Rose, in *Gypsy* and Betty in *Breezeblock Park*. In 1996 I brought my *Shirley Valentine* here for five wonderful weeks. I remember that Richard Williams had to beg a new kitchen and although Bill Kenwright was expecting the kitchen to go into his store, even as I was taking my final bow I could hear the crew drilling and firmly planting that kitchen in to the green room. It's still there and whenever I go in to that room I smile at "my" kitchen. When the theatre reopened I had the wonderful job with Micky Starke of painting the gold star on the front of the theatre. All went really well – then Micky made me laugh and I slipped. So there is a gold blob just below that star that is forever mine.

PAULINE DANIELS, ACTOR

Youth theatre: from Liverpool to the Ukraine

I wrote *Man Made* for the Playhouse Youth Theatre, based on the seven deadly sins and we called it an opera – it was like a mix between Greek Drama and wild cabaret spectacle – the music score had a lot of dance beat mixed in with the slightly east European melodies. The idea of the show came from Kate Willard, director of The Youth Theatre, who was very dynamic and responsible for creating Brouhaha which is now such an integral part of Liverpool's culture. Kate built up a brilliant network of contacts with youth theatres all over Europe and beyond: it was her idea to bring so many foreign theatre companies to Liverpool. It was a real

187

Gypsy by Arthur Laurents, Jule Styne and Stephen Sondheim, directed by Ian Kellgren; with Pauline Daniels as Rose, December 1987

achievement and I will never forget the night when she stood alone on the Main House stage addressing young people from all over Western and Eastern Europe and being almost submerged in wilds cheers and applause.

The Youth Theatre also strayed abroad, including a trip to Ternopol in the Ukraine. This was an extraordinarily ambitious, project and I was asked to create a music-theatre piece with a cast of about thirty and then take it to an International Drama Festival in the Ukraine. Again I chose a Dostoyevsky novel, *The Gambler*, because of its theme of obsession and addiction to gambling. We called it a Greedy Pantomime and it was staged like some wild graphic novel, full of energy and high octane ensemble playing. The music was a hybrid of Russian music, funk, cabaret and the blues. The cast were quite terrifying at times as the chorus of totally driven gamblers prepared to sacrifice everything for their addiction. Rosalind Henderson created the wildly expressive set and costumes – it was undoubtedly the most unrestrained show I have ever worked on. And so we headed east with our attempt to re-interpret a great Russian novel. We flew to Moscow – just after the fall of The Berlin Wall and you could feel the lingering sense of censorship in the air. When we arrived, it was late at night. I remember how empty the city centre was, with only one piece of neon, like a starfish on a deserted beach and the occasional figure scuttling through the darkness like a figure from a Gogol novel. The trains at Moscow station seemed as if they were from the 1930s. At Ternopol Station we were met by a group of actors wearing beautiful traditional Ukrainian costumes and dancing with huge puppets. We were whisked away to an opening party lit by lanterns and a huge bonfire. We saw some fascinating work – a genuine folklore drama, an edgy and highly sophisticated version of *The Good Woman of Schezwan*: I was worried about our presentation of *The Gamblers* ... but it was well received. I met some real characters out there. I also quickly learnt that many great ideas were automatically toasted with vodka!*

PATRICK DINEEN, COMPOSER

Red Star Brouhaha was an international youth theatre festival planned to run in 1990 but postponed until the following year which was inspired by a visit of the youth theatre to Hungary in 1988. It was to lead to the foundation of Brouhaha International, the arts and cultural development agency, which organizes (amongst other things) international collaborations, festivals and community celebrations.

'It's too good to lose'

> How has it come to pass that a celebrated and justly famous playhouse now faces a bleak future? Have people stopped wanting it? No, the figures are there. The people are here. Has this theatre been profligate, recklessly spending huge sums of public money? No, the figures are there. Compared with similar sized theatres in similar sized towns and cities, this playhouse has for years been scraping by and existing on the absolute minimum. There is no fat to trim. For a major theatre in a major city you cannot get leaner than that.
>
> WILLY RUSSELL, QUOTED IN LIVERPOOL ECHO, 18 JANUARY 1991

Willy Russell was speaking at the launch of the campaign to save the theatre from closure. They had twelve weeks to solve the cash crisis.

> Don't despair. Something will save the theatre even if it is only the ghost of Maud Carpenter.
>
> BERYL BAINBRIDGE, QUOTED IN LIVERPOOL ECHO, 18 JANUARY 1991

> Liverpool without the Playhouse is unthinkable. To think of it dark, turned to other uses is insufferable. Liverpool will be much diminished.
>
> GEORGE MELLY, QUOTED IN LIVERPOOL ECHO, 18 JANUARY 1991

> It is horrifying to hear of the possible closure of the Playhouse. It is the most important repertory theatre in the country. Michael and I loved the Playhouse and had we not met there, there would have been no Vanessa, Lynne or Joely.
>
> RACHEL KEMPSON, QUOTED IN LIVERPOOL ECHO, 18 JANUARY 1991

'It's too good to lose' campaign

> From 1986 the funding of the Liverpool Repertory Company was severely affected by the loss of Merseyside County Council and the introduction of the five distinctive boroughs now known as Merseyside. Conflict arose as to who now had responsibility for the Playhouse. By 1991 the Playhouse was

threatened by closure as debts grew. The financial fight was led by John Stalker the theatre manager, Caroline Parry and Rebecca Farrar. The greatest support came firstly from the ceaseless work of the *Liverpool Echo* and *Daily Post* followed by the local radio and the public.

So great was the response to the *Echo*'s "It's Too Good to Lose" appeal that within weeks 100,000 individually signed postcards were posted to The Arts Council. Each card had to have a stamp, which a member of the public paid for and, by law, if addressed to Lord Palumbo personally, he was obliged to send a reply, regardless of his need for further secretarial staff, never mind the cost of postage. Using the press and media, he asked to be allowed to not spend the extra money sending individual replies. It felt like a triumph; it was merely a blip in the fight. Thus it was that young people who had been almost daily in the forefront of the campaign set about the hiring of a mini bus to take the campaign to London.

A further signed 20,000 cards were collected by the many volunteers who manned the table in the foyer of the theatre. Meantime Dougie organized the mini bus and I was given the task of selecting six people eighteen or over to ride with us. Nearly all the Youth Theatre wanted to go, so I was obliged to restrict the team to Gill, Geoff, Beverley, Corinne, Rodney and Gary.

Packed lunches and cans of pop were in abundance; though we had promised ourselves a hot meal on the route home. We were strangely quiet and watchful of the traffic on the road. For some it was a new experience, the thought of visiting the Arts Council and the Houses of Parliament must have been weighing heavily upon them.

Charles Hart received the group very graciously. Then we trooped over to the House where we split into two groups. Each choosing to ask for an interview with their MP or just to watch from the Gallery. Then three of us went over to the Lords to speak with Lord Tordoff. He gave us some helpful advice as to whom we might write to further our campaign.

There seemed to be so much to-ing and fro-ing that at one point I was fearful of losing them. But at six o'clock sharp they all turned up at the mini bus. We made it home sometime after midnight. I still feel very proud of all of them.*

PELHAM MCMAHON, WRITER

Architect's impression of the Gallery level bar

Bill Kenwright, 1991–1996

❝ The Playhouse is now run from London. I will eventually be involved in the colour of the tea that's poured out, but there are more important things right now. Like the sort of theatre people want. ❞

BILL KENWRIGHT, QUOTED IN *LIVERPOOL ECHO*, 24 SEPTEMBER 1991

❝ In 1911 the reps grew up because of the failings of the commercial managers. Today however there seems to be the need for a healthy marriage of the subsidised and the commercial. We have such a union here and this may well be the way back to seasons as rich as that of 1911. ❞

IAN KELLGREN, PROGRAMME NOTE, *AN AWFULLY BIG ADVENTURE*, MARCH 1992

Ian Kellgren stayed until January 1996.

A view from the executive producer

❝ The Liverpool Playhouse has played a huge part in my life …

The first words I ever heard on a stage were from *The Merchant of Venice* when a young Trevor Baxter uttered to an even younger John Stride, "In sooth, I know not why I am so sad …"

That moment, and that memory, has lived with me forever. With my friend Howard Kay, I became a very young regular on the front row of the balcony. Same seat – every third Wednesday. In those days a thriving Liverpool Playhouse Repertory Company would play to packed houses for a three week run.

Not long after my Shakespeare experience I found myself on the stage of The Playhouse appearing as a stoat amongst twenty or so local kids in their Christmas production *Toad of Toad Hall*. My first line uttered, as opposed to heard, was the equally memorable "How the happy little stoats laugh when he is off his oats. Down with Toad." After that debut as an eleven year old, I worked on and off at the theatre throughout my teens playing small roles, making tea, shifting scenery, and in fact doing anything else they wanted me to do. I was in love with the place. Its auditorium, its stage, its nooks, its crannies – its magic!

An Awfully Big Adventure
by Beryl Bainbridge,
directed by Ian Kellgren;
March 1992. Rodney
Bewes as Vernon and
Eithne Brown as Lilly

Several decades later, when I had extraordinarily, and without any planning, become a theatrical producer, I was approached by The Playhouse to see if I would like to mount some co-productions with them. When I had originally become a producer, in the late sixties and early seventies, there was an absolute divide between commercial and subsidised. Supposedly different ideals and definitely different bank accounts! I found this odd, and began to question the logic of subsidised theatres mounting shows for a very limited period often without thinking of giving them a longer life. My company's strategy was welcomed by most subsidised houses, and it was a real joy to be approached by The Playhouse.

The first major success we had together was Alan Bleasdale's epic *Are You Lonesome Tonight?* I remember as if it was yesterday, standing on the second floor landing with Alan introducing Martin Shaw as the man we had asked to play Elvis Presley – to a somewhat a startled northern press!

The choice proved to be the perfect one, though, as Alan went on to pick up the *Evening Standard* Best Musical of the Year Award.

A few years after *Lonesome* I was approached in turn both by Ian Kellgren, the artistic director, and Frank Taylor, "the official administrator", to see if I could help The Playhouse which was in danger of closing its doors as its financial problems had mounted to near breaking point. The following five years were some of the highest highs and lowest lows of my life. In the main the board were supportive, and Ian was a wonderfully loyal and energetic partner, but somehow the "awfully big adventure" (extraordinarily the title of the first show that Ian and I

Diana Rigg in *Medea*
by Euripides, directed
by Jonathan Kent;
September 1993
(Phil Cutts)

mounted together, an adaptation of Beryl Bainbridge's much-loved book which Ian had always hoped to see on The Playhouse stage) wasn't as successful as we had all hoped. A massive campaign had been undertaken in 1991 to "Save the Playhouse" and when the board and myself sat down the first urgent need was to find an audience again. We undoubtedly did this, but probably at too high a cost – to both sides. I think the greatest gift I've ever given any theatre was the production of *Blood Brothers* with Stephanie Lawrence that graced the stage for Christmas in 1992. The Empire had pleaded with me to stage it there and obviously enjoy the benefits of a near 2,400 seater theatre as opposed to one a quarter of that size. But Ian and I were desperate to give The Playhouse something special – and we did. I loved seeing *Blood Brothers* back on The Playhouse stage, just as I hugely enjoyed the world premieres of *Good Rockin' Tonight, Ferry Cross the Mersey, Only The Lonely, No Trams to Lime Street* and plays like *Dancing at Lughnasa* – but my greatest moment was probably when the curtain came down on the opening night of Diana Rigg in *Medea*. I was standing at the back of the auditorium when a couple approached me.

Toad of Toad Hall by Kenneth Grahame (adapted A.A.Milne); Bill Kenwright is the little white stoat, towards the front and bending over, fifth from the left; December 1958

Imagine: The John Lennon Story, devised by Keith Strachan and Ian Kellgren (from an idea by Bob Eaton), above: Andrew Schofield and below: Mark McGann; directed by Ian Kellgren; July 1992 and June 1994 (Phil Cutts)

The man asked "Billy lad, were you responsible for that" I responded that I was – in a way. And he said, "I'm a docker – and I didn't want to come here tonight – she made me – but I can't remember ever having had such a good time. I'm going to come again." A great moment – and another of The Playhouse memories I will take to my grave.

The audiences came, and the place undoubtedly buzzed again, but it became more and more difficult to mount productions that would not only excite an audience, but also support the heavier production costs that were necessary, and the support of both the powers that be and my bank balance, finally ran out of steam. I was told – very pleasantly – that the Arts Council had asked the board to make a decision – did they want a commercially-run theatre or a subsidised one? Which, in hindsight, was absolutely the right question at that time. And looking back, although I had been proud of what we had done at The Playhouse, I was relieved to hand it over once again.

I had some wonderful times at The Playhouse during my formative years watching and then working alongside such talents as John Thaw, Rita Tushingham, Caroline Blakiston, and Hilary Crane, and later some unmissable years as a director, and a producer – but times change. What The Playhouse in its partnership with The Everyman has pioneered now is exactly what the standard bearers of repertory theatre in Great Britain should be doing to keep their flag flying proudly. Exciting, innovative theatre, which on many occasions is the result of mutually beneficial partnerships with other subsidized theatres and organisations. The Playhouse has got it right again, and I salute the Spirit in everyone involved.*

BILL KENWRIGHT, EXECUTIVE PRODUCER

An Awfully Big Adventure by Beryl Bainbridge, directed by Ian Kellgren; March 1992

This had been scheduled to open in March 1991 but was postponed when closure threatened.

6 Never-Never Land is always yesterday, and each of us describes it the way we wish it had been.*

BERYL BAINBRIDGE, PROGRAMME NOTE

6 It touches on three bygone worlds ... Liverpool of 1950 when there was still the old market, the Oyster Bar, Brown's Café and Reeces. The bygone world of rep theatre which in the sense of a permanent company for a

season is no more. And the bygone world of all our childhoods seen in the resonances in *Peter Pan* that the company is producing in the young girl's life.'

One Fine Day by Dennis Lomborg; a one man show directed by Bob Thompson with Joe McGann; August 1994

'Beryl's father used his influence to get her a job as an acting assistant stage manager, aged sixteen. She used her experiences in her novel, *An Awfully Big Adventure*, which was set in the Playhouse. It seemed like a good idea to have the novel adapted into a stage play and to put it on at the Playhouse. I approached a playwright whom I had commissioned work from before. To my surprise, he declined my offer to adapt the book. He seemed to be saying that Beryl's quirky style, perhaps, should be left to her to adapt.

As a result I found myself at Beryl's Camden Town house, squeezing past a full sized, stuffed buffalo in the narrow hall, before entering what Melvyn Bragg described as "a cluster of artefacts whose centre of gravity lies somewhere between an extravagantly decorated Romany caravan and a collector's item museum of curios and works of art".

She was a fascinating raconteur although her daughter, whom we cast to play the Beryl character when we did produce the play of the book, felt that her mother's story telling talent tended to blur the distinction between fact and fiction. Beryl did claim, for example, that in her days at the Playhouse the audience were still permitted to smoke and as a result the actors on stage could sometimes not see the audience for the cigarette fug.

As with anyone returning to a place of their youth, Beryl found the Playhouse smaller and altered in ways she could not always identify. Of course, the Liverpool surrounding the Playhouse had changed even more and like a guide in a dream land she took me round trying to place where things had been. We went to the restaurant in George Henry Lee's, which was still there then, but lacked the grandeur of her memory.

Beryl died in the summer of 2010 and so one more connection with an era when actors could learn their craft in the company of other actors is gone too.'

Stepping Out by Richard Harris, directed by Martin Connor; September 1991
'The Playhouse is stepping into the future with apparent confidence. Their back-from-the-brink season opened last night with a new coat of paint on the outside of the building and plenty of fun within …
Bill Kenwright commissioned the script as a small-scale seaside entertainment seven years ago. He then transferred it to the West End, where prophets of doom said it would flop because the production had no 'star names'. They were wrong. *Stepping Out* ran for four years and travelled the world. Why? Because, I suggest, it is about the triumph of the spirit.'
(Joe Riley, *Liverpool Echo* 19 September 1991)

Medea by Euripides, directed by Jonathan Kent, September 1993

Greek theatre   Bill Kenwright's decision to revive Jonathan Kent's production of *Medea*, provoked some positive responses from critics who had been disparaging over his choice of plays. Robin Thornber, who'd had harsh words for Kenwright's management of the theatre, was forced to admit that it was the most 'intellectually honest and compelling production I've seen of a classically awkward text and a dazzling display of sheer theatrical virtuosity'. (*Guardian*, 21 September 1993)

❛ I was obviously very aware that we had already done one Greek plays this season, when Jonathan Kent and Diana Rigg sat down with me to discuss a re-launch of their Almeida production of *Medea*. However, from one who does more productions that most, you can believe me that you don't often get the opportunity to work with something you really do believe could be classed "definitive" – and I really do believe that this production will be the yardstick that all future productions of this great play will be measured against … Jonathan Kent has in a very short time at the Almeida Theatre established himself, and his company, as probably the most artistically successful production house in Europe. When I saw the Kent/Rigg *Medea* originally, I was overwhelmed by the power of Diana's performance, and I am simply thrilled that the Playhouse has now joined forces with the Almeida to remount this production before it goes to the

West End. I am quite confident that tonight you will see a performance that you will never forget.'

BILL KENWRIGHT, PROGRAMME NOTE

The other Greek production was Peter Hall's *Lysistrata* which had been performed in May.

Summer musicals

While critics objected to a string of summer musicals, Kenwright was unapologetic: 'If you've got it, flaunt it. Just as Stoke capitalises on its potteries, so we must capitalise on our musical past. If we don't, we're fools. It's a key to our ability to thrive again.' (*The Times*, 17 February 1996)

' The musical rock and roll biography has become a standard summer feature at the Liverpool Playhouse.'

DAILY POST, 27 JULY 1993

' I make no excuse for presenting these "rock 'n' roll musicals" during the summer at the Playhouse. I passionately believe that the theatre has a right, even a duty, to celebrate every aspect of today's society. The rock 'n' roll of the fifties helped enormously to shape that society. Almost

Ferry Cross the Mersey by Maggie Norris & Guy Picot, directed by Carole Todd; with Gerry Marsden as himself and Carl Kirshner as his younger self, February 1996

overnight, barriers of nationality, language and custom were broken, uniting a generation divided by politics, religion and oceans. One of the greatest thrills of my time at the Playhouse has been to witness the heaving, swaying, clapping, full houses that have greeted these summer productions – at a time when normally our theatre has been closed. Rock 'n' roll has filled the houses, filled the coffers, and sent a lot of people home very happy.'

BILL KENWRIGHT, PROGRAMME NOTE, SEPTEMBER 1993

Musicals included:

Good Rockin' Tonite (October 1991)
Imagine (June 1992 and July 1994)
Only the Lonely (July 1993) – appeared 3 times by August 1994
The Sound of Fury (June 1995)

The 19th Hole by Johnny Speight, directed by Tony Craven; Eric Sykes as the Club Secretary, September 1992 (Phil Cutts)

Thank you, Willy

Blood Brothers by Willy Russell, directed by Bill Kenwright and Bob Tomson; December 1992

6 Dear Theatregoer –

1983 – it was business as usual on Merseyside – Liverpool top of the League and at Wembley AGAIN – but the word was that Everton could be on the way back – and the hottest ticket in town was not for the Derby game but for a musical called *Blood Brothers* at the Playhouse.

I had loved Willy Russell's *John, Paul, George, Ringo … and Bert* and adored his *Rita* but nothing quite prepared me for my first confrontation with Mickey and Eddie, his *Blood Brothers*. If every theatre was "total" for me, if ever an experience was truly overwhelming, it was that night at the Lyric Theatre, Shaftesbury Avenue when I was drained but uplifted by the sheer theatricality of an epic musical set in my beloved home town.

Like many other theatre lovers, I mourned the original productions premature demise – and, not so secretly, set about planning what I hoped could be my part in its return.

Blood Brothers by Willy Russell, directed by Bill Kenwright and Bob Tomson; Con O'Neill as Mickey, December 1992

Over the following three years *Blood Brothers* built up a successful reputation in repertory theatre throughout Great Britain and in 1987 Willy and Bob Swash decided that the time was right for me to take it on an extended national tour.

After a year of astonishing receptions from Glasgow to Liverpool (of course) to Chichester we decided that the moment had come to take a chance on a return to the Capital. On July 28th after two sold-out weeks of previews *Blood Brothers* received one of the most extraordinary standing ovations in West End theatrical history. I am not a man of envy but like millions of other Merseysiders, I suppose I had always envied a Kevin Ratcliffe or a Phil Thompson for that wonderful feeling they must have had as they held the F.A. Cup aloft in front of their fellow scousers. Victory is always sweet, but victory alongside your own has to be more special than probably most of us can put into words. All I can say is – this was my moment! I was sitting in a packed London theatre next to my own brother, mother and father, just behind me was my author and friend and his family, in front of me was my co-director and friend and his family, and on the stage was my magnificent company – and all of us were glorying in the triumph of our home town – while a thousand London first nighters leapt to their feet and cheered the roof down!

The following morning *Blood Brothers* was welcomed "back to the West End where it most assuredly belongs" by Jack Tinker of the *Daily Mail*. Sheridan Morley wrote that not before time we had turned *Blood Brothers*, "from a cult success into a huge critical and box office winner" and welcomed it as "one of the great musicals of the decade". So here we are, ten years later, in many ways back at the beginning! The production that you will witness tonight has been specially mounted for a *Blood Brothers* invasion of Canada and New York. I don't think there has ever been an occasion when a "mega hit" West End musical has returned to its original subsidised home before embarking for Broadway, but as far as Willy, Bob and myself were concerned there was only one place where we wanted to start this final tilt at the championship, and that place was the Liverpool Playhouse ... Willy alone amongst writers of musicals in the world today has had the courage to tackle the way we live now – on a grand, musical scale. Ten years ago Willy gave me the theatrical experience of a lifetime – an experience that continues to thrill me every day that I work on his *Blood Brothers*.

Thank you Willy.

BILL KENWRIGHT, PROGRAMME NOTE

In this version of the play, Mrs Johnson was played by Stephanie Lawrence, and it was to be the musical's only return to the Playhouse.

Alun Owen

No Trams to Lime Street by Alun Owen, directed by Bill Kenwright, music and lyrics: Ronnie James Scott and Marty Wilde (dedicated to Alun Owen who had died in 1994); October 1995

The town I was brought up in is an active part of my plays. I think it is highly individual, but then everyone's home town is, and Liverpool has the added advantage of having a multi-racial population. It's a Celtic town set down in Lancashire. Its people evolved an accent for themselves that they've borrowed from their Irish and Welsh grandfathers. The problem of Identity, which is to me one of the greatest the twentieth century has produced, is exaggerated in Liverpool, and the exaggeration makes it dramatic.

ALUN OWEN, 1961, QUOTED IN THE PROGRAMME

Alun Owen ... was the first to capture for theatre and television that peculiar Liverpool mixture that can scoff and hope in the same breath. It is an eagerness to believe that rides in tandem with an irresistible urge, mostly born of experience, to debunk. Willy Russell and Alan Bleasdale acknowledge their debt to him. He wrote about what he knew of life on the Liverpool streets, about the religious tensions and the tramcars, about the pubs and churches, chapel and synagogues and all those who rode, drank and prayed in them ... When *No Trams to Lime Street* was being prepared for television at the beginning of the sixties, a casting director told him, "People don't make love with a Liverpool accent." "No?" said Alun, "where do you think all those fuckin' babies come from?"

DAVID NATHAN, PROGRAMME NOTE

Studio 3

Watching by Jim Hitchmough, directed by Tony Mulholland; February 1986.

Starting out: Jim Hitchmough

❛ *Watching* was the first and only play I did in Liverpool so I won't claim to be a Playhouse veteran or any kind of expert on Liverpool. However, it was clear from the start of rehearsal that *Watching* was very much a "Liverpool" play, written by a local and examining themes that were reminiscent of the work of Willy Russell and Alan Bleasdale – class, love, aspiration, survival – and, above all, shot through with bitter sweet comedy.

Jim Hitchmough, a thoughtful and gentle man, who sadly died in 1997, created this gem of a two-hander. He invented two mis-matched characters: stuffy mummy's boy Malcolm from Meols and brash gobby Scouse Brenda, and threw them into outdoor scenes that offered, through the relentless one-liners and tragi-comic set-ups, something of the "heady essence of being alive", as one critic wrote. It had a simple premise, boy meets girl, boy takes girl bird-watching, girl turns boy's world upside down. In doing so, he learns to be assertive and more of a match for her, and she learns to connect with her own vulnerabilities, and their mutual consciousness-raising leads them towards love by the end. For all their dissimilarities, Malcolm's bird-watching hobby and Brenda's one of "people-watching" has actually left them both more as "observers" of life and as a result they have far more in common than they first realise.

The play opened in the Playhouse Studio in February 1986. Featuring Cheryl Maiker and myself, it had a simple set of fake grass and plastic seagulls to represent, for the most part, the windswept Wirral. Brenda teases and provokes Malcolm constantly, battering at his peace of mind, ridiculing his hobbies, job and background and severely testing his patience. Over time, Malcolm's confidence grows (after a temporary separation), and when they meet again, his straight dealing and gentleness, and even ordinariness, starts to allow Brenda to reveal her own vulnerabilities beneath the brash exterior. All in all, they were two

True Dare Kiss by Debbie Horsfield, directed by Richard Brandon; October 1983

201

Changing Gear by Jim Morris, directed by Tim Fywell; Tom Georgeson, February 1987

extraordinarily well-drawn characters, full of contradictions and pride and the foolishness of real life.

I remember Jim's delight at the critical reception, especially the influential Joe Riley in the *Liverpool Echo* who gave it a terrific thumbs up, citing it as "a steadfast case for more plays about ordinary people". It is always a relief to be well received in a new work, not least for the theatre, but the real treat for us was the audience, who clearly enjoyed seeing these recognisable local characters perform their elaborate courtship dance.

When the show transferred to London's Bush Theatre, it had a similar reception. One or two critics thought it a little coarse, and some of the jokes a bit old-hat, but the tiny cast felt they had missed the point. Brenda's breezy humour was full of spirit but also had a ring of sadness to it, even desperation, which all seemed to reflect the state of Liverpool back in the difficult 1980s. The rest of the reviews were great seeing genuine charm and truth in the writing and acting and the run was a sell-out.

The play was later the basis for a very successful TV series. The first episode was essentially the first half of the play, with a lot of the same jokes, and it was a great to follow how Brenda and Malcolm's world developed over the next few years. It was a testament to Jim's great skill that the characters maintained and spread their appeal so well from stage to screen.

ADAM KOTZ, ACTOR

I went to work at the Playhouse around Easter time, 1985. Jules Wright had just taken over as Artistic Director and she brought me in as director of the Youth Theatre. I had some background in Theatre in Education having directed and written plays at the Theatre Workshop in Edinburgh and I looked forward to carving out my own "territory".

Jules was about to embark on an ambitious season in the Studio backed by Granada TV and she chose a number of plays, new work, reflecting her own background in new work at the Royal Court in London. I favoured the same approach. Amongst the scripts lying around on my desk when I arrived was a piece called *Down the Soc*, a lively comedy about young people in a social security office. Jules gave me the studio to put it on. The youth theatre was fragmented and I along with local woman, Brigid Benson, worked hard to bring some sense of identity to the group. I named it *Upstart!* and was fortunate to find myself working with a terrific and talented group of young people several of whom went on to make a career in theatre and TV.

Watching, Jim Hitchmough, directed by Tony Mulholland; extended and transferred to Bush, Adam Kotz and Cheryl Maiker, February 1986

Jules liked my production of *Down the Soc* and thought I could handle a new play which had been sent to her by a local ex-merchant seaman called Jim Hitchmough. It worked fantastically well in the intimate setting of the studio and sold out. Scouts from The Bush theatre in London came along and the next thing I knew it was transferring. The restaging was relatively straightforward and it repeated its success in London. Jim Hitchmough found himself courted by Granada TV. Jim was one of the nicest men I have ever met and he deserved all the success he found late in life. Good guys don't always come last, and he was the proof of that.

It was an exciting season, 1985–86. Sometimes the chemistry comes together and a combination of elements really make something work. We often talk about such episodes in "mystical" terms as if we are unsure how to replicate such good times, but in truth there is no secret. Jules gave enthusiastic people a chance and they – I include myself – took it with both hands. She surrounded herself with hungry people; she took chances, knowing that not everything was going to work out, but less afraid of failure than hopeful of success and in that last phrase lies the formula for the successful "chemistry" I referred to. She chose to look to future talents and build on them and Liverpool responded, especially because in plays such as *Down the Soc* and *Watching* it saw itself reflected. I was sorry when she left, and I regret that I was too young and inexperienced to give her more support. ,

TONY MULHOLLAND, DIRECTOR

While Jules Wright was at the Playhouse, the studio also premiered:

Ourselves Alone, Anne Devlin; a co-production with Royal Court Upstairs where it transferred (October 1985)
And the Name of the Daughter was Rose, Roxanne Shafer (November 1985)
Short Change, Terry Heaton; transferred to Royal Court Upstairs where it was the first of three plays about 'the north' (January 1986). Terry Heaton became writer in residence in 1988
Shamrocks and Crocodiles, Heidi Thomas (April 1986)

Taking on Thatcher   *Fears and Miseries of the Third Reich/Fears and Miseries of the Third Term* directed by Kate Rowland; January 1989

Writers for the *Third Term* included: Kay Adshead, Nick Darke, Noel Greig, Catherine Hayes, Terry Heaton, Debbie Horsfield, Frank McGuiness, and Jim Morris.

❛ Isn't it asking for trouble when the Playhouse is fighting for funding and the Arts Council is now run by Conservatives?❜

ROBIN THORNBER, *GUARDIAN*, 7 JANUARY 1989

❛ We would not want rate-payers money used for what we consider very offensive political propaganda ... If any analogy is attempted between the Prime Minister and Hitler we would regard that as a gross insult. We will be calling for an immediate cessation of any money from Sefton going towards this production and an apology from those responsible.❜

COUNCILLOR RON WATSON, CONSERVATIVE LEADER OF SEFTON COUNCIL, QUOTED IN *DAILY POST*, 3 DECEMBER 1989

❛ Members of your Board were saddened by the notorious but unfounded publicity which this production received prior to its first performance, as a result of an initial unsubstantiated report from a journalist. We were greatly surprised by the speed with which local and national politicians felt able to jump onto the publicity bandwagon without checking the veracity of their sources. Needless to say, as soon as these productions opened for public scrutiny, the public debate ceased ...❜

CHAIRMAN'S STATEMENT TO 1989 AGM

A playhouse company

❛ I joined the Liverpool Playhouse in the mid-80s from the Everyman Theatre. At the time such a move was tantamount to an act of betrayal. Both theatres had strong identities, competitive instincts and this combined with their individual creative visions made the move a real challenge. Ian Kellgren had invited me to join, and under his leadership I was encouraged to take risks, broaden my own knowledge and take charge of the studio

Fear and Misery of the Third Reich by Brecht with *Fear and Misery of the Third Term*, directed by Kate Rowland; transferred to Young Vic Studio, January 1989

205

space. I was passionate about making the literary department a vital conduit for new writers, particularly regional talent. I wanted to explore new ways of working, re-invent the studio space and build on the Playhouse Studio's reputation by creating a hothouse that nurtured not just new writing talent but directors, actors, designers, composers. From Stephen Daldry's ground-breaking production of *Rat in the Skull* to the creation of the Studio Company in 1988–89 with its amazing repertoire of new and classic work it was an exciting time. In the main space I directed Beth Henley's *Crimes of the Heart* designed by Eve Stewart with the most wonderful cast of women, and Peter Nichols *Passion Play*. But it was my time in the Studio where I worked with so many talented individuals. *Leave Taking* by Winsome Pinnock premiered in the studio and then went down to the Royal Court. The Studio Company was a unique enterprise, an acting company of young regional talent, who stayed together for a whole season of work, from Shaun Duggan's *A Brusque Affair* to Andrew Cullen's *North*, *Beaux Stratagem* to Claire Macintyre's *Low Level Panic*, readings, workshops and experiments.

The company tried many things but the one that properly changed me was the production of Brecht's *Fear and Misery of the Third Reich* alongside the contemporary work *Fears and Miseries of the Third Term*. Thatcher's Britain was a miserable and difficult place for many so the commissioning of eight short dramas from original writers like Frank McGuiness and Debbie Horsfield aimed to reflect that time. Shaped by an extraordinary poem *The Shadow Man* from the much missed Adrian Henri, it was a potent counterpoint to Nazi Germany with its parallel structure and anatomy of fear. Designed by Hannah Mayall, who was the resident designer for the Studio, with music from Patrick Dineen, it was a force to be reckoned with and went on to win awards, and travel down to The Young Vic. The impetus of this and the studio season eventually led me to found Altered States, a new writing national touring company, and cemented my total dedication and obsession with working with and developing writing talent both in the theatre and now at the BBC. You can't think of the Playhouse without remembering Alan Bleasdale's championing of writers, the odd production that went wrong, the pub across the square and of course Mathew Street.

If I look back at that time the legacy is one of finding and nurturing talent, great theatrical adventures and finally and most importantly friendships that have lasted a lifetime.*

KATE ROWLAND, ASSOCIATE DIRECTOR

A composer in residence

*I remember the moment vividly, I was sitting in the kitchen, the sky was grey and so was my life. I was going through the *Guardian* Jobs column when suddenly I saw this tiny advert … "Composer-in-Residence wanted

for The Liverpool Playhouse". Something made me reach for the pen.
I didn't expect to even get an interview. In fact, in typical fashion, I
almost jeopardised the whole thing, by posting my application at the last
available moment.

But two weeks later, I was on a train to Liverpool.

It was a beautiful early autumn day when I arrived at Lime Street
and as I walked toward the Playhouse I felt incredibly elated, I couldn't
believe it, Liverpool, mythical city of the North, home of The Beatles!
Citadel of music, politics, Strawberry Fields forever …

In a small room four directors surrounded me, each of them fiercely
intelligent and probing me with their questions. It was like something out
of a Pinter play. I fielded questions which ranged from my views on Brecht
and Weill's collaboration, my ability to write music on found objects to
what was referred to by one young director called Julian as "my dubious
choice of shirt". That was it, the man had insulted my shirt. There was no
way I wasn't going to get the job.

A few weeks later I was standing at Lime Street Station with one
suitcase and a box full of books. This was 1988, and Thatcher was still
"she who must be obeyed". We had been through The Poll Tax, The
Miner's Strike: this was a time when you simply had to have an opinion
of Margaret Thatcher, where it still meant something to hold deep held
political beliefs and where the State's involvement in education and health
was, for many of us, still something to be applauded rather than despised.
I mention all this, not only because Liverpool was such a city with an
enduring political consciousness, but also because the person who hired me
as composer-in-residence was intensely political and believed in theatre as
a means of protest and articulating the injustices and prejudices of society.
Her name was Kate Rowland and she was to go on to become Head of
Creative Writing on BBC Radio, but at this time she was Artistic Director
of The Playhouse Studio. She was tough-minded, creative and driven and
she created a fantastically provocative programme of plays and events for
the Studio Season.

I was asked to write the music for every show in that studio season.
This was learning on the job, for you had to be versatile – it was then
that I appreciated what I had already learnt on my all my theatre jobs
in London as well as learning the most important lesson of all – "how
to interpret a director's brief" – "Patrick I'm hearing gamelan cymbals
careering towards Prohibition Jazz with maybe a touch of baroque …"

It was such an exciting time, things moved at such a pace and I felt
very fortunate to be at the heart of it working with so many talented
individuals. The production that was closest to my heart at the time was

Self Catering by Andrew Cullen, directed by Kate Rowland; September 1992 (Phil Cutts) Jane Hogarth as Meryl Streep, Andrew Schofield as Clint Eastwood and Paul Broughton (below) as Henry Fonda

Fears and Miseries of The Third Reich/Third Term, a hugely ambitious concept critiquing the political climate. Apart from being the musical director for Brecht's songs, I was asked by Kate to write a set of songs for the contemporary half: my brief was for them to be direct, fierce, darkly comic and to add a further critical dimension to the writing. After the years of struggle, it felt fantastic to be given the opportunity to do this work and to express in music and lyrics the feeling that many of us shared at the time. The production got so much press attention that it transferred to the Young Vic and went on to win *Time Out*'s Best Fringe Show Award.

The rest of the season, although not so overtly political, was equally challenging including a very fine production of Brecht's *Drums in The Night* directed by Tal Rubins. This was an early work by Brecht full of raw political statements, roughly hewn characters and it was a gift for music. Looking back now, that season was a little like being in a band; here was a group of actors, and a creative team working together constantly – like all groups, there were the usual highs and lows and heartaches and moments of conflict – but on the whole, it was an uplifting, invigorating experience; and we were a strong and united team. Best of all, there was an audience hungry for the work, shows were extended and that little studio became an arena for excitement and debate and when it was over, I felt proud to have been involved.

Kate moved on to form her own company. It took a while to get used to her being gone, because she brought such a determination and edge to the work. The second Season again was built around a repertory company but already the landscape was changing and, within six months, Thatcher would be gone. In addition to writing the music to all the shows for the season, I was also given the chance to stage my own production. I chose *The Double*, a short novel by Dostoyevsky which I adapted as a music theatre piece – I felt that the absurdity, the desperation and the dark comedy at the heart of Dostoyevsky's work leant itself to an adaptation and the story of a little man completely overwhelmed by the hypocrisy and cruelty of his society seemed perfect for a score of cabaret songs and lyrics that commented not just on the action but on society in general. The set and costumes were created by Rosalind Henderson, the resident Designer for this season; apart from her absolute originality and immense visual flair, she also had an ability to get to the psychological heart of the characters. Ros and I went on to form our own music theatre company, Base Chorus.

Writing this has made me realise how that period was in a way the last flourish of overtly political theatre. For a brief moment, the Playhouse seemed to have the absolutely perfect combination – a populist main house, a thriving outreach and Youth Theatre Department, a provocative and stimulating studio seasons. Looking back now, it seemed natural to be producing political theatre; not agitprop but work which so consistently articulated the deep and natural sense of unfairness that was in the air. It is incredible to think now that there was a group of actors, directors, a designer and a composer who were hired to work together over an entire season. It's, almost, unthinkable now.'

PATRICK DINEEN, COMPOSER

The Studio in the 90s

'As we celebrate the centenary of the Liverpool Repertory Company, theatre is under severe financial pressure. When my play *Self Catering (A Short History of the World)* premiered at the Liverpool Playhouse studio in the 1990s, concern about funding was also a critical issue. It's a reminder that the campaign to protect the arts isn't a passing inconvenience; it's a permanent battle for anyone who understands that the wealth of a nation can't just be measured in pounds and pence.

"I became a playwright because it rained in Liverpool on a particular Wednesday in 1989. I went to shelter in the Open Eye photography gallery and found a leaflet advertising the Liverpool Playhouse Young Writers Award. I was already a published writer – I had a letter in *SHOOT!* magazine when I was eleven – but I hadn't written for the stage. *North* won a £1,000 cheque and was performed in the Studio Theatre. It wasn't badly received except by a friend's mother who resented the admission price of £3. She said, 'it was only worth £1.50.'

I was very pleased to come back to the Studio Theatre with *Self Catering (A Short History of the World)* … and fortunate that there was a Studio Theatre to come back to. There has been a permanent theatre on this site since 1866; it would have been an indictment of today's Britain if we allowed a 125-year-old theatre to die. Salman Rushdie has spoken about the importance of allowing writers to have access to 'the arena of discourse'. That access is being threatened by economic, as well as religious, fundamentalism.

Theatre, unlike cinema or sport, has so far escaped the most conspicuous interventions of commercial sponsors. I hope we'll never get to the stage where Macbeth is obliged to drink Heineken in the banquet scene and Hamlet has to wear Adidas training shoes and smoke Marlboro. The more insidious and sinister effect is that companies, sensitive about their public image, will neglect plays which, for reasons of style or substance, lack mass appeal. This

is the sham and the shame of the free market approach to arts
funding. Sponsorship can lead to censorship.

Too many theatres are producing bland musicals or stage versions
of television programmes. George Bernard Shaw said that art is the
food of the soul; *'Allo 'Allo* is the fast food of the soul. Increasingly
it's left to studio and fringe theatres to provide a more varied menu.

The people at the Liverpool Playhouse have helped me a lot while
I've been trying to achieve my long-term ambition. To write a play
worth more than £1.50.*"*

I wrote those words nearly twenty years ago. They were printed next to the
cast list for the premiere of my first full-length play, a comedy called *Self
Catering (A Short History of the World)*. It was put on stage by Kate Rowland,
Artistic Director of the Liverpool Playhouse Studio, who had a bold and brave
policy of commissioning young unknown writers. After a successful run in the
Playhouse Studio and a tour of England's eclectic theatrical venues, including
Runcorn Library, *Self Catering* was filmed by Channel 4 and published by
Warner Chappell. Thanks to the Playhouse, I had a lucky start.

One of the oddities about taking *Self Catering* on tour was learning
that you can't watch the same play twice. Every night was different.
The scene that made people laugh in Brighton barely raised a titter in
Tamworth. When the play appeared at the Liverpool Playhouse Studio,
some nights it was ten minutes longer, simply because the audience was
laughing so much.

I'm very fond of that Grade II listed building in Williamson Square,
a distinctive synthesis of 1860s and 1960s architecture which is like
seeing Brahms jamming with the Beatles, but when we celebrate the
Liverpool Playhouse we're really honouring all the amazing people who've
contributed to its history. Not just the dedicated theatre workers, onstage
and offstage, but also the open-minded and open-hearted audiences.

For a hundred years, thousands of shows attended by millions of
people have created a legacy of a trillion personal memories. Here are a
few of mine.

When we were rehearsing *North* in Mathew Street, I attended a
planning meeting and listened to a debate about whether we could afford
to buy a loaf to rehearse the sandwich scene. Even in those days there
was never enough bread to go around. The opening night coincided with
a heatwave. The audience provided air-conditioning by wafting the cast
list vigorously while the poor actors on stage, who were supposed to be
stranded on a train in a frosty forest, were sweating desperately inside
woolly jumpers and thick coats.

I saw the studio theatre transformed into a broken train, a wintry wood, a desert island, and for my third play there, *Pig's Ear*, a suburban house. On one night two actors slipped accidentally into dialogue from the last scene of the play. Unfortunately they were half an hour early. Their fellow actors began to giggle. I was sitting on the back row of the auditorium with the director, Ramin Gray. I considered ending the play there and then, but Ramin wisely decided to let things continue. The flummoxed actors got to the end of the final scene and then looked confused when the play carried on. Half an hour later they performed the final scene again, with exactly the same dialogue. Nobody in the audience seemed to find this odd, even the local critic. He wrote the best review I've ever had from the *Liverpool Echo*.

It's thanks to the Playhouse that I've never had what my folks called "a proper job" and for that I am grateful, most of the time. As a full-time writer you don't have the benefit of sick pay, holiday pay, and, quite often, pay. I often see advertisements in newspapers with the headline "Why Not Be a Writer?" Some days I can think of a dozen reasons. But somehow over the years I've written plays, films, short stories, non-fiction books for adults and picture books for children. Everything was made possible by the opportunity, the freedom and the confidence that I was given by the Liverpool Playhouse. The next generation of writers, directors and actors deserves the same opportunity.

ANDREW CULLEN, WRITER

Andrew had 3 plays performed in the studio:

North, directed by Kate Rowland, May 1989 which won the Liverpool
    Playhouse Young Writers Award.
Self Catering (A Short History of the World), directed by Kate Rowland,
    September 1992. It was commissioned by Altered States Theatre
    Company and was filmed for television in 1984.
Pig's Ear, directed by Ramin Grey, November 1995.

Proud of our track record

For many theatre people, their first experience of professional work is in a Studio theatre – there is nothing quite like being a member of the audience on the first night of a new play in a Studio theatre where everyone else feels a member of the family and part of an exciting experience. The Liverpool Playhouse is proud of its track record in Studio work – many well-known writers and actors had their first taste of a Liverpool audience in our second venue, indeed some productions which were first seen in the Studio are now "household names", both *Watching* and *Self Catering* went on to appear on television, and *Night Collar* and *99 Heyworth Street* enjoyed great critical success at bigger venues.

Watch this space ...'

PROGRAMME NOTE, NOVEMBER 1996

Happy birthday playhouse

'On 11/11/2011, the Liverpool Repertory Theatre will be a hundred years old. Of course the building itself was built in 1866 as a music hall and the company has undergone many physical and philosophical changes, not to mention a name change, but the spirit that underpinned those original pioneers who sought to bring high-quality, home produced theatre to Liverpool, lives on. As a quick perusal of this history of the Playhouse will reveal there has always been a creative courage and a desire to nurture the next generation of forward thinking artists at the kernel of every artistic vision since its inception.

For several years the Playhouse housed a small studio in what is now our rehearsal room. It was the compact crucible for many a fledgling writer and performer. Many of our most celebrated theatre practitioners took their first steps as artists in the safe yet utterly daring Playhouse Studio. "Safe" because the budgets were small and the audience numbers none too exposing but "daring" in its essence for the very freedom that lack of box office pressure released.

How many times have we been asked if/when we could bring it back?

Well the answer is the renaissance of the Playhouse Studio is our birthday present to the theatre. Whilst we will still have to use it as a rehearsal room, we have fitted it out to allow public access and technical support for use as a studio theatre whenever we can.

Its opening production will be the world premiere of a new play by Liverpool writer Lizzie Nunnery.

All the best birthday presents should encapsulate the receiver and take them into the future. We like to think that everyone who has truly understood the personality of this great theatre and the principles upon which it was founded will understand why this safe yet daring space is the perfect present for an old lady with a lot of spirit.'

GEMMA BODINETZ, ARTISTIC DIRECTOR

Richard Williams 1996–1998

Trouble ahead

❝ It is vital that all those people who believe in the Playhouse, and want it to have a future actually turn out to support us. The Arts Council will be reviewing our future next month and a substantial part of that assessment will depend on audience numbers ...❞

RICHARD WILLIAMS; QUOTED IN *LIVERPOOL ECHO*, 13 SEPTEMBER 1996

❝ We'll do what we can to help ... but ultimately it's down to local people to show that they *WANT* the Playhouse.❞

ARTS COUNCIL STATEMENT; QUOTED IN *LIVERPOOL ECHO*, 13 SEPTEMBER 1996

❝ Dear Patron,

As you are probably aware from the press, this Theatre has been going through a number of changes and has had a difficult time financially. The continuing support of our public funders will rely directly on the support we get from you, the theatre-going audience of Merseyside. We have been told that the Arts Council support, upon which the future of the Liverpool Playhouse is dependent, will depend on our achieving good Box Office figures. All the decisions will be made early in November so can I please urge you, if you enjoy tonight's show to tell your family and friends and persuade them to come along to this production ...❞

RICHARD WILLIAMS, PROGRAMME NOTE

Music theatre

The Magic Flute, book by Simon Nicholson and Richard Williams; music arranged by Joanna Macgregor; lyrics by Simon Nicholson; directed by Richard Williams, January 1997

❝ When Simon Nicholson, Richard Williams and I first had a conversation about presenting *The Magic Flute*, we agreed that our production had to have two objectives: firstly it had to entertain and delight an audience who know the opera well, and had seen and heard it before; secondly, it would fire the imaginations of those who hadn't yet come across Mozart's last opera and maybe were sceptical about opera as an art-form.

The Magic Flute by Mozart, libretto adapted Richard Williams and Simon Nicholson, musical arrangement by Joanna Macgregor, directed by Richard Williams; January 1997 (Phil Cutts)

It's often said that the music in an opera can compensate for a ridiculous plot, wooden characterisation and frankly unbelievable denouements; and the plot of *The Magic Flute* twinned as it is with gorgeous music and, at times, heartstoppingly simple and direct melody, can be baffling. It's a glorious mixture of high art and low comedy, mixing together slapstick and deadly serious masonic ritual ... Our idea in updating the plot to contemporary New York was to provide a coherent story to present without in any way being untruthful to the original libretto; to present all major arias and ensembles sung by operatic singers, and at the same time to make it a theatrically strong experience ... Although updating dictates some startling changes, our plot and characters remain faithfully true to the original. In terms of the music, I was determined to keep all the famous arias, ensembles and incidental pieces of music. Obviously I had a major challenge as there wasn't an orchestra at my disposal and I was told I could have three players!

JOANNA MACGREGOR, PROGRAMME NOTE

215

Second season

‘ *She Stoops to Conquer* marks the end of this, our first, revived repertory season ... Between the end of its run and the beginning of our next repertory season in September, we shall be playing host to a number of productions from other companies, starting with Arthur Miller's towering drama, *All My Sons*, starring Liverpool's own Jean Boht. Although Jean is perhaps best known for her recent television appearances as Ma Boswell in *Bread* and one of the stars of *Brighton Bells*, she began her theatrical career here at The Playhouse, so it will be an immense pleasure to welcome her back.

The hilarious adventures of a Liverpool taxi driver are celebrated in *Night Collar*, a comedy by two Liverpool-based writers, Tony Furlong and Jimmy Power, which started life at the Studio here at The Playhouse and has reached a larger audience through its run at the Everyman and which we are delighted to welcome back here on the main stage so that even more people can get to see this wonderful new theatrical treat ...

A Midsummer Night's Dream by Shakespeare (adapted by Andy Rashleigh), directed by Richard Williams with music by Joanna Macgregor; October 1996

August places the focus firmly on Liverpool with a new play called *I'm Marrying Robbie Fowler* – a great new comedy that will go on national tour immediately after its premiere here, followed by a celebration of the life and music of the Beatles – *Sergeant Pepper's Magical Mystery Tour*.

I am particularly pleased to have directed this production because I performed in the same play on the stage here when I was a junior

Assistant Stage Manager in 1965. I remember the director, Kay Gardner, giving me a good dressing down in front of all the other actors because, as one of the servants, I had been foolish enough to follow the urgings of other members of the cast to put in extra bits of business. Although it was painful at the time, I can now fully agree with her …*

RICHARD WILLIAMS, PROGRAMME NOTE

Closure The audience may have continued to support the Playhouse over the summer months and into the following autumn season when Richard Williams directed Godber's *Bouncers* and *Shakers*. But by then, years of funding cuts from both the Arts Council and the local authorities (particularly as a result of the abolition of the metropolitan county council in 1986), which had at one point left the theatre on monthly funding, were taking their toll.

A night at the Playhouse for the Playhouse, 15 December 1997

*Your support, as ever, is valued and never more so now as Liverpool Playhouse faces another crisis. Ironically we are currently enjoying our best success for some time. Barbara Dickson in *7 Ages of Woman* and The Royal Shakespeare Company's production of *Cyrano de Bergerac* were both sold out, our own production of Daphne du Maurier's *Rebecca* exceeded our Box Office target, and *The Wizard of Oz* is currently a hit with our audiences. For the first time in years, our productions are making a surplus.

However, despite these successes, old debts have caught up with us. The Company is in Administration and our future is uncertain. Behind the scenes we are working with our funders on a rescue package to ensure that The Liverpool Playhouse … will continue … Whatever the outcome of the present talks, I sincerely hope that the chosen solution will put Liverpool producing theatre on a firm footing. Crisis and threat of crisis have come all too often in recent years to all our cities' theatres. I believe that if our theatres could flourish … then the real benefits would flow through … Tonight's Benefit Concert is an important part of keeping the tradition of theatre alive in Liverpool.*

RICHARD WILLIAMS, PROGRAMME NOTE

We cannot say when it will reopen. It depends what ideas come forward. But I am cautiously optimistic and I believe that people will not let the Playhouse die … Preliminary discussions have begun with the Playhouse's funding partners. The Everyman has entered into discussions to merge the Playhouse and the city's Everyman while retaining the separate artistic identities and approaches of both theatres.

TREVOR BIRCH, ONE OF THE TWO ADMINISTRATORS;
QUOTED IN *GUARDIAN*, 9 OCTOBER 1997

217

The Mystery Plays adapted and directed by Richard Williams with music arranged by Joanna MacGregor; February 1997 'Further proof of Richard William's great good taste and equal daring in providing a season which while not overtly commercial is actually all the better for being different.' (Joe Riley, *Liverpool Echo*, 15 February 1997)

6 The funders are committed to a producing theatre in Liverpool but what remains to be seen is whether the city can support two producing venues. 9

PATRIC GILCHRIST, DIRECTOR OF PERFORMING ARTS, NORTH WEST ARTS BOARD, QUOTED IN *GUARDIAN*, 9 OCTOBER 1997

6 Theatre is a people business. It's about dreams. But sometimes you have to shatter those dreams. 9

JANE DAWSON, ADMINISTRATIVE DIRECTOR; QUOTED IN *LIVERPOOL ECHO*, 26 JUNE 1997

Supporting the Playhouse: Playhouse Circle and Friends of the Playhouse

The Playhouse Circle started in 1922, running, with some breaks, until the late 1960s with the object of supporting the theatre and stimulating interest in the Repertory movement and drama in general and holding seasons of lectures, play-readings and discussions. It was later replaced by the Friends who also raised money to support the theatre.

6 The Friends of the Playhouse during the 1980s was mainly a theatre appreciation group very similar to the current play reading circle. From

1991, and with the fight to save the theatre, things had to change to a more political fundraising movement. Elizabeth Christie was chair and William Fulton and others were committee members. John Stalker and Pelham McMahon quickly signed up nearly five hundred members.

Thus it was that a group prepared to roll up their sleeves to raise money and to support staff with clerical work became a fixture for the next seven years. We raised money from auctions, bazaars, outings, coffee mornings, raffles and numerous other projects. By the time I was elected to the Chair, the favourite were the open days, when Friends joined me to act as guides. Altogether over £40,000 was raised to support the Theatre, the youth theatre, studio productions, drama students, framed photos to dress up the plainness of the foyers and main staircase and other smaller products.

Night Collar by Furlong and Power, re-staged by Richard Williams from the original direction of Marie Higham; Margi Clarke and Gerry White, May 1997

219

I'm Marrying Robbie Fowler by John Chambers and Dave Simpson, directed by Richard Williams; August 1997
'It's 2-1, tempers are rising and chaos reigns when Frannie, a football orphan, is torn between mum, who supports Liverpool and dad, who is absolutely ball-istic over Everton – pandemonium ensues when Frannie walks in and announces she is going to marry Robbie Fowler. Dad rules it off-side, mum thinks it's a match made in heaven!' (Flyer)

My happy memory was helping Pelham and others cooking hot meals for the cast of *Blood Brothers*. They only had a 40 minute turn around on Matinee days. We earned a reputation for excellent gravy.

No matter how much we did by way of mail-outs or later as cleaners, we were rewarded by the "Cast Nights" when we dressed up and mingled with stars of screen and stage. For such occasions we provided refreshments and a glass of wine for our guests.

I was devastated when in 1997 it became apparent that if financial reasons weren't enough to close the theatre, Health and Safety rules were. The theatre was going to go dark. And dark it was for two whole years. At first the core group mentioned above were going in and keeping the place clean. We soon discovered how much was missing from the different rooms and fought the administrators concerning this matter. As a result the theatre was locked up tight with access denied and temptation removed from all who felt they had a right to electrical goods or theatre posters. Most importantly the Friends kept their Bank Account and made themselves ready for when the theatre reopened. A monthly meeting still takes place and all enjoy remembering the old days.

JEAN MILLS, CHAIR, 1993–98

The Theatre was closed on 3 January 1998.

Jo Beddoe, 1999–2003

The re-opening of the theatre in December 2000, was seen by many as a sign of the resurgence of the city. 'If the Playhouse's success is important to regional theatre,' argued Lyn Gardner, 'it is crucial to the future of Liverpool.' The entire city seemed to be in a state of transformation; hotels were springing up, the waterfront was receiving a £200 million facelift, and the city centre population, which had fallen to under 3,000 in the 1990s, was on the increase. 'This financial buoyancy,' she continued, was also 'reflected in a cultural optimism of which the Playhouse is the most obvious symbol'. (*Guardian*, 31 January 2001).

A view from the executive director

❝ In 1982, I came to Liverpool Playhouse to be General Manager with the Gang of Four, (after a year as a teacher at Croxteth Secondary Modern in 1965) and there renewed my passion for Liverpool and its theatre. It is not the magnificence of the river, or the buildings, or even new shopping opportunities or Liverpool Football Club, which I cherish most about Liverpool. It is the voices that tell the stories.

The Gang of Four, Alan Bleasdale, Chris Bond, Bill Morrison, and Willy Russell were the artistic directors during my time, and they were four very special writers and directors whose voices were distinctive, vibrant and important. Each of them, particularly Bill Morrison in his Studio programming, nurtured and supported emerging writers and gave opportunities to writers like Jimmy McGovern, Debbie Horsfield, Caryl Phillips, Jim Morris, Peter Whalley, Catherine Hayes, Claire Luckham, Adrian Henri, Jim Hitchmough, and Carol Ann Duffy who wrote *Take My Husband* for the Studio and later, *Cavern of Dreams* for the Main Stage. In the 1980's, although in recession, Liverpool was a city of strong and remarkable voices, from its writers, musicians, artists, performers, poets, comedians, supporters, audiences, and politicians, to the dockers and bishops, and luckily for the Playhouse, the Board of Directors. With the courage, support and dedication of its Board members, particularly Carl Hawkins, Elizabeth Christie

Repainting the building in preparation for the re-opening

221

Brassed Off by Mark Herman (adapted Paul Allen), directed by Neale Birch; a co-production with Birmingham Rep, with Bernard Kay as Danny, May 2003

and William Fulton, the Playhouse became a theatre known for the strength and quality of its writing.

I always remembered the words of Henry Cotton, a former Chair and then Vice President of the Playhouse reminding me, that, on taking up my post, I was privileged to have, in my hands, a duty of care for this most prestigious theatre, with its unrivalled history of achievement. He also reminded me that I was in good company, as there had been more than one female General Manager including the formidable Maud Carpenter who had been the General Manager for over fifty years. She came out of the ether to me on more than one occasion, in a dark and empty auditorium, when things looked impossibly difficult. Unlike Maud, I only lasted two years before leaving for the Royal Court Theatre in London. Liverpool Playhouse was my first proper theatre job. It was a wonderful and exhilarating rite of passage, working with the most extraordinary writers, directors, designers, performers, technicians and the wider Liverpool theatre community. It was a golden time and those two years taught me, above all, respect for the writer, which I have never lost.

It was, therefore, an overwhelming sense of gratitude and a commitment to writers and the future of the Liverpool Playhouse, which brought me back from my theatre job in New York in 1999 to lead the new Liverpool Playhouse and Everyman operation. The Playhouse had been dark for three years and my first task was to manage the £3 million refurbishment of the Playhouse and get the theatre opened within the City Council's timescale. Against all odds, and due to the magnificent endeavours of the new staff team and the *Christmas Carol* Company, the theatre opened only a day late in December 2000.

As a precaution, the official re-opening was held on February 3rd 2001. During the refurbishment, a member of the public had sent me programmes of the original opening in 1911 and the Golden Jubilee in 1961, both of which included poems specially written for the occasion by John Masefield, who became the Poet Laureate in 1930. Reading the poems gave me an emotional sense of history and responsibility, and I thought it was only appropriate, therefore, to commission a poem for the re-opening. I decided to ask Carol Ann Duffy (who herself later became Poet Laureate) if she would write a poem to celebrate the Playhouse. On that special reopening night, on the stage, after the production of *Twelfth Night*, actors Tony Booth and Neil Pearson, both associated with the Liverpool Theatres, read the Masefield poems and Lesley Sharp, who had appeared in *Cavern of Dreams* and is now a widely acclaimed stage and television actress, read Carol Ann's beautiful, and hauntingly moving, new poem. For me it was, and remains, a very personal and precious moment.

Thanks to the efforts and commitment of many, including Liverpool City Council, the Arts Council, Chairman, Professor Simon Lee and the Board and the support of the staff and theatre makers and audiences of Liverpool and Merseyside, we had honoured the duty of care and once again Liverpool Playhouse was a stage for voices and telling the story. At the end of the evening, in the empty auditorium, I swear I saw Maud Carpenter smile.

Jo Beddoe, General Manager, Liverpool Playhouse 1982–84; Executive Director, The Liverpool and Merseyside Theatres Trust (Playhouse and Everyman) 1999–2003

'A Liverpool Theatre': Carol Ann Duffy

You heard a voice of water and air and light
Down by the pier head, from the river's opening throat
As hundreds disembarked from a ferry-boat

You followed the crowd. The boast and brag of stone
Clamoured under your feet; glamorous, northern –
The tall dark handsome streets of the place you were born in.

A seagull screamed, trapped in the mouth of the wind.
A woman cried, tramping the streets while it rained,
mourned by cathedral bells, for love or money.

You walked down the hill to the city, one of many,
hearing the stories the buildings blagged – slavery,
bravery, knavery, fame, tell tales of stone birds spreading
their wings. You heard a voice of leather and metal guitars
sing from a backstreet, fade like a ghost, like a light from a star
that took years to arrive. Ships on the water moaned.

You hunted it down, the sound of the soul of the voice,
of the bricks and the mortar, the doing and the dying, the staying
or leaving. You reached for a shape for the drama

and shadowed the crowd to a square where a playhouse stood
like a ship of stone and glass. You took a seat in the darkness,
the sound of applause like talent thinking aloud, embarked

on a listening voyage of words. This was your theatre now.
A girl on the stage was telling you how, tonight,
She heard a voice of water and air and light

COMMISSIONED FOR RE-OPENING OF THEATRE, 3 FEBRUARY 2001

What's going on? ‘ The bringing together of the Everyman and Playhouse into a new single operation begs many questions …

How will the two theatres work together? The Liverpool and Merseyside Theatres Trust is the name of the new limited charitable company formed to run both theatres. We will be known as the Liverpool Everyman and Playhouse … We are one staff in two buildings …

What kind of work are you going to do? We will produce our own productions and we will present the best national and international touring companies. We will offer a range of quality productions, from Shakespeare to the classics, from new writing to work for young children. We will look at new ways of presenting established work. The selection of work is the responsibility of Jo Beddoe and three Associate Directors. Rose Cuthbert programmes the visiting companies, and James Kerr and Robert Delamere, established, talented young directors, both originally from Merseyside and with emerging national reputations, will inform and inspire the vision for the future and direct in-house productions. James and Robert have begun a workshop programme for locally based actors, and together the team will develop a policy for new writing …

Will the theatres retain their individual distinctiveness? What audiences, actors, directors and designers love about the theatres is their distinctiveness, the most important element of which is the two very different stages and auditoria. The Playhouse, with its proscenium arch, lends itself to epic work but retains a close relationship with the audience. The Everyman has a semi-circular thrust playing area, which the audience wraps around, offering a special intimacy. We will programme each theatre with productions which are right for the space … The distinctiveness of the two theatre spaces will inform the passion of our directors.

Will you be mainly presenting or producing? We will aim to get a balance. We are keen to produce more in-house work and we will be maximising resources to do that. We are delighted to be presenting James Kerr's *Twelfth Night or What You Will* as our opening production of this joint season …

We want to play our full part in Liverpool's renaissance, to contribute to the quality of city life, and to make a difference. Making all of this work is probably the most exhilarating challenge any of us has ever had.

NOTE IN SEASON BROCHURE, SPRING 2001

The Play What I Wrote, by Sean Foley and Hamish McColl, directed by Kenneth Branagh; September 2001

National success

The play is about us and a reflection of Morecambe and Wise and the gag of the show is that we're not doing a tribute show but somehow we use all of their material. So when we go back to Hamish and Sean's flat it looks exactly like Eric and Ernie's flat from the TV series.

It should be a great show that tries to capture what was so brilliant about them. It's a celebration of them … It's the combination of absolute willing daftness and that fantastic thing they have with guest stars. In the very, very nicest way they're taking them down a peg or two, like asking the stars to "get off" the stage because only professionals are allowed up there. And of course, there are guest stars in our show and we hope they surprise the audience. The main thing is to make people laugh and allow our double act to be a reflection of what might have gone on between Eric and Ernie. A real life behind the double act.

We always have great fun playing to Liverpool audiences, which is partly why we wanted to open the show here. People in Liverpool seem to have that quality of life; being able to laugh and have a good time. We find when we come up here that people tune straight into our style of comedy …

SEAN FOLEY (ONE PART OF THE RIGHT SIZE, THE OTHER BEING HAMISH MCCOLL), PROGRAMME NOTE, SEPTEMBER 2001

The Play What I Wrote was scheduled for a two week run in Liverpool, prior to a transfer to Wyndhams in the West End where it won an Olivier Award for best comedy. In 2003, the show transferred to Broadway. In true Morecambe and Wise style, the show included guest stars.

Phil Willmott's first Playhouse show

Around the World in Eighty Days, written and directed by Phil Willmott, December 2002

'My first production at Liverpool Playhouse resulted from a discussion with Jo Beddoe about the kind of Christmas show that might draw an audience to the venue. It's always a tricky question, the holiday market can be lucrative but it's hard to lure people away from the big commercial pantomimes or indeed the rightly celebrated rock and roll pantomimes at the Everyman. My response was not to try to compete on a panto level but to present a lively alternative for older kids and people who wanted to enjoy a classic story. We decided I'd direct a revival of my own musical of *Around the World in Eighty Days*.

I'd already staged it with a huge cast and a tiny budget at London's Battersea Arts Centre and here was the chance to take a different approach. This time the scenery would be lavish but instead of a cast of 25 and a band now everything, all the characters, all the puppetry, all the music were to be generated by twelve clever actor musicians. The core cast came from the original BAC production but were augmented by performers who could also play the musical accompaniment.

Around the World in Eighty Days by Jules Verne (adapted by Phil Willmott; score Annemarie Lewis Thomas), directed by Phil Willmott; the production was dedicated to the life and work of John Thaw (1942–2002) who had appeared as Passepartout in February 1967; December 2002

John Thaw in *Around the World in Eighty Days* by Jules Verne (adapted by Pavel Kohout), directed by David Scase; February 1967

The rehearsal period was great fun as so many of us knew each other from previous productions and we all shared a big and Christmassy house in Kensington that made me feel like an enthusiastic Big Brother contestant. Cleo Pettitt designed a stunning set inspired by the inside of Fogg's pocket watch and the gigantic cogs would turn to bring on the next international location – usually one simple piece of additional scenery trucked on from the side so it looked rather like one of those toy theatres where you slide elements in on sticks from the wings. Mervyn Miller, now recognised as one of the world's puppet experts, following his work on the National Theatre hit *War Horse*, designed the beautiful life size elephant on which our heroes could cross the jungle.

It was a fast moving show of constantly changing costumes and scenery and I was amazed by the Playhouse's hard working and ingenious backstage crew who'd also sometimes appear as part of the onstage action. Mikey would get a nightly round of applause for operating the model train leaping across a collapsing bridge at the show's climax. The show sold well considering the competition, and the fact that the Playhouse was dwarfed by a huge billboard advertising the rival show at the Empire. As I made my way to the London train following the opening night I looked in on the Schools' matinee. There were several hundred kids sat in rapt anxious silence as Phileas Fogg expressed his concerns that the expedition would fail – so I knew we'd done a good job! Following a successful run at the Playhouse we toured the whole elaborate production – elephants, dragons, hot air balloons and even Mikey and his model train crash – to Windsor, Richmond and Guildford.

PHIL WILLMOTT, DIRECTOR

Gemma Bodinetz and Deborah Aydon, 2003–

❝ What do you do with a theatre steeped in history? Whose stage has launched some of our country's finest talents? Whose past encompasses the gentry in their velvet-lined boxes and the "ladies of the night" heckling from the back of the gallery?

We think you go to its roots and then take it somewhere it has never been before. Take the essence of this glorious building and spin it into the future. Make it what it's always been: something that everyone can be a part of.❞

SEASON BROCHURE, SPRING–SUMMER 2004

Inspired by the past

The Mollusc by Henry Hubert Davies, directed by Gemma Bodinetz; May 2006

❝ Being the Artistic Director of any theatre requires an intimate knowledge of its audience, its city and its history. Only once you've rolled yourself around in this can you begin to fall in love with all that's best about it and to clear away all that prevents "your" theatre from shining … My respectful relationship with The Playhouse turned into a romance when I read a dusty book that was already on my office shelf when I arrived. Printed in 1935, *The Liverpool Playhouse Theatre* by Grace Wyndham Goldie is a charmingly evocative history of the Playhouse from the inception of the repertory company in 1911 until 1934.

It lovingly recounts the highs and the lows of a theatre company taking its first steps; the seasons that were huge successes, the shows that failed to catch the public imagination. It lists all the actors that were part of the ensembles, most of whom had lush names from another time: *Baliol Holloway*, *Drury Channell* and my own personal favourite, *F.Pennington Gush*, to name but a few. They worked incredibly hard, rehearsing one play during the day and performing another at night.

Above: Gemma Bodinetz and Deborah Aydon (Stephanie de Leng)

229

Corin Redgrave as Archie Rice in *The Entertainer* by John Osborne, directed by John Tiffany; January 2004

The Lady of Leisure; or The Mollusc by Henry Hubert Davies, directed by Gemma Bodinetz; Tessa Churchard as Dulcie, May 2006 (Stephen Vaughan)

It also lists all the plays that were performed each season, and as I read these lists I was struck by how many of those listed I had never heard of. One such play was *The Mollusc*. Now, not only did this play have a rather ridiculous title but it did seem to be rather popular and had been a hit in 1912 and 1922. I was titillated and ventured into our archives to find and read a copy.

What I found is what you will see tonight with only its title changed (few people nowadays seemed completely sure what a mollusc was). I can't pretend to have unearthed a great classic of early 20th century literature, but it is very well constructed ... and is, I think, delightfully funny.

It's also like nothing we tend to see at the theatre anymore and I think that makes it worth doing in itself. I also owe *the Lady of Leisure* a huge debt of thanks, because it is now inextricably linked with my passion for the Playhouse and the great and eccentric actors that trod her boards.

GEMMA BODINETZ, PROGRAMME NOTE

Made in Liverpool

The observant among you will have noticed the "Made in Liverpool" stamp that appears on this and other production images. Last season saw a huge increase in the number of home-grown productions and an incredibly positive response from the critics and you, our audience, to these productions. Home-grown work is still the cornerstone of our artistic policy and the "Made in Liverpool" stamp is a shorthand that tells you that your theatres have produced this work and that you can trust the quality, passion and integrity of a home-grown production. You can also congratulate yourself that your attendance at one of our productions is a positive act of support for your local theatres and part of them taking centre-stage nationally. Last season proved unequivocally that "Made in Liverpool" was not a sign of parochialism but confirmation of quality.

GEMMA BODINETZ AND DEBORAH AYDON, PROGRAMME NOTE

Christmas in Liverpool

The Flint Street Nativity by Tim Firth, directed Matthew Lloyd; December 2006 and 2007

❝ Sometimes a theatre presents a play. Sometimes it produces one. In rare cases it creates the idea for one out of nothing. Such was the case with *The Flint Street Nativity*. The potential of turning my own television play into a piece for theatre had gone spectacularly unseen by me for years since its initial broadcast. Out of the blue I got a call from an alert member of the Playhouse team who had chanced to meet the original director of the TV play, and hadn't realised that *Flint Street* was written by the same guy who wrote *Neville's Island*, which the Playhouse had presented some time previously.

Had I ever thought of adapting *Flint Street* for stage? The answer was no. The television play was far too short for a theatre play and even though it had a temptingly theatrical setting and an attractively small number of sets, something was still missing. Somehow the stool lacked a third leg.

The offer did however set me thinking.

As a child I had often undertaken the epic journey from my Victorian redbrick primary school in distant Warrington to see Christmas shows at

The Flint Street Nativity by Tim Firth, directed by Matthew Lloyd; December 2006 and 2007 (Stephen Vaughan)

the Playhouse. These were my very first experiences of theatre. Of course we'd had groups come into school to do plays; we'd had beardy guys on stilts do something about Rumpelstiltskin which had scared the living daylights out of me ... but the Playhouse was a *theatre*. It looked like a theatre. It had fancy bits on the outside. It had columns. In fact it had columns on the inside that got in the way sometimes but that didn't matter because they were *theatre* columns. It was like a church only with wine gums and the genuine prospect that someone special was actually going to turn up.

These are the experiences that form your desires as a kid. Of course you don't know it at the time. All you sense is a quickening of the heart. At nine, the idea that one day you would have a play performed in this building could not even be comprehended.

But here I was with that theatre on offer and two legs on my stool. Ultimately it was the Playhouse itself that forged the solution. The play should not be a play. It should be exactly the kind of show I came to see as a kid – a cocktail of words and music. The children of the story should sing carols, but their minds should wander, as children's minds are wont to do when confronted with abstruse Victorian lyrics about the abhorring of virgins' wombs. They should sing their thoughts.

This was of course an element the television play never had, an element of pure theatre generated by the theatre's own legacy on a child. The following Christmas saw the first night of *Flint Street* performed by the finest Liverpudlian actors and set in a redbrick Victorian primary in Liverpool. As a traveller from a distant land I set out with my own kids to witness a very different nativity.

TIM FIRTH, WRITER

6 Firth's play is part of a theatrical renaissance on Merseyside. Attendances at the Playhouse and the Everyman have gone up by 45 per cent in the three years since Gemma Bodinetz and Deborah Aydon took over ... They haven't got there by being timid. 9

SUSANNAH CLAPP, *OBSERVER*, 24 DECEMBER 2006

A view from the executive director

6 The first time I became properly aware of the Liverpool Playhouse it was as a "beleaguered regional theatre". There were a lot of them about in the early nineties. Arts funding was being cut nationally, and the break-up of larger local authorities like Merseyside meant that many theatres were being squeezed from more than one direction. Every now and then a mass gathering of artistic and executive directors was convened to shout "down with this sort of thing" for three or four hours and from one of those meetings I picked up the theory that the Arts Council had "a little list" of theatres to be allowed to fail.

Whatever the reality of a very complex situation, by the time it re-entered my consciousness, the Playhouse had gone through voluntary liquidation and been dark for two years. Mercifully, the Arts Council, City Council and board members of both theatres had then managed to create a model for the Playhouse to merge with the Everyman and it was due to reopen its doors. Working in Dublin at the time and having an over-developed appetite for a challenge, I was sorry it wasn't me having a go at that; I'd always liked Liverpool.

A few years later, when Jo Beddoe decided to move on after setting up the new company and reopening the Playhouse, the job came up again. By now, Liverpool was bidding for Capital of Culture and, while we all knew Newcastle would get it, there was a real sense of optimism about the city, something it hadn't had a chance of grasping for far too long.

In the summer of 2003, Gemma Bodinetz and I were appointed on the basis of a hugely ambitious shared vision for where we would like to take the Playhouse and the Everyman. When Liverpool was announced as Capital of Culture 2008, our bluff was called. We'd have to do it.

The lead-up to 2008 was all-consuming. In our first season, we almost doubled the programming, with six new productions across the two theatres in the first six months of 2004. We learnt very quickly that the closure had taken its toll and the audience base – never something the Playhouse could take for granted – had dwindled away. Box office receipts in our first year were less than half those of similar theatres in other cities.

And yet. The mantra that rings in our ears from those early days is Hold Your Nerve. While the figures told us to turn back, we were continually urged to keep going. The quality and range of the work; our efforts to build an audience which would be artistically adventurous, financially sustaining and as socially mixed as possible; investment of time, energy and care in bringing on new talent – everyone wanted this to succeed.

The Arts Council had increased its funding as part of a transformative investment in regional theatre across the country and wanted to see a return. The City Council backed the new model as it readied Liverpool for the international spotlight in 2008. Our team – from the senior management to the bar staff and ushers – seized ownership of the vision and worked tirelessly to make it happen. The board never wavered in their faith that we were on the right course. Theatre colleagues around the country and arts colleagues around the city were invaluable networks of mutual support and creative collaboration. And most importantly, Liverpool buoyed us along – from the city's press and media to the people who stopped us in the street to talk animatedly about the show they'd just seen.

This was a time of extremes. Of despair as an audience of 75 arrived for a beautiful production with four-star national reviews, tempered by delight and relief as a capacity house roared with laughter at Sheila Hancock's grotesque mother-in-law in *The Anniversary* and the coffers were replenished. The tightrope between adventurous programming and popular appeal, between box office income and access for all, is walked by every subsidised theatre. In these early years it felt as if we were walking it in a force nine gale, while juggling.

Every Capital of Culture has, we learned, gone spectacularly wrong before (in the fortunate cases) going right. Liverpool was certainly no exception. But by the time we lined up with Liverpool's finest to emerge from a cargo container on the steps of St George's Hall at the opening ceremony in January 2008, the city was ready. As the year went on it became clear that Liverpool had pulled it off. Across the city the programme was worthy of that international spotlight; people from all walks of life and of all ages were getting involved with culture in unprecedented numbers, and there was a sense of real pride at home and a fresh image abroad. It was Liverpool's time again.

Of course, this glorious new dawn collided with the worst recession in living memory. The investment by national and regional funders which yielded such a great artistic and social return is now being reversed. It's cold out there. But so far we have managed to sustain bold programming; audience numbers have held strong and new talent is continually coming through.

As this book goes to press we are no less excited or terrified than we have been for the last eight years. After a ten-year fight to make it happen, the Everyman is about to be transformed by a two-year, £27m redevelopment. The Playhouse's birthday season will begin with Roger McGough's glorious version of *Tartuffe*, which will then tour around the country; a muscular new version by Liverpool writer Stephen Sharkey of a timely Brecht classic; a new production of *The Ladykillers* with a fabulous cast will open here before heading into the West End; the utterly joyous Rock 'n' Roll Panto will invade the Playhouse at Christmas and, perhaps most excitingly, we will relaunch the Studio with a new play by one of Liverpool's finest young writers.

With each new season we take another deep breath and walk out onto the tightrope. Put our faith in our artists and our audience despite the economic chill in the air. And night after night we learn something new about what a theatre can mean to its city. What can we do but hold our nerve? 〞

DEBORAH AYDON, EXECUTIVE DIRECTOR

Capital of Culture 2008

〝 Celebrate Liverpool, celebrate Culture, celebrate 08 – and beyond. 〞

〝 The whole European Cultural Capital title has been extraordinary. It's as if Liverpool has entered a new era, a different age, and with it has come a sense of possibility. A high proportion of the city's immediate future is pegged on culture ... 〞

DEBORAH AYDON, QUOTED IN *INDEPENDENT*, 15 JANUARY 2004

Once Upon a Time at the Adelphi, written and directed by Phil Willmott; June 2008

> Whenever I direct in Liverpool I love staying amidst the shabby Edwardian grandeur of the Adelphi Hotel and it felt like this could be a great backdrop for a romantic musical. It seemed appropriate, given the nostalgic subject, to turn for inspiration to the old-fashioned musicals I'd loved as a kid. These classic shows of the 1950s and 60s have a deceptively simple formula. More often than not they centred around a sparky on-off romance between opposites, secondary comic lovers, a really simple plot – usually based around a misunderstanding – but above all a big hearted sentimental passion for their setting (Chicago, Oklahoma, Bali Hai, London – why not Liverpool?)

> So *Once Upon a Time at the Adelphi* had all of these elements plus I also wanted to try mixing in contemporary singing styles and incorporating my favourite Adelphi legends – that a cowboy once stayed with his horse (true, I've seen pictures) and that Hitler once worked in the kitchens (alas, not true but fun to imagine). Real life Adelphi love stories I researched formed the basis of Alice and Thompson's epic on-off romance and the song *Once in a Life Time* is an unashamedly sentimental hymn to the spirit of Liverpool. It was a big thrill when it became a sort-of unofficial anthem to the city's year as Capital of Culture.

Once Upon a Time at the Adelphi by Phil Willmott, directed by Phil Willmott; June 2008 (Robert Day)

It's the story of present day receptionist Jo's meeting with elderly Alice on the roof of the Adelphi hotel. The older woman tells her of how she met and fell in love with a petty thief, Thompson, in the 1930s. They built a life together as he found respectability as a hotel employee amongst the eccentric characters that populated the Adelphi in its heyday, including chamber maid Babs forever looking for love amongst the Hollywood guests. But Thompson's chequered past is never far from the surface, the two lovers split dramatically over a misunderstanding and Jo begins to see parallels in her own troubled relationship. Happily everyone becomes reconciled in a dramatic climax that celebrates the hotel's past and present.

The show opened at the Playhouse on a spectacular award-nominated set by Christopher Woods, a beautiful revolving skeleton of architectural pieces that spun into place evoking ever changing locations in the hotel over three decades. It played to nightly standing ovations over a sold out extended run. Local and national critics warmly recommended it and some months later, it received a T.M.A award for best musical in the UK and a *whatsonstage* nomination for the year's best regional production.

PHIL WILLMOTT, DIRECTOR

Once in a lifetime

The stars are calling out our name
It's Liverpool's time again
At last the world is waking.
Shout the news across the sky
Tonight it's you and I
Who'll choose the road we're taking.
For tonight
The world will dream along with us.
We waited long enough, now is the right time.
If we fail then we fail but at least we chose to fight
Don't waste tonight's
Once in a lifetime.

PHIL WILLMOTT

2008 was a great year for the Everyman and Playhouse. We were part of an exceptional year for this city and we like to think we played our part and did it proud. But the Capital of Culture was never an end in itself, it was always the gateway to on-going cultural confidence and creativity. We hope that as we stride beyond 08 you will share our pride and commitment for all we do and our desire to build upon your faith in us.

GEMMA BODINETZ AND DEBORAH AYDON, PROGRAMME NOTE, FEBRUARY 2009

Canary by Jonathan Harvey, directed by Hettie Macdonald; a co-production with Hampstead Theatre and English Touring Theatre, April 2010 (Helen Warner)

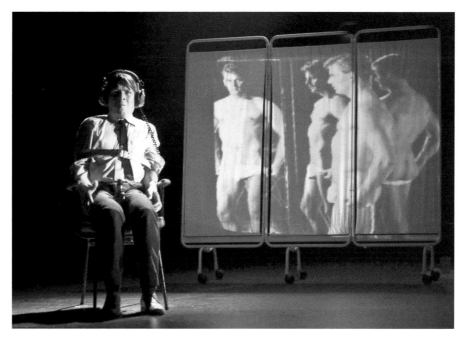

Canary by Jonathan Harvey; directed by Hettie Macdonald; April 2010

Starting out: Jonathan Harvey

' I have always had a great fondness for the Playhouse, as my first play *The Cherry Blossom Tree* (I was going through my Chekhov period) had been produced in the Studio as part of the Young Writers Festival in 1987. From then I'd gone on to write many plays, some of which had come to the Everyman on tour, but I'd not written a play specifically for Liverpool, and for the majestic stage of the Playhouse.

I took a break from playwriting to concentrate on the big bad world of telly, from 2001, but when Liverpool was awarded the Capital of Culture status in 2008, I was keen to make my return, onstage in my home city. I could think of nothing more exciting.

I met with Gemma Bodinetz to discuss my idea. Big, bold and a little bit crazy, I wanted to tell stories about what it has been like for gay men living in this country since the 50s and 60s. It was going to be an ambitious piece and Gemma was thrilled. And what's more she commissioned it! (It's always nice to be paid to work …) Now I just had to write the blooming thing!

That took a lot longer than I thought. Earlier drafts of the play were workshopped, and after a lot of hair tearing and soul searching I missed my golden opportunity to open the play during the 2008 festivities. It's hard work writing plays!! But by 2010 there was a version that everyone was happy with.

Rehearsing and realising *Canary* was one of the happiest periods of my career. I got to work with the delightful and far-too-clever-for-her-own-good director Hettie Macdonald, and we had the most wonderful cast imaginable. And we premiered this big, bold, and I think brave play in Liverpool. What more could I ask for? So often there is a snobbery in theatre … the only decent plays can be seen nowhere but London. Bollards to that, say I. (Bollards is the polite version!) Why can't brilliant theatre gestate and be born in "the provinces"? Well, there was certainly nothing provincial about *Canary*. And there is certainly nothing provincial about the theatre(s) that Gemma and Deborah run. They are vibrant, exciting spaces full of ideas. Big ideas and big emotions and politics and humour and anarchy and love. The essence of Liverpool, really. So I guess they must be doing something right … and doing it in the right place.

Canary changed my career. Suddenly TV commissioners remembered I could do stuff other than light, frothy, camp comedy. It opened new doors for me. So I will be eternally grateful to Gemma and the theatre for not running a mile when I knocked on her door and told her about my new idea. Thank you Gemma. And thank you Liverpool.

JONATHAN HARVEY, WRITER

Antony and Cleopatra by William Shakespeare; directed by Janet Suzman; October 2010

Why Cleopatra?

A few years ago, my transnational friend Kim Cattrall said to me: Can I play Cleopatra? Is it the most difficult part you've ever done? Even if I have done very little Shakespeare before, do you think I could do this one? And to all of her sweetly humble queries my answer was "yes".

And so being Liverpool born, Canadian nationalized, American domiciled, British by temperament, she scanned her world, and we pondered where we should begin this experiment in – what? – courage? You may wonder why actors bandy that rather important word – but actually it is rather courageous to pit yourself against the greatest dramatic creation of the known canon if all you are famous for is a man-eating fashion icon called Samantha. Courageous because you are asking for every scribbler earning their bread off your pitiful attempts at being taken seriously, to knock you toppling with scorn and derision, or worse still, faint praise.

A certain element of modesty informed our thinking; she is a star and we could easily have taken the idea to more West Endy producers, but we both felt that a provincial start would suit us both. Kim is a remarkably

humble and pragmatic person, well aware of the silliness that colours most of the performance scene.

We first took our plan to her Canadian base, to the famous Shakespeare factory at Stratford, Ontario – where they were more than willing to host us but only if Kim were to also play the glorious Ranevskaya in a *Cherry Orchard* the same season. Not only the same season, but to open the Chekhov ten days into the rehearsals for the Shakespeare. A plan that displayed a surprising ignorance of the demands of either great part. I'm afraid I lost it, exasperated by the thoughtlessness of the proposal. They lost it too, exasperated, I think, by me.

The logical next step was to move nearer home, and when Kim suggested her birth-place everything just slotted into place. Of course!

Why not have our phoenix re-born as a classical actress on the banks of the Mersey? Gemma Bodinetz thought the same way; every one of the marvellous team that run the Liverpool Playhouse and Everyman did too. Sure, there was an element of risk, and maybe not least me as director, but what lay securely behind our suggestion was the fact that I had played that Old Serpent and had the clearest idea of what I would seek to bring out in the play, and I felt as sure as I ever have that I would be able to help Kim find that elusive queen because I had been there and knew the way. She – curious, hard-working, sparkily intelligent, something of a truth-seeking missile – trusted me. It's wonderful to work with trust, I tell you. So rare.

The public reaction to the return of the Prodigal Daughter was tremendous: a six-week run swiftly booked out to the gunwales. Even up in the gallery, you could hear a pin drop, and even more gratifying was the fact that the majority of punters were seeing Shakespeare for the first time; Samantha had pulled in a whole new constituency. Maybe they imagined they would be watching a sex-mad clothes-horse queening it over the Nile, but – and here's the rub – they did not leave at the interval, and that's a sign if ever there is one that this great play was exerting its magic. Poetry was winning over pop-culture. I hope they'll become theatre-goers now.

I have been to Liverpool, and did know something of the warmth and embracing individuality of your average scouser, but there was no way of predicting what a happy time we were to have from beginning to end of this thrilling adventure. It was the perfect place for Kim to begin her new career as a serious actress – not that she wasn't before, but perception is everything, isn't it?

JANET SUZMAN, DIRECTOR

2003–04 *The Entertainer*, John Osborne, directed by John Tiffany
The Astonished Heart & Still Life, Noel Coward, directed by
    Philip Wilson
Ma Rainey's Black Bottom, August Wilson, directed by Gemma Bodinetz

2004–05 *The Anniversary*, Bill MacIlwraith, directed by Denis Lawson
The Odd Couple, Neil Simon, directed by Matthew Lloyd)
Dr Faustus, Christopher Marlowe, directed by Philip Wilson
Who's Afraid of Virginia Woolf, Edward Albee, directed by
    Gemma Bodinetz
Chimps, Simon Block, directed by Wilson Milam

2005–06 *The Tempest*, Shakespeare, directed by Philip Franks
Season's Greetings, Alan Ayckbourn, directed by Nikolai Foster
Billy Liar, Willis Hall, directed by Phil Willmott
Hedda Gabler, Ibsen (translated Michael Poulton), directed by Matthew
    Lloyd (co-production with West Yorkshire Playhouse
The Lady of Leisure; or The Mollusc, Henry Hubert Davies, directed by
    Gemma Bodinetz

2006–07 *All My Sons*, Arthur Miller, directed by Gemma Bodinetz
The Flint Street Nativity, Tim Firth, directed by Matthew Lloyd
Our Country's Good, Timberlake Wertenbaker, directed by Edward Dick
Much Ado About Nothing, Shakespeare, directed by Phil Willmott
Noises Off, Michael Frayn, directed by Philip Wilson

2007–08 *The Flint Street Nativity*, Tim Firth, directed by Matthew Lloyd
Tartuffe, Molière (adapted Roger McGough), directed by Gemma Bodinetz
Once Upon a Time at the Adelphi, written and directed by Phil Willmott

2008–09 *Proper Clever*, Frank Cottrell Boyce, directed by Sirdar Bills
Boeing-Boeing, Marc Camoletti, directed by Matthew Warchus (presented
    by Sonia Friedman then on tour)
The Price, Arthur Miller, directed by Giles Croft (co-production with
    Nottingham Playhouse)
When We Are Married, J. B. Priestley, directed by Ian Brown (co-production
    with West Yorkshire Playhouse)
The Hypochondriac, Molière (adapted Roger McGough), directed by Gemma
    Bodinetz

Proper Clever by
Frank Cottrell Boyce
directed by Sirdar
Bills; October 2008
'A multi media
story for MySpace
generation'
(Robert Day)

2009–10   *Kes*, Barry Hines, directed by Nikolai Foster
The 39 Steps, John Buchan (adapted Patrick Barlow), directed by Maria
Aitken (by arrangement with Edward Snape for Fiery Angel Ltd and
Tricycle Theatre London and in association with West Yorkshire
Playhouse)
Ghost Stories, Jeremy Dyson and Andy Nyman, directed by Jeremy Dyson
and Andy Nyman (co-production with Lyric Hammersmith)
Canary, Jonathan Harvey, directed by Hettie Macdonald (co-production
with Hampstead Theatre and English Touring Theatre)

2010–11   *Antony and Cleopatra*, Shakespeare, directed by Janet Suzman
No Wise Men, Steven Canny and John Nicholson, directed by Gemma
Bodinetz; with Peepolykus

Twisted Tales, Roald Dahl (adapted by Jeremy Dyson), directed by Polly
 Findlay (co-production with Lyric Hammersmith and Northern Stage)
Oedipus, Stephen Berkoff (after Sophocles), directed by Stephen Berkoff
 (co-production with Nottingham Playhouse; transfer to Edinburgh)
Tartuffe, Molière (in a new version by Roger McGough), directed by Gemma
 Bodinetz; revived by English Touring Theatre for a national tour
The Resistible Rise of Arturo Ui, Bertolt Brecht (translated by Stephen
 Sharkey), directed by Walter Meierjohann (co-production with
 Nottingham Playhouse)
The Swallowing Dark by Lizzie Nunnery, directed by Paul Robinson for
 re-launch of the Studio (co-production with Theatre 503)
The Ladykillers, William Rose, adapted for stage by Graham Linehan, directed
 by Sean Foley (co-production with Fiery Angel; West End transfer)
Cinderella-Mop! In the Name of Love, Mark Chatterton and Sarah Nixon,
 directed by Mark Chatterton; (the Everyman rock 'n' roll pantomime
 reinvented arrives at the Playhouse)

**An artistic
director's view**

‘ I can't begin to encapsulate all this theatre has been to me over the last
eight years. As someone who has spent much of their life on the move my
office on the second floor next to the rehearsal room, has been the room I
have had the longest relationship with in my 44 years on this earth. With
working weeks that frequently exceed 70 hours, the Playhouse has become
both my artistic and in many ways physical home. I have auditioned in
that office, dozed off reading many a script on the pillar box red sofa,
listened anxiously through the wall at a rehearsal in crisis, worked on
board papers late into the night with the comforting sound of the show
relay as background noise, hung out its back door onto the patio with a
fag between my fingers trying to think of next season's Christmas show
and laughed and cried and discussed funding bids and eye-liner brands for
too many hours to recall with the one and only Deborah Aydon.

Tartuffe by Molière
(adapted Roger
McGough), directed
by Gemma Bodinetz;
March 2008
(Robert Day)

Deborah and I arrived in September 2003 with what we thought was a simple mission to produce great theatre that was of a world-class standard but that would be driven by the heart-beat of its region. We didn't want to be slavishly parochial but neither did we want a ubiquitous theatre that could be found in any city in the country. My own knowledge of The Playhouse was patchy; essentially a Londoner I think back then you could have probably accused me of a London centric view of theatre. If a theatre outside London had had a good review in *The Guardian* it would have crossed my consciousness; if it hadn't for a while, then I think I would have assumed it was failing in some way. I was aware of some purple patches in the Playhouse's distinguished history but I was also aware that it had gone through some lean times and much was expected of it now. I was its first artistic director for a few years and in 2008 Liverpool was to be the European Capital Culture. Like the city itself, Deborah and I had our work cut out.

I really had my work cut out because unlike Deborah this was the first time I had ever "run" a theatre. I look back on that ambitious yet hideously ignorant woman in her middle-thirties with a mixture of embarrassment and affection. I really had no idea all it would entail to be the custodian of such a treasured cultural icon. I believed fervently that artistic excellence would draw audiences no matter what. I had little appreciation of either the region or the existing audience, just a blind belief that a great play realised with passion and skill would be a winning formula. If plays/seasons had failed to catch the public imagination in the past, why then they can't have been very good. I wince even as I type these words because the journey from then to now has been such an extraordinary one and whilst my belief in artistic excellence has not diminished an iota, my appreciation of a regional theatre's relationship with its audience and place has grown immeasurably.

The last eight years have been the most creatively productive of my life but they have involved a lot of listening and a constantly evolving relationship with Liverpool. I have discovered that a beautiful and critically acclaimed production of two rarely performed Noël Coward one act plays failed to capture the imagination of a Playhouse audience but that a full-bloodied (less critically acclaimed) *Dr Faustus* with an incredible set that would burst into flames in the final moments was an unexpected box office hit that was met with standing ovations each night. My own production of *The Mollusc* a little known, never performed Edwardian comedy unearthed from the Playhouse archives centred around an upper – middle class lady who contrived to do nothing by hilarious and ridiculous means. A wonderful set, an extraordinary cast (Greg Hicks,

Kelly Bright, Colin Tierney and Tessa Churchard) and some great reviews could not persuade Liverpool that an exploration of the frivolous was anything but that. Commissioned for the Capital of Culture a new musical by Phil Willmott *Once Upon a Time at the Adelphi* had them packed to the rafters and standing every night. Yes, there was much in it that was silly and camp and downright bonkers but at its heart was a pounding story about love against all odds (not to mention some great tunes and spectacular dance routines). It mattered. To the characters. To our audience.

There's no winning formula to finding a show that will hit the spot with a Playhouse audience (if only there were!) but as long as artistic ambition and excellence walk hand in hand with passion and a full-bloodied sense that nothing in life is to be taken for granted, you're in with a good shot. Nor can you only define success by the box office return. *Canary* a bold and beautiful play by Jonathan Harvey about the gay experience in Liverpool failed to set the box office alight but was met with cheers every night and my desk was piled high with letters of appreciation from those that felt their lives were reflected in it.

If the Playhouse were a painting it would be in vibrant oils, not water-colours. It began as a music hall and whilst its history encompasses every example of "high art" theatre, even now its very foundation stones, its fabulous relationship between the stage and the circle, seem to whisper "forget the extremes of human emotion at your peril. Make 'em laugh. Make 'em cry. Make it matter." I may not have walked into this office with its bright red sofa eight years ago understanding any of that, but the happy coincidence for me is that I agree whole-heartedly with our audience. Theatre isn't an intellectual exercise, it's an experience and it should be a memorable one.

Our opening show at the Playhouse starred Corin Redgrave as Archie Rice in John Osborne's *The Entertainer*. Interesting to recall that our first production set in a music hall saw one of our greatest and most sadly missed actors so perfectly capturing the searing bitterness and pathos of an old Vaudevillian playing to an indifferent audience who could smell his lack of commitment and contempt for them. Maybe even back then, somewhere I knew that the Playhouse has a big heart that must never be taken for granted. Sentiment is always to be eschewed but "heart" whether devastatingly packed into the centre of Arthur Miller's *All My* Sons or laced with the dazzling, wit of Roger McGough's adaptation of Molière's *Tartuffe* is the beating centre of the Liverpool Playhouse.

Cynics beware.

GEMMA BODINETZ, ARTISTIC DIRECTOR

Bibliography

John Belchem (ed.), *Liverpool 800: Culture, Character and History* (Liverpool, Liverpool University Press, 2006)

Basil Dean, *Seven Ages: An Autobiography, 1888–1927* (London, Hutchinson, 1970)

Kate Dorney and Ros Merkin (eds), *The Glory of the Garden: English Regional Theatre and the Arts Council 1984–2009* (Newcastle-upon-Tyne, Cambridge Scholars Press, 2010)

G. Walter George, *The Land Where Your Dreams Come True: A Review of the Theatre since 1946* (Liverpool, private publication, 1994)

Grace Wyndham Goldie, *The Liverpool Repertory Theatre, 1911–1934* (Liverpool, Liverpool University Press, 1935)

Pelham McMahon and Pam Brooks, *An Actor's Place: The Liverpool Repertory Company of Liverpool Playhouse, 1911–1998* (Liverpool, Bluecoat Press, 2000)

Rex Pogson, *Miss Horniman and the Gaiety Theatre Manchester* (London, Rockliff, 1952)

Michael Redgrave, *In My Mind's Eye: An Actor's Autobiography* (New York, Viking Press, 1983)

Charles Herbert Reilly, *Scaffolding in the Sky* (London, G. Routledge & Sons, 1938)

George Rowell and Anthony Jackson, *The Repertory Movement* (London, Cambridge University Press, 1984)

Olivia Turnbull, *Bringing Down the House: The Crisis in Britain's Regional Theatres* (Bristol, Intellect, 2008)

Colin Voake, 'From Diamond Jubilee to Seventieth Birthday', in brochure for the gala performance of *A Tale of Two Cities* (1981)

The Hypochondriac by Molière (adapted by Roger McGough), directed by Gemma Bodinetz. Lucinda Raikes as Angelique and Leanne best as Toinette, June 2009 (Robert Day)

Index

249